*John Smeaton, FRS
(engraving by W. Holl, after
portrait by Mather Brown)*

)HN SMEATON, FRS

JOHN SMEATON, FRS

Edited by
PROFESSOR A. W. SKEMPTON
Department of Civil Engineering
Imperial College of Science and Technology
University of London

Thomas Telford Limited
London, 1981

Published by Thomas Telford Ltd, Telford House, PO Box 101,
26–34 Old Street, London EC1P 1JH

© A. W. Skempton, 1981

ISBN: 978-0-7277-0088-9

Photoset, printed and bound in Great Britain by
REDWOOD BURN LIMITED
Trowbridge, Wiltshire

Acknowledgements

Many people have given help on particular points and are acknowledged in the Notes and References. Thanks are due especially to Miss Joyce Brown for transcribing Smeaton's letters to Benjamin Wilson, Mr Robert Matkin for finding the report on Dysart harbour and providing information as well as copies of some original documents on Ramsgate harbour, Mr William Bunting for clarifying several matters on Hatfield Chase and the River Don, Mrs A. W. Skempton for assistance in field and archive research on Potteric Carr and Adlingfleet Level, Mr Rodney Law for checking Chapter 8, and Mr A. P. Woolrich for providing new material on John Farey.

Little progress could have been made without facilities freely granted to work in various record offices, archives and libraries. These too are mentioned in the appropriate places, but a special word of thanks is due to the library staff at the Royal Society and the Institution of Civil Engineers.

Miss Anne Lane made the tracings, Mrs Brigette Cahalane typed with exemplary patience the numerous revisions which appear to be inescapable in a work of this kind, and Miss June Troy prepared the index.

Acknowledgement for permission to reproduce photographs is due to the Council of the Royal Society for twelve of Smeaton's drawings, to Mr Jonathan Gibson for Coldstream Bridge, to the Royal Scottish Museum for the model of the Eddystone masonry courses, and the Newcomen Society for the page from Smeaton's diary.

Abbreviations

Smeaton's drawings in the Royal Society collection are referenced throughout this book as *Designs* followed by the volume and folio numbers. His collected reports, published in 1812, are similarly referenced as *Reports* with the volume and page numbers. *Machine Letters* refer to the letters copied by Smeaton on Watt's copying machine and now in the Institution of Civil Engineers. All other abbreviations are explained at relevant places in the Notes and References.

Contents

Introduction

John Smeaton was the earliest of the great British civil engineers and the first to achieve distinction as an engineering scientist. It is also to him, more than any other person, that credit is due for laying the foundations of the civil engineering profession in this country; foundations on which his successors, very notably Thomas Telford, built the superstructure.

Smeaton started his career as a maker of scientific instruments, in London. He retained a keen interest in science throughout his life, but this ran parallel with an even stronger interest in engineering and by 1753 he had turned to engineering as the source of his livelihood. Gifted with exceptional intellectual and practical abilities and a remarkable capacity for study and application, he developed an extensive practice, unrivalled in the eighteenth century, as a consulting engineer.

The Eddystone Lighthouse is of course his best-known work, and this noble structure has so captured the imagination of engineers and the public alike that most of Smeaton's other achievements are almost forgotten by comparison. His major works include the River Calder Navigation; three fine masonry bridges at Coldstream, Perth and Banff; the Forth & Clyde Canal (from Grangemouth to Glasgow); substantial improvements of the Lee and the Aire river navigations; harbours at St Ives, Eyemouth, Portpatrick and Cromarty, and the north pier at Aberdeen; a lighthouse on Spurn Head; fen drainage schemes at Potteric Carr, Adlingfleet Level and Hatfield Chase; and the sluicing basin and Advanced Pier of Ramsgate harbour.

In addition to other, smaller civil engineering works, more than 50 watermills and several windmills were built to his plans. Indeed the design of watermills, for a wide variety of industrial purposes, was a subject to which he devoted much attention; they constituted the

1

main source of power in his day. He also made a close study of steam engines and at least a dozen were designed by him, including the most efficient (at Long Benton) and the most powerful (at Chacewater) of any before James Watt came on the scene.

It is fortunate that practically all of Smeaton's drawings have survived and are in the Royal Society library. This large collection, part of the national heritage of England, covers every aspect of his work. The quality of draughtsmanship is of a high order and reveals in particular his mastery of engineering details. The overall scheme, whether for a harbour, bridge or watermill, is obviously of essential importance and has to be the main consideration, yet its success will depend on getting the details right. Some of these, and the methods of executing them, could be and were left to the craftsmen on site; but in many instances Smeaton provided detail drawings of the utmost clarity.

As for Smeaton's personal involvement with site work, this varied greatly. He almost lived on the Eddystone job; he visited the Calder as often as once a week during the working season; and to Ramsgate, after his appointment as engineer, he went about four times a year with extra visits when new or difficult operations were involved. At the other extreme he assigned the entire supervision of a job to another engineer, including preparation of working drawings, though the scheme was to be carried out according to his master plan. This is known to have been the case at Adlingfleet where his friend John Grundy took charge, on the River Lee with the experienced Thomas Yeoman as engineer, and on the River Aire where the works were executed under the direction of his former pupil and assistant William Jessop.

A more typical arrangement was for Smeaton to produce a report and the necessary drawings, after examining the site, and then to leave construction in the hands of a resident engineer, millwright or engine erector, with one or two further site visits during progress of the work. On the bigger jobs, of course, such visits had to be made at fairly frequent intervals and additional reports and drawings would be required from time to time. The Forth & Clyde Canal is a good and rather well-documented example of this procedure. In all cases, except perhaps the most straightforward mill or small bridge, there is no doubt that he kept in touch with his site representative by correspondence. On Cromarty harbour, for instance—a job of only middling size and difficulty—well over a dozen letters passed to and from Smeaton and the resident engineer John Gwyn, together with some revised plans. Land surveys were made by a specialist but Smeaton took the levels himself as part of the site investigations.

His office organisation was simple, and he remarked that his work was as personal as that of any artist. From about 1760 he operated mainly from his home at Austhorpe, near Leeds, where he had one assistant: William Jessop followed by Henry Eastburn. Smeaton made the drawings and calculations, the drawings then being fair-copied by the assistant, and he wrote the reports and letters in his own hand, with copies entered in books by a clerk. Generally he moved to London for the first 4 or 5 months each year, attending meetings of the Royal Society and committees on Bills in Parliament and, after 1771, meetings of the Society of Civil Engineers. He must have had the services of a clerk in London, but the drawings made there seem nearly always to have been sent to Austhorpe for copying.

His fees were normally charged on a daily basis, never as a percentage of the cost, and on three jobs (the Calder, Forth & Clyde and Ramsgate) he was paid an annual salary as chief engineer.

Smeaton's scientific interests developed at an early age. In the 1740s he made electrical experiments with his friend Benjamin Wilson and had already adopted astronomy as the hobby he was to follow throughout his life; to such good effect that he published no less than five papers on this subject in the *Philosophical Transactions (Phil. Trans.)*. But he started on his first, and indeed his most important, contribution to engineering science in 1752; research which culminated in the celebrated paper, read to the Royal Society in 1759, on "An Experimental Enquiry concerning the Natural Powers of Water and Wind ...". Written with a clarity matching the elegance of the experiments and the practical significance of the results, this paper was awarded the Copley Medal and established Smeaton's reputation within the Royal Society, of which he had been a Fellow for several years, as one of their most valued members.

The fame of the "Experimental Enquiry" tends to overshadow Smeaton's other scientific work. It was he, however, who discovered by simple chemical analysis the essential components of hydraulic limes; he made the first accurate measurements of head loss in the flow of water through pipes; he defined power in correct terms, and made the first systematic experiments on steam engines, and engine trials, using a correct definition of efficiency; he thoroughly understood the significance of hydraulic mean depth in open channel flow, applying his knowledge in practice by 1765, if not earlier, while in two further *Phil. Trans.* papers he threw light on the then still obscure subjects of the relation between work and kinetic energy, and the loss of energy in non-elastic impact.

Moreover, on his jobs he took opportunities of gauging streams, measuring the head loss through outfall sluices, determining the work actually performed by men or horses, for example in pumping water, and observing with a sharp eye and intellect such natural phenomena as the formation of bars at river mouths, the silting up of estuaries, the erosive power of rivers, and so on. Often his reports—though directed towards a very particular object, such as improving a harbour entrance—start with a discussion of the general principles involved, and it is from these that he derives the practical solution.

He was, as has been said, a philosopher among the engineers; but he was also an engineer among the philosophers. For it is critical to an understanding of Smeaton's character to realise that he was as much at home on a construction site, working on the drawing board or discussing a job with his clients or his resident engineer, as in making scientific experiments or reading a paper to the Royal Society. He was so able in all these things that his workmen, his fellow engineers and his scientific friends in their different ways all recognised his genius.

Here we begin to see how Smeaton played such a vital role in the civil engineering profession. This, in the early part of his career, was coming rather hesitantly into being in response to a rapidly increasing amount of work. For its full recognition by society and its own sense of vocation, however, someone was needed of his intellectual powers, practical skill and personal integrity, working as an engineer and commanding respect on site, in boardrooms, in Parliament and in the scientific world. These requirements he met more completely, by far, than any engineer before him.

Smeaton was well aware of what was going on in this respect. In relation to his largest job, the Forth & Clyde Canal, he drew up a pattern of management still familiar today, and defined with precision the functions of the chief engineer and the resident engineer, the latter term being introduced for the first time. This was in 1768; the same year, as it happens, in which he first described himself as a "civil engineer" on the title page of one of his printed reports. Thereafter he made several references to the profession of civil engineering, a phrase not previously encountered in the writings of Smeaton or anyone else; and from his letters it is clear that he considered himself, rightly, to be as much a professional man as any doctor or lawyer.

Further, Smeaton and some of his colleagues in 1771 founded the Society of Civil Engineers. A typical eighteenth-century dining club, it continues to flourish today and has for many years very properly been known as the Smeatonian Society. Not a learned or "chartered" body, the club nevertheless clearly demonstrated the strong feeling of association and common interest among the leading engineers of the day.

There is little room for doubt, then, that by the 1770s the civil engineering profession existed, if still in a state of infancy, and that it owed much to Smeaton's example and presence. These were certainly the views held 20 years later, by men such as Jessop, Mylne and Rennie who proceeded to honour the memory of their predecessor by publishing a collected edition of his reports: an act unique in the history of engineering.

No man is infallible, and in 40 years of practice it is not surprising that Smeaton made a few mistakes. The earliest of his steam engines, at New River Head, was a disappointment. But it led him to undertake research which proved highly beneficial in his later engines. When planning a radical new scheme for improving the drainage of Hatfield Chase he held back from taking his designs to their logical conclusion. He did so partly to minimise cost, and it is arguable that the clients, if presented with the full scheme, might have been deterred from even starting; nevertheless the fact remains that the successfully completed works owe almost as much to plans by the executive engineers as to those of Smeaton himself. Then of course there are cases where no-one could have foreseen all the consequences and some remedial measures were required. This happened at Aberdeen harbour. Smeaton's north pier admirably served its main purpose of reducing the bar at the entrance; but later he had to design a small deflecting pier to reduce wave action within the harbour. In a different category is the failure of Hexham Bridge. This was destroyed by an exceptional flood in the River Tyne 2 years after completion, and there is no doubt that Smeaton misjudged the magnitude of a possible flood at this site, and its effect on the foundations. These examples of failures or partial failures simply emphasise the problems inherent in engineering. The bridge at Hexham was not the first, and it was by no means the last, to collapse.

Civil engineering has to be both an art and a science, and the engineer's responsibility is to develop both aspects to the limit of his powers in order to fulfil the clients' requirements as safely and economically as possible. Smeaton steadfastly based his practice on this principle, to the immense benefit of his country and profession.

No biography of John Smeaton has been published since the

account given by Samuel Smiles in *Lives of the Engineers* in 1861. This fact reflects not a lack of interest in the subject but rather the difficulty of dealing adequately with a career covering such wide and varied fields of activity. The present book is therefore a collaboration. It is based on research mostly carried out during the past 10 years and chiefly by the authors of the following chapters.

Imperial College   A. W. SKEMPTON

I
John Smeaton
TREVOR TURNER AND A. W. SKEMPTON

Smeaton was born on 8th June, 1724 at Austhorpe Lodge in the parish of Whitkirk, 4 miles east of Leeds. His father, William Smeaton (1684–1749), had a practice as an attorney in Leeds and the house, built by John's grandfather, was part of a modest estate of some 6 acres mostly rented, presumably, to farmers.

The family originated in York where Smeaton's great-grandfather, John, was a well-known watchmaker and freeman of the city. His grandfather, too, was named John and it was he who left York, set up in business in Leeds and eventually prospered to the extent that he could finance the building of Austhorpe Lodge in 1698.

William Smeaton had married Mary Stones from Beal, a hamlet on the southern bank of the River Aire, in 1722. John was their eldest child, followed by a brother William in 1728 and a sister Hannah in 1732; but William died at the age of 4, so John must have led a rather lonely pre-school childhood in a quiet country house and from all accounts he was a serious-minded little boy.

When 10 years old he went to Leeds Grammar School and stayed until he was 16. Already he had a home workshop, and on leaving school devoted himself wholeheartedly to mechanical pursuits. His distant cousin John Holmes has this to say:

"In the year 1742 [when Smeaton was 18], I spent a month at his father's house, and being intended myself for a mechanical employment, and a few years younger than he was, I could not but view his works with astonishment; he forged his iron and steel, and melted his metal; he had tools of every sort. . . . He had made a Lathe, by which he cut a perpetual screw in brass, a thing little known at that day, and which I believe was the invention of Mr Henry Hindley, of York. . . . Mr Hindley was a man of the most communicative disposition, a great lover of Mechanics, and of the most fertile genius. Mr Smeaton soon became acquainted with him, and they spent many a night at Mr Hindley's house till day light, conversing on those subjects."

This momentous meeting with Henry Hindley, a clock- and instrument-maker of genius, took place, as Smeaton records, in the autumn of 1741. Despite the difference in age between them Hindley treated him as a friend and practically as a colleague from the start; thus demonstrating clearly for the first time the feeling of confidence and respect which Smeaton generated among all who knew him. Great minds think alike, it is said, and they recognise one another very quickly. This explains why, as an instrument-maker of apparently no remarkable distinction, Smeaton was elected FRS when only 28 years old and why, with little engineering experience, 3 years later, he was selected without hesitation as the man most suitable to undertake the daunting work of rebuilding the Eddystone Lighthouse.

However, this is to anticipate our story. Smeaton's father could only have viewed the mechanical proclivities of his offspring with some alarm. His family was slowly improving its social position and his own son was apparently turning full circle by consorting with tradesmen and showing every sign of becoming one himself. The chance of an 18-year-old obtaining an apprenticeship was slim, and the living eventually to be made was nothing compared to that of an attorney.

In these circumstances Smeaton was sent to London in the autumn of 1742 to receive a legal education. That he returned home in the summer of 1744 does not mean that his time had been entirely wasted, for apart from studying law books he made, or renewed, his acquaintance with Benjamin Wilson. Three years older than Smeaton, he too had gone from Leeds to London to become a lawyer. He obtained a clerkship in Doctors Commons but was soon to abandon his career to become a notable experimentalist in electricity and a successful portrait painter, and it was probably due to him that Smeaton was introduced to Watson, Gowin Knight, and other members of the Royal Society who widened his horizons in natural philosophy.

On returning to Yorkshire Smeaton had to wait 2 months for his books and papers to reach him at Austhorpe (they came by sea) and from a letter to Wilson written in October we see that he was settling down to a 3- or 4-year programme of building up a set of mathematical instruments; the first intimation that Smeaton was thinking, doubtless inspired by Hindley, of becoming a professional instrument-maker.

Part of his time at Austhorpe was spent in making apparatus for Wilson to use in his electrical experiments, some of which were carried out at Austhorpe in 1745. It was in these that Smeaton investigated the "maximum effect" when several variables were present. He was to use the technique with great success in his future investigations into water, wind and steam power.

Much of his correspondence with Wilson concerned astronomy, an interest that stayed with him for the rest of his life, and he was busy making a telescope. By 1747 he could tell Wilson that he was counted quite an artist at grinding and polishing lenses. He was also spending 3 days a week in Leeds having French lessons; his Latin was already fairly good from schooldays, but French was essential as well for science as for engineering.

By 1747 he had made the acquaintance of a young lady in Leeds (could this explain the frequency of the French lessons?) to whom he eventually proposed marriage. We first hear of her in a letter to Wilson, where Smeaton says he hopes to be in London that winter:

"I have three powerful reasons to draw me hither: in the first place (and I hope you'l allow me to put that in the front) I believe my favourite (Oh she's a charming Girl, but I hope you'l excuse these wild Digressions for as you know folks in Love are never like other folks) will go to London this winter; in the second place I want badly to see what you and the Philosophical World are a doing; and lastly I hope I shall have some small Business there."

After a long dissertation on telescopes, astronomy, and a paper that Wilson is planning to publish, the letter resumes:

"She is your townswoman and the daughter of a thriving Tradesman . . . and withall a friend of Philosophy and the Mathematicks, but as he has several Children besides, and for that reason she is something inferior to me in point of fortune, you may be sure that this circumstance renders her not quite so agreeable, as she otherwise would be, to my father and mother. As to herself she is neither a Beauty nor a Witt, but yet above the Medium in both. She's a young lady of excellent sence prudence and virtue and such a peculiar sweetness of temper and behaviour as render her beloved to all who know her . . . and has charmed my very Soul from me. Prithee now my Friend in your turn tell me if I be not going mad; and indulge this piece of Frenzy that I have plagued you with."

Three weeks later things were not going well:

9

"I am now [he writes to Wilson] in a likely way to be as great a Philosopher as yourself, tho I must confess it is sorely against my will; my Father and Mother show themselves extremely adverse to my Love affair . . . my dear Girl is now in London, and you may believe me my heart is there too. When she went up, I set her as far as Ferrybridge where she took coach, but the next morning my mother came into my bedchamber before I was awake and discharged me from ever writing a line to her upon pain of being turned out of Doors and forfeiting Austhorpe Estate. I am at my witts end what to do . . . We ought all of us to be philosophers, but I don't know that we should be all of the Stoical Sort."

Eventually Smeaton's parents relented and agreed to the marriage if he went to live in London; but then Miss Banks' father proved reluctant to have her live at a distance. Faced with this impasse Smeaton had no alternative but to withdraw his offer of marriage. A rather serious row developed and he found himself unpopular with his friends. He considered entering a university but Gowin Knight, to whom he turned for advice, dissuaded him from such a course and instead apparently advised him to come to London and set up as an instrument-maker.

Philosophical instrument-maker, 1748–52

So with his parents' blessing, at last, Smeaton set off for London in 1748. His first success was an improved vacuum pump or, as it was known at the time, an air pump. This he completed in 1749 and, though a year or two later he improved it still further, the original design gave rarefactions several times better than anyone else achieved in comparative trials. It was used by Wilson, Watson and other experimenters in studying electrical discharges at high vacuum.

To help him, Hindley in 1748 sent one of his equatorial telescopes to London for sale and wrote (in November of that year) a long account of his method of dividing, or graduation, of instruments. In this early period Smeaton assisted Dr Knight in the development of a mariner's compass and presented an account of it to the Royal Society in July 1750. He made several of these compasses and accompanied Knight on sea trials in HMS *Fortune* in 1751, presumably to gain approval of the Navy Board, which was finally obtained, and the compass became standard in the Royal Navy.

During the voyage of the *Fortune* to Kingston-upon-Hull, Smeaton took the opportunity of carrying out trials of a ship's log consisting of a brass spinner driving a counter mounted on the taffrail. In fact it was almost identical with commercial models still available today, but did not perform very well in heavy seas and he did not pursue further development. However his workshop was kept busy; by 1751 he was employing three craftsmen and in December of that year moved from Great Turnstile, off Holborn, to larger quarters nearby in Furnival Inn Court. It was there in 1752 that he began his classic experiments on the power of water and wind. Also at this time he completed a telescope for John Ellicott and a precision lathe for William Mathews, to mention but two of his clients.

Successful though he was in this activity, there is no question that Smeaton could rank with the great instrument-makers of the day. Rather he was valued for the power and clarity of his intellect, and it was these qualities which led to his candidature for Fellowship of the Royal Society. The proposal form, dated 14th December, 1752, and submitted by Lord Charles Cavendish, reads as follows:

> "Mr John Smeaton maker of Philosophical Instruments, a Gentleman well known to the Society for his great skill in the theory and practice of Mechanicks . . . being very desirous of the Honour of being elected a Fellow of the Royal Society: we do therefore, from our personal aquaintance, recommend him as duly qualified to become a useful member of this Society; both on account of his abilities in Mechanics, as also in being well versed in the knowledge of the mathematicks and natural Philosophy."

Supported by William Watson, John Ellicott, Gowin Knight and James Short, among others, Smeaton was duly elected on 15th March, 1753.

Engineering career, 1753–59
His experiments on water and wind, now nearing completion, may be regarded as a first step towards engineering. The invention of a new form of pulley tackle in 1752 was another, and indeed so early as 1748 he submitted, on his own initiative, a design for a cofferdam to be used in repairing one of the piers of Westminster Bridge (see Chapter VII). By 1753, however, he had decided to make his career in engineering or "engineery" as he usually preferred to call it. Here he probably realised there were wider possibilities and more scope for his particular abilities.

How he obtained his first commission, to design a watermill at Halton in Lancashire, is not known. In fact the whole affair is rather surprising. Without previous experience as a millwright it is remarkable that he could have been asked to undertake the job. Moreover he had, so far as we are aware, no connections with Lancashire. Nor had he even been in Yorkshire for several years. His father having died in 1749, it seems that his mother and sister came to live with or near him in Holborn, and Austhorpe Lodge remained closed until after his mother died in 1759.

Nevertheless his first watermill was certainly built at Halton in 1753 and a second, at Wakefield for Sir Lionel Pilkington, in 1754. A windmill, also at Wakefield, followed next year for a Mr Roodhouse and possibly there had been two somewhat earlier windmills at Barking and Nine Elms.

Also dating from 1753–54 are the first of Smeaton's designs for masonry bridges, in this case for the projected Blackfriars Bridge. In May 1754 he read a paper to the Royal Society on some experiments, using an apparatus of his own design, on the thermal expansion of a wide range of materials. Then, in September 1754, we find him in Scotland drawing up a very logical scheme for draining a large tract of peat land known as Lochar Moss, near Dumfries. As we learn from a letter to Wilson, written from Dumfries just before completing the Lochar report, he was about to go to Hopetoun House, near Edinburgh, for several days. That Smeaton had now headed his career in a different direction is clear from the tenor of this letter, which goes on to set out the principles on which his future was to be based:

> "I must freely say, that as to any little success that I have met with I plainly see it all, some how or another, connected; one thing well done recommends another: and if I am likely to expect any future success, I can only build it on this principle, which I always had and intend steadily to pursue: that whether I gain more or less never to meddle with any Business whether great or small, without Endeavouring to bring it to the utmost perfection in my Power; and to give my employers satisfaction. This being the case, I please all I have to deal with, who together with the work itself involuntarily, undesignedly, and may be unknowingly, are the best recommenders to future Business."

To his credit he never, in the whole of his professional life, wavered from the tenets just enunciated.

Already well read in science, Smeaton had also studied some of the famous Dutch mill books and Belidor's great work, *Architecture Hydraulique*, which gives by far the most comprehensive view of civil engineering as practised in the early to mid-eighteenth century. He now decided to obtain first-hand knowledge of Continental engineering by making a trip to the Low Countries. On Sunday 15th June, 1755, he sailed from London and arrived in Dunkirk on the Tuesday, where he inspected a sluice which was having to be rebuilt because of faulty foundations. This was to be used to deepen the harbour by using water, stored in a canal, to carry away the mud and sand. He saw other schemes of a like kind during his visit, and it was a method he approved of very much and recommended frequently in his subsequent career. On his first day in France he also remarked on an inverted syphon used to carry the water of one channel under the bed of another. This appears to have been the first inverted syphon or "fox" he had seen, but he was to use the idea later in some of his land-drainage schemes.

On his journey, which lasted 5 weeks, he visited many of the places of engineering interest in what is now Belgium and Holland. Much of his travelling was by boat, which gave him ample opportunity to inspect most of the civil engineering works on a waterway system. Some of the larger works he was already familiar with from his reading of Belidor, and it is clear from his comments that he was quite up to date with current practice. Again, when he visited a mill, whatever its purpose, he shows himself to be perfectly familiar with the state of the art in England.

He took the opportunity of calling on Professor Musschenbroek in Leyden, one of the most distinguished scientists in Holland and an early investigator into the strength of materials. They spent a pleasant hour together and there is in Leyden Museum a mariners' compass by Smeaton which he probably gave, or later sent, to the professor.

After having difficulty in finding a ship to return to England he eventually found one at Schiedam. Setting sail early on the morning of Sunday 13th July, the ship encountered contrary winds and it was Tuesday afternoon before the ship's master got her over the bar at the mouth of the River Maas. By Friday they were off the Yorkshire coast, where Smeaton was hoping to disembark at Scarborough, but the wind made it impossible to get ashore and they had to continue to Blyth.

From Blyth he set forward directly to Edinburgh where he had some undisclosed business, perhaps again with Lord Hopetoun. In September 1755 he was still in Scotland, surveying the state of the River Clyde below Glasgow, at the time a shallow, shoaly river almost hopeless for navigation by any but the smallest ships. Also in 1755 he reported on fen drainage in the manor of Haldenby, part of Adlingfleet Level near the confluence of the Ouse and the Trent.

Early in 1756 Smeaton was in Northumberland designing a bridge at Hexham for Sir Walter Blackett. This design was not adopted;

instead the job went to John Gott. Meanwhile an event occurred in December 1755 which was to set him on the path to the top of the profession; it was the destruction of the lighthouse on the Eddystone Rocks.

Smeaton, writing in his *Narrative of the Building . . . of the Edystone Lighthouse*, records the reply of Lord Macclesfield, President of the Royal Society, to the enquiry from Robert Weston, the major shareholder in the lighthouse, for a proper person to take charge of the rebuilding:

> "Lord Macclesfield told him, that there was one of their Body whom he could venture to recommend to the business . . . [who] for about three years past . . . had wholly applied himself to such branches of mechanics, as he [Mr Weston] appeared to want; that he was then somewhere in Scotland, or in the north of England, doing business in that line: that what he had to say further of him was, his never having know him to undertake anything, but what he completed to the satisfaction of those who employed him; and that Mr Weston might rely on it, when the business was stated to him, he would not undertake it, unless he clearly saw himself capable of performing it."

That Smeaton did undertake this great work to the entire satisfaction of all concerned is now enshrined in our engineering heritage.

He returned to London on 23rd February, 1756, and had discussions with Mr Weston. The weather not permitting a visit to the site, he took the opportunity of preparing a second design and estimate for Blackfriars Bridge. These formed the basis of a successful application to Parliament by the Corporation of London for the necessary Act. Then, in April, Smeaton surveyed the Eddystone rock, visited various stone quarries in May, came back to London to make the designs and models demonstrating the methods of construction proposed, which were approved, and returned to Plymouth on 23rd July to start work; but this time as a married man.

For Smeaton had fallen in love again; the lady being Miss Ann Jenkinson, youngest daughter of James and Faith Jenkinson of York. Her father, who died in 1742, was a merchant tailor and freeman of the city. The families were already connected as Ann's eldest sister Sarah had married Joseph Broadbent, the son of Smeaton's aunt and therefore his first cousin. When they became engaged we do not know, but the Eddystone job probably provided a welcome sense of security, after what must have been a couple of lean years, and the marriage took place at St George's, Hanover Square, on 7th June, 1756.

The 4 years 1756–59 were largely devoted to the Eddystone, and the story of that work is given in Chapter IV. The winter months, however, when storms prevented landings on the rock, gave opportunities for other undertakings and so in November 1757 he was surveying and drawing up a scheme for making the River Calder navigable from Wakefield to Salter Hebble near Halifax; in April 1758 he reported on Dysart Harbour in Scotland, and also gave evidence in the House of Commons on the Calder Navigation Bill—the first of many appearances before parliamentary committees; in December of that year he reported again on the River Clyde; early in 1759 he was in the North East, looking at Seaton and Cullercoats harbours and the problem of rendering the River Wear navigable to Durham. In March and April he gave evidence to Parliament on this scheme, as also on the Clyde proposals.

Nor did Smeaton neglect his scientific interests. Among further papers to the Royal Society was an account of the damage by lightning to Lostwithiel church in Cornwall. These observations led to the Eddystone Lighthouse being one of the earliest structures protected by a lightning conductor. Another paper concerned the variation in weather conditions between the Eddystone and Plymouth, which may have led to the construction of his first hygrometer; an instrument that he improved upon some years later. One of these later models was kept in the Royal Society's rooms for many years, and the readings of another one, kept at home at Austhorpe, were occasionally quoted in the Leeds papers. It was while working on the Eddystone job that Smeaton also began his research into cements and hydraulic limes, although the results were not to be published until many years afterwards.

But the chef-d'oeuvre of this period was the preparation and presentation of his paper on "An Experimental Enquiry concerning the Natural Powers of Water and Wind to turn Mills, and other Machines, depending on a circular Motion". Based chiefly on the experiments made in 1752–53, and partly on practical experience with mills in the next 3 years, this is one of the greatest contributions to engineering science made in the eighteenth century.

The paper was read at five evening meetings of the Royal Society in May and June 1759, during a short return to London from Plymouth. Immediately afterwards Smeaton resumed work on the Eddystone, which was now nearing completion. The last stone bears the date 24th August, 1759 and the light was permanently exhibited from 16th October in that year. He then prepared revised plans for the Blackfriars Bridge, an open competition for the design of which had been advertised and was, a few weeks later, won not by Smeaton but by the young Robert Mylne. This disappointment, however, received more than adequate compensation in the award, on 22nd November, of the Copley Medal for his Experimental Enquiry paper; an event celebrated by his dining at the Royal Society Club that evening.

This marks the end of the first part of Smeaton's engineering career. He had built at least three mills; reported on two land-drainage schemes, a harbour project, two bridges and three river navigations one of which, the Calder, was about to be constructed; he had received the highest award in England for original research; and had completed what was immediately recognised to be a work of quite outstanding importance. Visitors flocked to see the model of the Eddystone which, he proudly remarks, was shown and explained to them by Mrs Smeaton.

John and Ann Smeaton had lost their first child, Hannah, who was born in December 1757; and John's mother died in London in October 1759. Austhorpe Lodge had probably been deserted for most of the time after his father's death 10 years earlier and needed a great deal of renovation. It was to this house that he brought his wife and baby daughter Ann whose baptism, at St Andrew's church, Holborn, took place in May 1759 during Smeaton's visit from Plymouth to read the paper to the Royal Society. Just when they moved to Austhorpe is not clear; perhaps it was in the summer of 1760. By that time work was well under way on the Calder Navigation, and Smeaton himself had come to Yorkshire some months earlier to get the job started. It was also towards the end of 1759 that William Jessop, then a boy of 14 (whose father, Josias Jessop, had been in charge of the Eddystone operations) joined Smeaton as a pupil.

Engineering career, 1760–64
Had we not to hand ample documentary evidence it would be difficult to believe that one man, working alone or with a single assistant, could possibly have investigated and reported on so many projects of such diverse types, or that he could have been responsible for the design of so many bridges, mills, harbours, river and canal navigations, steam engines, and fen-drainage schemes. Merely to list Smeaton's professional papers is a hopeless task in a single chapter; he wrote about 200 reports and produced over 1,000 drawings. Very fortunately, most of his reports written after 1760 were published (after his death) in three large volumes and practically all his drawings have survived intact; they are in the Royal Society library and have been

catalogued. The history of these and other Smeaton papers, and of the reports printed in his lifetime, is given in Chapter XI. As for the works carried out in accordance with his plans, a list is given in Appendix III. It is possibly not quite complete, but even so runs to over 100 items.

To trace the whole of Smeaton's career cannot therefore be attempted here. We shall continue the chronological sketch up to 1764; then mention only some of the highlights to 1780, and describe in a little more detail the period 1781–83 which is partly covered by three surviving diaries. The last 9 years of his life fall into a rather different pattern, and are considered briefly in the final section of this chapter.

Starting in 1760, then, the Calder Navigation was Smeaton's main concern. He made all the necessary drawings for locks, weirs, flood gates and so on. For the first 18 months Joseph Nickalls was resident engineer, but Smeaton had to make frequent site visits during critical stages of the work, and from the autumn of 1761 he was in full charge of construction with two superintendents of carpentry and masonry. This state of affairs continued until the end of 1764, by which time the navigation had been opened from Wakefield to Brighouse: a distance of 18 miles with seventeen locks on the most difficult river navigation yet attempted in England or, perhaps, anywhere else.

However there were periods in which his presence on site was not required, when he could carry on his work as a consulting engineer. In August 1760 he first made the acquaintance of John Grundy, having been called in to give a second opinion on his scheme for the Louth Canal; in October he visited Scotland, again going to Dumfries and Glasgow; in November he met James Brindley in connection with proposals for what was to become the Trent & Mersey Canal. Reports on these jobs followed in due course. Also in 1760 Smeaton produced designs for a masonry bridge at Stockton on Tees, a fulling mill at Colchester and a copper mill at Hounslow Heath, and published an interesting pamphlet on his design for Blackfriars Bridge.

The next year, 1761, seems to have been a particularly busy one on the Calder, but some further mills were designed and he was again associated with Grundy, this time in planning major improvements in the navigation of the River Witham from Boston up to Lincoln and in drainage of the adjacent low grounds.

By the end of 1762 the Calder works had reached about 12 miles from Wakefield. During this year Smeaton attended Parliament on the Bills for Stockton Bridge and the Bridgewater Canal, designed a mill at Stratford, in Essex, and made visits to, and reported on, Christchurch harbour, the River Chelmer, the drainage of Potteric Carr (near Doncaster) and the Fossdyke Navigation in Lincolnshire.

Early in 1763 he received an urgent call to advise on means to secure the foundations of London Bridge; then came a visit to Rye harbour, followed in the summer by a very important trip to the north result-ing in designs for bridges at Coldstream and Perth and the first plans for the great Forth & Clyde Canal; and in the autumn he was examin-ing proposals for fen drainage in Holderness (east Yorkshire) yet again in association with his friend John Grundy.

Work was continuing in 1764 on the Calder where for the past 2 years the faithful John Gwyn and Matthias Scott had been the two superintendents. Both of them, after their experience on the Calder, were to serve Smeaton as resident engineers on various jobs and, indeed, Gwyn remained as Smeaton's principal site engineer for the rest of his life. From 1765 he worked successively on Perth Bridge, Portpatrick harbour, Aberdeen harbour, Cromarty harbour, Hull North Bridge, and Ramsgate harbour; a truly wonderful record and one that is notable for the friendship existing between Smeaton and Gwyn.

To complete the story of 1764: the Calder Navigation reached Brighouse, as already mentioned; long reports were written on the Forth & Clyde project, on improvements of the southern part of Hat-field Chase and Misterton Soss (later to play a vital role in Jessop's drainage of Gringley Carrs), and on a new scheme for draining Adlingfleet. The latter involved a large map surveyed by Charles Tate, with levels taken by Smeaton himself. Also in 1764 he prepared extremely detailed specifications and estimates for the outfall sluice of Holderness Drainage, as well as writing several short reports and designing the waterwheels and machinery for Kilnhurst forge, near Rotherham.

Meanwhile at home Mrs Smeaton had been busy putting the house in good order and looking after the family, now increased by the arrival of Mary, born in 1761, and about to be further increased by the birth of Hannah, who was baptised at Whitkirk in January 1765. Ann Smeaton's elder sister, Miss Mary Jenkinson, was living at Austhorpe and of course so was young Billy Jessop, now a pupil of 5 years' ex-perience, aged 19, and capable of assisting Smeaton with drawing, levelling and so on.

Billy's father having died in 1760, his mother found difficulty in paying for his board and lodging. On learning of her plight, that good

Fig. 1.   Austhorpe Lodge (engraving by James Cooper after sketches by Percival Skelton and Thomas Sutcliffe: Smiles' Lives of the Engineers, *Vol. 2)*

man Robert Weston wrote to Smeaton saying "I chuse to make myself the Staff of his Support", and he made the necessary payments until Jessop completed his apprenticeship in 1767.

It may seem odd that Smeaton could not afford to waive whatever sum was involved. However, the fact is that the family found themselves in somewhat straitened circumstances. Renovations at Austhorpe appear to have been expensive, and included the building of Smeaton's workshop and office (Fig. 1); the Calder salary was fairly generous but he was still charging the usual consulting engineer's fee of 1 guinea a day and, even so, experiencing long (in some cases unforgivably long) delays in getting his fees paid. To economise, he gave up his quarters at Furnival Inn Court, staying while on visits to London with John Holmes in the Strand.

In short, it had become desirable for Smeaton to find an extra source of income and, from his experience on the Calder, he was averse to taking another job involving constant supervision of site work and the distracting arguments (however necessary) with committee members, contractors and suppliers of materials.

Fortunately at this time one of the receiverships of the Greenwich

Hospital Derwentwater Estates in Durham and Northumberland fell vacant. In the face of stiff competition for such a congenial post he succeeded, with the support of the Earl of Egmont and Robert Weston, in obtaining the appointment, the date being 30th December, 1764. The annual salary was around £400–500 and the duties were not onerous. Nicholas Walton, the other Receiver, lived at Farnacres near Gateshead and saw to the detailed running of the very large estates, while Smeaton would be required only to attend, for about a month each time, the twice-yearly rent collections which involved travelling from Berwick on Tweed in the north to Keswick in the west and to Hartlepool in the east. Despite the unequal responsibilities he and Walton became great friends and Smeaton's advice on engineering matters helped to improve many of the watermills and other works on the hospital's estates, the lead-mine drainage adit known as Nent Force Level being a notable example.

As things turned out the Greenwich appointment came in the nick of time; for just a month afterwards, following a radical change of membership on the Calder committee, Smeaton lost his job as engineer to the navigation. He came back later, as related in Chapter V, and successfully completed the whole scheme. As a consultant, however—and indeed for the rest of his career, from 1765, he held only two salaried engineering appointments: on the Forth & Clyde Canal and, much later, on Ramsgate harbour.

Many of Smeaton's private letters of 1764 have survived. Extracts from four of them are given below.

The first, written on 27th February to John Holmes, is mostly about financial affairs including the selling of some Stock, probably to pay for the building of the office and workshop at Austhorpe, and continues:

"I begin to think (and I may honestly say to hope) that I shall not see London this Spring; but if it should take place will give you all the notice I can as I mean to quarter myself upon you under the conditions you stipulate viz. to let me do as I please. You will say *hope* in the place I putt it is an unkind word, but stop a little, when I do come I should chuse to be a little less in a hurry than I must be at this Season . . .

"Last week we had very pleasant mild weather and were in hopes that the incessant Storms which have beset us were at last exhausted, but this Day the Surface of the Earth is covered with Snow and once more puts on the hoary face of Winter. I won't tell you how well we wish you and Yours and how glad we are to hear of the welfare of our Friends; for as I expect a Female pen will be employed I will not take this subject out of her hands, by whom it is likely to be handled in a superior manner. I am Dear Coz.

Yours most sincerely, J. Smeaton.

"P.S. dont make any more Apology's about being in a hurry, for I always know you are so; and I have been so for several years; but hope to see the time when I have leisure to mend my pen before I write."

The second letter, dated 17th April, chides Benjamin Wilson for the long delay in sending several pictures to Austhorpe from London; one is a portrait of Smeaton painted in 1759. They finally arrived in July:

"Dear Friend. That we begin to condemn you is most certain, my wife says she is out of all Patience with you, her house having been putt to right and everything in its' place for almost a twelve month the pictures excepted. It happens very lucky for you that you happened to get the first word; for I believe this very post would have born a letter to you, if I had not received one, consider what a World of Scolding it has saved: yet you must permit me to refresh your memory with matter of fact: 'tis now almost a twelve month since I wrote desiring you to send the pictures with all possible speed; and receiving no answer . . . what could we think? but that you had forgot your rusticated Friends. I should have wrote sometime ago but that I was in doubt whether I might not see you in London . . . Pray how does Dr Knight? I hear he has been in an ill state of health this Winter past. [Then follow some news of the Calder works, a note on a solar eclipse and an invitation to stay at any time at Austhorpe.] My Wife joins me in respects to you & enquiring Friends & I am, Dear Sir, your most humble Serv! J. Smeaton."

The next letter, dated 26th April, is to Langley Edwards, engineer in charge of the Witham and now building the Grand Sluice at Boston.

"Dear Sir. It gives me great pleasure that my recommendation of Stone for the Grand Sluice gives Satisfaction. I fancy the last Winter will make the Country believe it is a necessary work; from what you describe I can readily conceive your Situation last Winter, and indeed upon the falling of the last great Snow I gave over expecting you [at Austhorpe] and found it highly necessary to be upon my Guard at home, having 3 times in the Compass of 5 Days had the Water over the top of the Lock Walls at Wakefield which are 14 feet above common Water, and the Water going in a sheet of 7 feet over the Dam heads of 200 ft long, and 8 feet over those of 150 ft besides what made its way over the Surface of the Meadows . . . however the snow went away in the mildest manner imaginable; and I think the damage upon the whole Winter has been less than we have ever had since we have had any part open . . . We are now open to Coopers

Bridge, that is 14 Miles and includes 13 Locks; we propose opening 4 Miles which includes 4 Locks more up to Brighouse, and then there will remain 4 Miles including 4 Locks now in hand which we propose, God willing, to open about this time twelve months . . . It will give me great pleasure to hear how you go on . . . Dear Sir. Your most humble Serv! J. Smeaton. *P.S.* the progress you mention in the spadework surprizes me."

The fourth letter, dated 4th June, was written to John Grundy after hearing of his wife's death:

"Dear Friend. Your letter of the 10th ult gave my Wife and me great concern; and we most truly and sincerely, sympathize with you; when I opened your Letter I ceased wondering at your long silence, which much too well accounted for it. My Wife fully intended accompanying me to Spalding as mentioned in my last and nothing could have prevented her but the decrees of Providence which frequently interfere and prevent our Schemes of Pleasure in order to oblige us to think humbly of ourselves, and to curb the idea that we are apt to entertain of our own Power, will and pleasure . . . however thank God she is now better; I therefore leave it to your determination whether you will accept of a Visit from me alone this Summer, or stay till my Wife can accompany me to wait upon Miss Grundy.

"About this time twelve months . . . I hope we shall have completed the Calder, and then I propose to commence Master of my own time; at present tho' we are advancing with proper Speed, yet there is always some point of difficulty that needs particular attention; and when not that, the Trustees always think the Business neglected if I am not there once a week . . . The month of May I am sensible is already elapsed, but the incessant troubles of the Winter so nearly exhausted my time, that I have Capital Business now in my office, that was ordered in August last, which with some other outstanding since Christmas I must dispatch before I set forward. [Then follow details about arrangements to meet on the Holderness Drainage job at Beverley and a complaint about the difficulty of getting fees paid.] . . . Since my last my two Girls have been inoculated and thank God have got well over the same. My Wife joins with me in sincerest Compliments to you and Miss Grundy & I am, Dear Sir, Your most humble Serv! J. Smeaton."

In this letter Smeaton is delicately referring to his wife's pregnancy. "Miss Grundy" is Grundy's sister Polly.

The years 1765–83

During the next 18 years Smeaton was engaged as a consulting engineer to an extent which had no precedent in Britain. This arose partly from his own pre-eminence, but also from the rapid expansion in the number and scale of public and industrial works throughout the country.

It would be an exaggeration to say that civil engineering existed as a profession before 1760. Works of a civil engineering nature had obviously been undertaken, even if not yet described by that term, and there were men such as William Lellam, Charles Labelye and John Grundy who had worked as professional engineers; but they were isolated individuals, and depended on a salaried position from which base they carried out occasional "extramural" consulting. There were also some engineer–contractors, of whom John Perry is an example. They, too, wrote reports from time to time but made their somewhat hazardous living from design-and-build "package deal" jobs. Bridges, in particular, were often built in this way, and usually by masons who would not have laid claim to the title "engineer".

By contrast, in the 1770s a profession of civil engineering had come into being. By the end of that decade at least half a dozen men were well-known consulting engineers and a number of others had regular employment in charge of works; there were scores of resident engineers and land surveyors engaged on canals, fen drainage, bridges and harbours; contractors were emerging from the older gang-piecework system; and the pace of industrial development demanded an ever-increasing number of mills, iron-works, coal mines and other enterprises requiring expert designs for watermills, steam engines and machinery.

Nothing symbolises the emergence of a profession more neatly than the formation of the Society of Civil Engineers in 1771. In true eighteenth-century style this was a dining club, and as such exists to the present day, but it provided (and still provides) an opportunity for engineers to meet one another in a friendly atmosphere to discuss their work and all manner of topics. As Mylne, one of the founder-members, said: "Conversation, argument and a social communication of ideas and knowledge ... were, at the same time, the amusement and the business of the meetings."

The first of these meetings was held on 15th March, 1771, at the "Kings Head", Holborn, when the following resolution was passed:

"Agreed that the Civil Engineers of this Kingdom do form themselves into a Society consisting of a President a Vice President, Treasurer and Secretary and other Members who shall meet once a fortnight ... at seven o'clock from Christmas or so soon as any of the country Members come to Town ... to the end of the sitting of the Parliament."

Smeaton of course was present, and for the next 20 years attended as frequently as anybody. In his diaries he usually refers to the Society as the "Engineers Club". Some years after his death it began to be called the "Smeatonian Society", or simply the "Smeatonians", and this name has stuck ever since. The society has in its possession the very fine portrait of Smeaton by Romney (see Appendix II).

Most of the leading figures in the profession, during the past 200 years, have been Smeatonians. It is interesting to mention some of the members who joined the club in its first 3 years:

Thomas Yeoman (c. 1708–81) FRS, the first President of the Society; consultant to several canals and river navigations, engineer in charge of the River Lee works, and for many years joint chairman of the Society of Arts committee on mechanics.

John Grundy (1719–83), of whom we have spoken as a colleague and personal friend of Smeaton; he succeeded his father in 1748 as engineer to the Deeping Fen Proprietors and started his own practice as a civil engineer a few years before that date.

Robert Mylne (1733–1811) FRS, distinguished as the engineer of Blackfriars Bridge, recently appointed engineer to the New River Company, and a leading consultant; also an architect of exceptional talent. Treasurer of the Society 1791–1811.

Joseph Nickalls (c. 1725–93), a millwright by training, built Stratford mill and the waterwheel at London Bridge to Smeaton's design; but he had been resident engineer on the Calder & Hebble Navigation and in 1771 was appointed engineer to the Thames Commissioners. President of the Society 1783–92.

John Golborne (c. 1724–83), engineer to the River Dee Company, consultant to the North Level of the Fens and the River Clyde where work carried out to his plans proved very successful.

Robert Whitworth (1734–99), chief assistant to James Brindley for whom he did much of the surveying and planning for the Coventry, Birmingham and Oxford Canals; he became the most able canal engineer of the late eighteenth century.

Hugh Henshall (c. 1734–1816), resident engineer on the Trent & Mersey Canal; after Brindley's death in 1772 he completed this great work and also the Chesterfield Canal.

John Smith (died c. 1783), engineer–contractor for the Nene Navigation and resident engineer on Smeaton's River Ure works.

Thomas Hogard (died 1783), succeeded Grundy as engineer of Deeping

Fen in 1764; commissioner of several fen drainage schemes in Lincolnshire.

Langley Edwards (died 1774), joint author with Grundy and Smeaton of the Witham report and engineer in charge of the works there, also engineer for the Black Sluice drainage scheme in south Lincolnshire.

John Gott (1720–93), designer and/or builder of several notable arch bridges, Surveyor to the West Riding, and resident engineer on the Aire & Calder Navigation.

John Longbothom (died 1801), engineer of the Leeds & Liverpool Canal.

William Jessop (1745–1814), joined the Society in 1773 a year after setting up on his own as a consulting engineer. After Smeaton's temporary retirement in 1784 Jessop became the most eminent practising civil engineer in England, a position he later shared with Rennie and still later with Telford.

Some of these men have now been forgotten by all except keen students of engineering history, but they and their immediate successors (the membership soon rose to about twenty), and a few others who for some reason never joined the Society, formed the civil engineering profession in its early days. Smeaton was the acknowledged leading spirit in the club. John Holmes, himself a member, writing just after Smeaton's death, said:

> "I have spent many evenings with him in the last twenty years, in a Society of Civil Engineers, which he was one of the first to promote, and where he was always heard with great attention and held in particular esteem."

As for any question whether or not Smeaton regarded himself as a professional man and practising within a profession, the answer can be given very simply: he did so, explicitly and with conviction. The evidence, from his own writings, is set out in Chapter X. It is also to be noted that the Eddystone Lighthouse has become the very symbol of civil engineering in Britain, as a representation of Smeaton's masterpiece appears in the crest of the armorial bearings of the Institution of Civil Engineers.

Thus we can picture Smeaton travelling around the country to various sites, working on his reports and scientific investigations, making designs for, and advising on, all kinds of projects, and giving evidence to parliamentary committees; proud to call himself an engineer, conscious of his position in the profession and accepted, as an engineer, in the highest scientific circles of the day. He was a man who met as equals Joseph Priestley and Henry Cavendish, who proposed James Watt for Fellowship of the Royal Society, who counted among his closest friends such distinguished men as John Michell and Alexander Aubert, and who had his portrait painted by Romney, Gainsborough and several other artists of note; but who, in turn, never failed to meet his fellow engineers at their club whenever he was in town, who saw to it that his resident engineers became members if this was a geographically possible proposition and, certainly in the case of John Gwyn, treated them in terms of real affection.

These are very significant aspects of Smeaton's life. That he also created many outstanding works can now be taken for granted. It is sufficient to mention the completion of Coldstream Bridge in 1766 (perhaps the most handsome of all his bridges), of St Ives harbour pier in 1770, and Perth Bridge in 1771; to note that by then another nine or ten mills had been built to his designs, construction had started on the largest of all his works, the Forth & Clyde Canal, and he was consultant to the Carron Company in Stirlingshire, one of the biggest and most efficient ironworks in Britain. Moreover, in 1767 he raised his fees to the then unprecedented figure, for an engineer, of 5 guineas a day when away from home.

Most of Smeaton's work for the Carron Company was undertaken in the 1770s, a decade in which he also completed another dozen mills and made major advances in steam engine design. The performance of his first steam engine, built in 1769, was disappointing. As a result, he characteristically determined to master the subject and carried out an extensive series of experiments on a large model engine, which he built at Austhorpe, and conducted systematic engine trials in the Newcastle area. These experiments and trials led to his famous engine at Long Benton colliery, set to work in 1774, and the equally memorable engine at Chacewater mine in Cornwall in the following year.

Both gave notably better performances, and the latter was far more powerful, than any engine previously erected. That Smeaton's contributions in this field were soon to be partially eclipsed by the brilliant inventions of James Watt should not detract from their merit; nor should it be forgotten that he went on to design some further excellent engines (including one exported to Russia) and that his designs for the associated machinery, especially for winding coals, were unsurpassed in the eighteenth century.

In 1773, accompanied by Jessop, Smeaton visited Ireland and gave valuable advice on the Grand Canal. Harbour works were completed to his plans at Eyemouth and Portpatrick, and the north pier at Aberdeen, which effectively created the harbour there, was an engineering triumph reflecting great credit on Smeaton's plans and Gwyn's execution of the work, dating from 1775 to 1780. At about the same time the lighthouse on the sands of Spurn Head was completed and improvements were made, with Smeaton as consulting engineer, at Ramsgate harbour and in the drainage of that large tract of low ground in south Yorkshire known as Hatfield Chase where, in the 1780s, Smeaton's scheme was extended by the able engineer Samuel Foster.

Meanwhile, as well as pursuing his astronomical observations and interest in scientific instruments, Smeaton had been contemplating some of the problems raised in his mind by the waterwheel tests. In 1776 he published in *Phil. Trans.* an experimental investigation on what was at the time a difficult and controversial problem: the relation between work, momentum and kinetic energy. In this paper he emphasised that work done (or "mechanic power" as he called it) was a basic parameter in mechanics and showed that it was proportional to MV^2. This was followed in 1782 by a paper describing remarkable experiments in which he actually measured the energy lost during the collision or impact of soft, non-elastic bodies. These three papers (i.e. the Experimental Enquiry of 1759 and the two just mentioned) are milestones in the development of mechanics. They were reprinted several times in England and, in a French translation, in Paris.

We see why he had to be his own master, as he put it in the letter quoted above, and why he simply had to have time, free from day-to-day distractions, to think, to compose his admirably clear reports, and to make experiments. Few truly great engineers have not in their character some leanings to scientific enquiry. In Smeaton's case they were singularly powerful.

The improvement in his financial position, allowing him rather more leisure, came about in the 1770s and was marked by the withdrawal from the Forth & Clyde job in 1773—after 5 years' work with everything now well under control—and by his resignation from the Greenwich Hospital appointment in 1777. As he wrote to James Watt in March 1778:

"I have already been at hard and incessant Labour for 30 years in which time I have had some Success for myself as well as others. But I never was of the Kind of enterprising turn, as to employ my head to the making a profit by the Labours of other mens Hands . . . and though I found myself in a way of improving my original fortune by very gradual and slow Steps

... my resolution was to continue the same unremitting Labour (in case God spared my Life and Health) till I was enabled to maintain my Family upon the income of my Fortune, in the same kind of frugal way, or plan, that was exercised during the raising thereof. This was accomplished about 3 years ago: and the first step to be taken, was to ease myself of a Degree of Hurry and fatigue, that I found must, if continued some years more, destroy me."

And he goes on to explain the need for carrying on with the Greenwich Receivership, until recently, in parallel with his "profession of a civil Engineer ... [to which] I have been strongly impelled by natural Inclination".

At Austhorpe, meanwhile, Jessop was still working as Smeaton's assistant up to 1772, and Henry Eastburn (1753–1821) had arrived as a pupil in 1768. He was the son of Mrs Smeaton's sister Faith, and in turn became an assistant in 1775; a position he held for 13 or 14 years. After his marriage in 1779 he and his wife settled in Whitkirk.

The Smeatons suffered the loss of their youngest girl, Hannah, in 1776. She was only 11 years old when she died. On a happier occasion Ann married John Brooke in August 1780. He was in the linseed oil business and Smeaton fitted out a windmill for him at Sykefield, close to Austhorpe Lodge where the Brookes lived after their marriage. In the following year—on 6th December, 1781, to be exact—Mary married Jeremiah Dixon. He became mayor of Leeds in 1784 and soon afterwards they moved to Fell Foot estate at Staveley near Windermere.

By a fortunate chance three of Smeaton's personal diaries or journals have survived, one kept at Austhorpe for 1781 and two kept at London for 1782 and 1783. From the first of these we learn that he visited the north in January and November, and spent 8 weeks in London during April, May and June. Otherwise, apart from a few short trips to York and one to Bawtry, he lived quietly at home with his family making occasional day visits to friends, such as John Michell at Thornhill, and to a local job at Seacroft Foundry. He also spent a good deal of time working on the nearby Sykefield mill, which was completed that year. Typical entries in the diary show astronomical observations in the early morning then, after breakfast, writing reports and making notes and calculations, followed by dinner around 3 p.m. and work at the mill or reading or both in the evenings.

The London diary for 1782 is full of interesting detail. Smeaton came up to town in February and remained there until May, with a week's visit to Wells harbour in Norfolk in March. He was no longer staying with John Holmes but lodged in chambers. From the daily entries we learn that he spent 30 hours writing the "Collision" paper, which was read to the Royal Society on 18th April. Letters took an hour or two most days; at least one letter a week went off to Mrs Smeaton, and as many came from her in return; the others were to various friends and clients, to Henry Eastburn at Austhorpe and to John Gwyn, then working at Cromarty harbour.

The mornings were usually spent in writing and the afternoons with professional meetings. In the evenings Smeaton enjoyed walking, talking to friends and going to the Royal Society and Engineers Club. He also enjoyed music; "concerto spirituale" is a fairly frequent entry. He went to one of the concerts given by Carl Frederick Abel at the Hanover Square Rooms, and he twice attended the opera.

It was on 20th March, on returning to London from Norfolk, that he learnt of the collapse of Hexham Bridge, 9 days earlier, in a sudden flood of unprecedented magnitude in the River Tyne. The bridge, designed with Smeaton's usual attention to principles and details, had been completed in 1780 with a good resident engineer in Jonathan Pickernell. It replaced an earlier structure, built at a slightly different location by John Gott, which suffered a similar fate in 1771. An analysis of the failure of Smeaton's bridge has recently been published by Mr Ruddock, and an outline is given in Chapter VII.

Smeaton had underestimated the maximum possible flood and its effect: the only serious practical mistake in his career (though there may have been an error in levelling in 1762 at Potteric Carr). However, it was a very costly one, to his client and to his own sense of professional pride. His feelings are summed up in a letter to Pickernell:

> "All our Honours are now in the Dust! It cannot now be said, that in the course of 30 years' practice and engaged in some of the most Difficult Enterprises, not one of Smeaton's works has failed. Hexham Bridge is a Melancholy witness to the contrary."

However much he suffered from this disaster, work had to continue. He went to Ramsgate harbour in August, to Liverpool (to study the dry docks there) in October, wrote long reports on the Fossdyke and on the Birmingham Canal, and spent most of December again in the north.

In 1783 he made his annual migration to London rather earlier than usual, arriving on 24th January, and with the intention of finding permanent quarters rather than lodgings. This he achieved 3 weeks later at Grays Inn, where he took a lease on a set of rooms or chambers. Here he soon established a work room with bench, tools, and so on; a load of things arrived from Yorkshire in July—probably drawings, letter books, etc.—and by September the furnishings were completed with the hanging of pictures.

The next 4 months up to May were full of activity: designing the steam engine and winding machinery for Walker colliery near Newcastle, preparing and giving evidence to Parliament on the Birmingham Canal Bill, making drawings and a report for Ramsgate harbour, visiting Gosport for designs for a mill, writing with great care, and after frequent meetings with Pickernell, his "memorial" or detailed account of the Hexham failure, discussing with the owner (Mr Hilbert) and the millwright (James Cooper) details of a mill at Carshalton being erected to his design, and sitting for his portrait by Gainsborough which had been commissioned by Samuel Whitbread.

The first 2 weeks of June were spent at Austhorpe, then came a trip to the north-east on Walker colliery and other business, followed, after a short return to Austhorpe, by a visit to Norfolk. Back in London, Smeaton had a bad attack of the "gravel". After recovering, he spent a few days' holiday with his relations, the Broadbents, at Nonsuch Park in Surrey. Then he resumed work, on the Walker designs and in connection with a mill at Deptford dockyard, and towards the end of August he went with Mylne to Norwich on the Wells harbour enquiry.

Mrs Smeaton was now seriously ill and she visited Bath in the hope of a cure, accompanied by her daughter Ann Brooke. Smeaton joined them there for a few days at the beginning of September, then returned to London for more work on the Walker engine and some other jobs, and to sit for his portrait by Mather Brown (commissioned by Mr Hilbert the millowner). He went to Bath again for about a fortnight, and spent a week travelling home via Gloucester, Worcester, Birmingham, Derby and Sheffield, arriving at Austhorpe on 9th October, 1783.

December saw him again in Northumberland. He visited Walker colliery on the 2nd of that month and then "viewed and surveyed the ruins of Hexham bridge". No other comments escaped from his taciturn pen, in his diary, but it must have been a sad day towards the end of an unhappy year as he stood on the banks of the Tyne, watching the water swirling around the ruins of his once fine bridge and carrying away, in his imagination, the reputation he had so hardly won of being Britain's foremost engineer. There was other work to be done, however. He stayed in the north until Christmas, visiting for a few days—as he always did on such trips—his friend Nicholas Walton at Farnacres.

Smeaton worked on to the very last moment, watching the trials of his coal-winding engine at Walker, and the final entry of the year in his diary, devoid of any hint of the misery he must have been feeling, reads:

> "Thursday, 25th December—Rode home from Wetherby, home to dinner."

He found his wife in a still worse state of health, and all attempts to save her life failed. She died on 17th January, 1784, on her 59th birthday.

The last 9 years

Ann Brooke now took charge of the household at Austhorpe. Smeaton continued to divide his time between Yorkshire and London. He had started writing the Eddystone book in October 1783; letters were sent off almost with their former frequency; he still attended meetings at the Royal Society and Engineers Club. But in 1784 he withdrew from engineering—temporarily, as it turned out, but effectively nonetheless for the next 3 years.

Shattered by Hexham and disenchanted with what then seemed a hard, demanding profession, he loyally helped Gwyn with designs for the North Bridge at Hull, produced drawings for some machinery at Carron, and carried out an engine trial at York waterworks: but very little else.

His intellectual power and manual skill, however, remained unimpaired. Early in 1785 Hindley's dividing engine came into his possession. This machine, which Smeaton had so much admired in 1741, was the first circular dividing engine constructed with any pretension to accuracy, but it had been neglected since Hindley's death in 1771. Smeaton immediately set about its renovation and, as we learn from a letter to Edward Nairne, the London instrument-maker, the job had been finished by March. A year later he sold it to Thomas Reid of Edinburgh, with detailed instructions. The presence of this engine in his Austhorpe workshop evidently directed Smeaton's thoughts anew towards the whole subject of precise graduation, and the result was a paper, read to the Royal Society in November 1785, giving a masterly review of circular dividing from the time of Tycho Brahe. This paper, of great interest in the history of scientific instruments,

31

has been fully discussed by Mr Law, and is one of Smeaton's best pieces of writing.

By 1787 his health and spirits had revived. Urgent requests for engineering advice could no longer be resisted, and Smeaton returned to work having doubled his previous fees to 10 guineas a day or 50 guineas a week. These were outrageously high, designed, as he said, "rather to save his time than to acquire money". Nevertheless on such terms he visited Plymouth dockyard and Ramsgate harbour in the summer. Later he went to Scotland, advising on a bridge at Montrose and spending several days at Aberdeen in order to draw up proposals for reducing wave action within the harbour. This he achieved by a small stone jetty or "catch pier" built out from the North Pier, which was constructed with admirable effect. However, the real tonic, fully restoring his enthusiasm for major civil engineering work, was a second visit to Ramsgate that year in December 1787.

A month earlier the harbour Trustees had asked Alexander Aubert to become chairman of the Board. Smeaton accompanied him to the site, and they clearly saw that the primary need, now the silting problems had been conquered, was to render the harbour "a place of quiet and safety for shipping". Mr Aubert also recognised the necessity of having an engineer responsible to the Trustees (rather than employing a consultant on comparatively rare occasions) and a full-time resident engineer. Smeaton agreed to take on this task, and happily arranged for John Gwyn to come down from Hull as resident. He (i.e. Smeaton) was to receive £250 a year.

Gwyn died in June 1789, aged 56, but already, after only 18 months' work, the dry dock had been largely rebuilt to a new, improved design and work was well under way on the "Advanced Pier" which reached completion, with great benefit to the harbour, shortly after Smeaton himself died in 1792.

Not content with throwing himself wholeheartedly into the Ramsgate job, and writing a long historical report on the harbour works, Smeaton visited the Channel Islands in June 1788 and Bristol in October of that year. In July 1789 he wrote a massive report, with drawings, on a comprehensive scheme for creating a "floating harbour" at Bristol, and made another site visit there in company with Jessop and Nickalls in September to decide, among other things, on the borings required.

It was also in this period that Mather Brown painted his second portrait of Smeaton, commissioned by Aubert. Aubert presented the painting to the Royal Society in 1799, saying:

"I beg leave to present to the Royal Society a Picture of my late most esteemed Friend Mr John Smeaton, Civil Engineer and Fellow of this Society, whose memory will ever be dear to all Lovers of Science and particularly to those who were aquainted with him. It was painted by Mr Mather Brown, a few years before his [Smeaton's] death & is allowed to be a striking resemblance of him... I present the picture to the Society because the members of it will have more frequent opportunities of seeing it than if I continued to keep it in my possession and because it may contribute to perpetuate the memory of so valuable & so amiable a member."

A year or two afterwards, that is in 1790, Mr Aubert had an engraving of the portrait made by William Bromley. This scarcely did justice to the very fine original. "However", as Smeaton wrote to Mary Dixon:

"this mark of my friend's esteem for me, with a view to give away amongst his friends, and mine, I cannot slight. The roughness of the manner is Characteristic and may serve as a memorandum."

The letter, written from Austhorpe in February 1790, goes on to say:

"I am summoned to attend the Visitation of Ramsgate Harbour the 1st of March, so my departure hence is settled for the 25th Inst. I am glad however that I am likely to have the pleasure of seeing my dear Daughter before I go; and it gives me great pleasure to find that you are to be accompanied by my favourite, the gentle Miss Walton whom, I shall be very glad to see here previous to my journey. I shall write to Mr Walton in a post or two ... I remain, thank God perfectly well, as well as the whole family [i.e. the Brookes]; all joining in tender affection to you ... I am your affectionate Father, J. Smeaton."

The journey to which he refers was to include a long trip, on behalf of Trinity House, studying sites for a lighthouse in the Scilly Isles and for another on the Owers rock off the Sussex coast. This he duly made, in June, and reported on a month later. It was his last big excursion, though followed by two or three further visits to Ramsgate harbour.

In 1789–90 he also returned to his first engineering love, the design of mills; and produced drawings for three watermills, all in Surrey; but there were to be no more.

By 1790 page proofs of the Eddystone book were arriving from the printer, and in checking them Smeaton had help from Dr Charles Blagden, another of his Royal Society friends and, indeed, Secretary of the Society at this time. January 1791 saw the publication, at last, of this magnificent folio volume. Shortly afterwards the Ramsgate report was printed. Meanwhile he had been enormously busy on the Birmingham–Worcester Canal, and gave evidence before the House of Lords in June. This, for practical purposes, may be taken as the end of his career. He formally took leave of the profession in October 1791 in a published circular which stated:

> "Mr Smeaton begs leave to inform his Friends and the Public in general, that having applied himself for a great number of Years to the business of a Civil Engineer, his wishes are now to dedicate the chief part of his remaining Time to the Description of the several Works performed under his Direction. The Account he lately published of the Building of Edystone Lighthouse has been so favourably received, that he is persuaded he cannot be of more service to the Public, or show a greater Sense of his Gratitude, than to continue to employ himself in the way now specified."

In London from January to June 1792, still living at Grays Inn, he may well have been working on a treatise on hydraulic machinery, which we know he started but never completed, and he attended seven meetings of the Engineers Club before returning to Austhorpe. There, while walking in the garden on a September day, he suffered a stroke and died 6 weeks later on 28th October, 1792, in his 69th year. Mary Dixon, who had come to join her sister, remarked:

> "The end he had through life deserved, was granted; the body sunk, but the mind shone to the last, and in the way good men aspire to, he closed a life, active as useful, amiable as revered."

Smeaton is buried at the little parish church of Whitkirk, where his daughters placed a memorial to him and their mother on the north wall of the chancel.

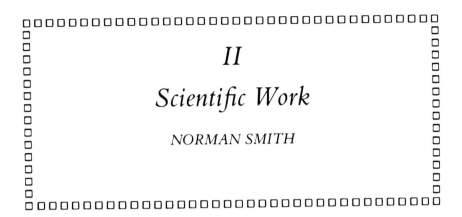

II

Scientific Work

NORMAN SMITH

In assessing John Smeaton's scientific work it is logical to begin by considering the main body of it, the papers published by the Royal Society during the 40 years or more that he was associated with that institution, first of all as an enthusiastic visitor to lectures and subsequently, from 1753, as a Fellow. In all, the Society published eighteen papers—the first in 1750, the last in 1788—and after Smeaton's death they appeared as a uniform volume in 1814.[1]

So far as their dates are concerned it is perhaps no coincidence that nine of the papers were read before 1760 and five after 1775. The 15 years between witnessed Smeaton at his most active as a civil engineer when he had little time for research. Yet even in this busy period he by no means neglected his scientific enquiries.

In the *Philosophical Transactions* of the Royal Society Smeaton expressed himself on, broadly speaking, three topics: instruments, astronomy and mechanics. Evidently scientific instruments, problems of measurement and astronomical observation appealed greatly to Smeaton and very likely it was these pursuits which, at various times, afforded him some of his greatest satisfaction and brought him the pleasure of the company of intellects impossible to find in the world of construction.

Smeaton's first six papers, published in quick succession between 1750 and 1754, reflect his chosen profession of scientific instrument-maker and they indicate clearly his association with men prominent in a variety of scientific and mechanical enquiries. The first paper, "On some Improvements of the Mariner's Compass" (1750), relates directly to an idea of Dr Gowin Knight, a friend of Smeaton's, and the subject of the next paper, "Improvements made in the Air-Pump"

(1752), was of value to William Watson in his examination of electrical discharges *in vacuo*.[2] "An Account of some Experiments upon a Machine for Measuring the Way of a Ship at Sea" (1754) extended an idea of an earlier contributor to the *Phil. Trans.*, the hydrographer Henry de Saumerez. Smeaton failed to calibrate his ship's log with sufficient accuracy and it was not, at the time, adopted. Nevertheless the account demonstrates his appreciation of correct and careful experimental technique; the same is even more apparent in the 1754 paper "Of a new Pyrometer".

Establishing precisely coefficients of thermal expansion of metals and other materials was not only an interesting challenge in technique, it was crucial to the search for a time-keeper featuring full temperature compensation, Harrison's marine chronometers for instance. In the measurements Smeaton undertook, the expansion of each 28 in. specimen was determined on a long-base lever micrometer developed from similar instruments used by Ellicott and Graham and improved by Smeaton to measure down to 1/20000 in. A water-bath, in which the whole apparatus was immersed, provided a temperature difference of some 150°F. The key problem here was to differentiate between the expansion of the specimen being tested and the unavoidable expansion of the whole, immersed, micrometer. Smeaton resolved the difficulty with the type of experimental elegance that appears time and again throughout his career. In this instance he used "a bar of straight-grained white deal, or cedar, which it is well known, are much less expansible by heat than any metal hitherto discovered" as a standard against which the "basis", a bar of brass which formed the frame of the complete instrument, could be calibrated. Thus when each specimen was tested the comparative expansion of the whole instrument could be allowed for.

Not all the materials which Smeaton investigated can be identified precisely in terms of their modern equivalents ("hard steel", for example, or "white glass barometer tube") but where a verification is possible Smeaton's coefficients of expansion prove to be very accurate.

Smeaton at an early age developed a taste for astronomy, and naturally enough his skill with instruments was an important component of a pursuit which occupied much of his time in his later years. His last three papers (1785/7/8) were all on astronomical observation and instrumentation.

The papers on instruments, measurements and astronomy show that perceiving a problem and investigating its explanation or solution afforded great satisfaction to an intellect that was fine by any standard and unique in eighteenth-century civil engineering. Yet, paradoxical as it may seem, little of Smeaton's work in these scientific fields was of great importance. In between the groups of papers on instruments and astronomy, however, he presented three which were of much wider interest and value because they dealt with subjects keenly debated at the time and of real scientific and technical concern. These were the papers on mechanics.

Experiments on waterwheels and windmills
It is generally claimed that the performance of watermills and windmills first attracted Smeaton's attention because of some commission he had received to build a mill. Perhaps not. The performance and efficiency of mills, especially those driven by water, were already controversial topics years before Smeaton began his experiments. Moreover it is certain, from his own account, that these were conducted in 1752 and 1753, and he cautiously decided to reserve judgement on the experiments until he had "an opportunity of putting the deductions made therefrom in real practice, in a variety of cases, and for various purposes; so as to be able to assure the Society that I have found them to answer". His first watermill was built in 1753.[3] In short it appears that his intellectual curiosity led to practical applications and not the reverse.

Between the early group of papers on instruments and "An Experimental Enquiry concerning the Natural Powers of Water and Wind to turn Mills..." (1759) there is an important distinction to be drawn. The work on instruments and measurement was, above all, constructionally intricate and in terms of technique exacting. With the mills, however, the emphasis was different; for here there were conceptual difficulties associated with quite fundamental questions in theoretical mechanics. Initially Smeaton did not realise that he was approaching key problems to do with the nature of momentum and energy and the concept of work. However the fact soon forced itself upon him, as the two later papers on mechanics prove.

Smeaton was not the first to conduct experiments on waterwheels. Christopher Polhem in Sweden had already tried such an approach earlier in the century and the possibility that Smeaton knew something of Polhem's work cannot be ruled out.[4] Smeaton was, to judge from his writings, well versed in the scientific and technical publications of the period and in any case he was of a mind to familiarise himself with the literature of any topic when the need arose.

Other European authorities had addressed themselves to water-wheels and generated some fundamentally conflicting views. In 1704 Antoine Parent had stated[5] that an undershot wheel would develop its maximum performance when the rim velocity was one-third of the stream velocity; and that the maximum efficiency of the machine could not exceed 4/27. Parent's analysis, its several defects notwithstanding, became well known and was widely quoted. Belidor amongst others accepted Parent's views in his *Architecture Hydraulique* and announced, moreover, that undershot wheels were six times as efficient as those of the overshot type. It was Desaguliers' opinion, on the other hand, that overshot wheels were ten times better than under-shot wheels.[6] "Monstrous disagreement", Thomas Telford was to call it, and clearly some explaining had to be done. In mid-century the issue was a lively one and Smeaton tackled it in a masterly manner.

His first approach to the problem depended solely on "experiments made on working models, which I look upon as the best means of obtaining the outlines in mechanical enquiries".[7] Such a view was entirely consistent with Smeaton's scientific work so far, although with the benefit of hindsight we can see that ultimately it limited the scope of his conclusions. A number of specific, and important, questions were resolved but simultaneously he was bound to exclude any possibility of examining, or even disclosing, some issues of a precise and fundamental nature.

Smeaton's apparatus, shown in Figs 2 and 3, is well known and requires no detailed explanation. Suffice to say that it was adaptable to test over- and undershot wheels and the closed-circuit water circulation, hand-pumped, was designed to supply a constant flow to the wheel. Performance at various heads and flows could be measured by recording the distance through which a weight was raised in a minute. It was a basically sound experimental rig, well designed for the job in hand.

Smeaton's experimental technique was elegant to a degree, and most impressive of all was his procedure for dealing with hydraulic friction losses in the sluice and flume and mechanical friction in the axles of the waterwheel and the pulley. What Smeaton wished to compare was the "power" of the water at the wheel and the useful "effect" produced by the wheel; i.e. the product of the weight lifted and the height to which it was raised. Calculating the water's velocity from the head registered in the cistern was no use because some of this actual head represented the energy required to overcome friction before the water reached the blades of the wheel. In addition, some of

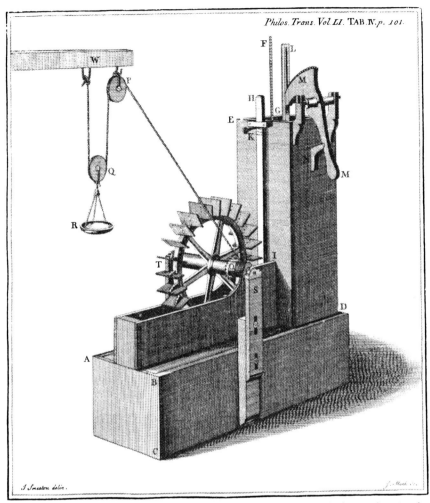

Phlos. Trans. Vol LI. TAB. IV. p. 101.

*Fig. 2. Waterwheel model tests, 1759, (engraving by J. Mynde from a drawing by Smeaton—Phil. Trans., **51**)*

the "effect" was bound to be wasted in turning the wheel and the pulley; and so, for a given head and sluice setting, Smeaton ran the experiment with various weights falling and assisting the waterwheel until the number of turns in a minute was the same whether water was flowing or not. All of this meant that he could calculate the water's velocity *at the wheel* (and hence determine an "effective" or "virtual" head) and also establish how much weight in the scale pan just balanced mechanical friction. It was a brilliant device which enabled him to measure efficiency of the waterwheel alone rather than the overall efficiency of the experiment. It is amazing that generations of writers have failed to appreciate this, the most perceptive part of Smeaton's technique. That is the reason incidentally why Smeaton's figure for the efficiency of undershot wheels is almost invariably quoted as 22 per cent (in fact the efficiency of the *experiment*) whereas the true value was, on average, 30 per cent.

Smeaton describes the waterwheel experiments in detail and at length. His conclusions can be summarised as follows:

(1) Overshot wheels are about twice as efficient as undershot wheels; in fact 66 per cent efficient as against 30 per cent.
(2) Overshot wheels are driven by weight only and very little is gained from any impact between water and buckets.
(3) For undershot wheels the optimum ratio of velocity between wheel and stream is at least 2 to 5 and can sometimes approach 1 to 2; Parent's figure of 1 to 3 was thus shown to be incorrect.
(4) Impact between a stream of water and a flat plate resulted in a marked loss of energy in the form of spray and turbulence.

Smeaton's demonstration of the superiority of overshot wheels guaranteed that in future British developments this would be the favoured type whenever possible. However, while the experiments answered the particular questions they could not by their very nature resolve certain basic issues. Only the purely mathematical enquiries of Jean Charles de Borda could do that and could prove rigorously that an undershot waterwheel was 50 per cent efficient at best, that the optimum ratio of velocities was 1 to 2, and that overshot wheels were in theory 100 per cent efficient. By enunciating two fundamental precepts—that entry should be shockless (as Smeaton had sensed) and that exit velocity must be zero—Borda laid the foundations for subsequent French developments in water power which culminated in the turbine.[8]

Nevertheless Smeaton's was an excellent piece of work meticulously and perceptively conducted. His opening remark that "in this case it is very necessary to distinguish the circumstances in which a model differs from a machine in large; otherwise a model is more apt to lead us from the truth than towards it" was to be, and is, a guiding maxim of all engineering model-testing. The early French work on waterwheels of Deparcieux and Bossut followed Smeaton's methodology exactly, and indeed in France Smeaton was the only British authority whose work was acknowledged in experimental mechanics.

When he turned his attention to windmills Smeaton could draw on

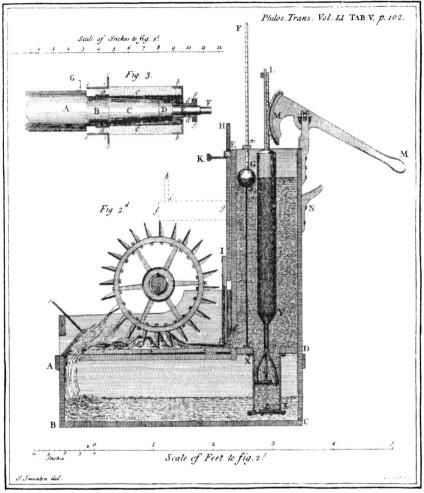

*Fig. 3. Section of waterwheel model (*Phil. Trans., **51***)*

a variety of sources for guidance. There was, in the first place, the mathematical work of Colin Maclaurin comparing the nature of wind action on a stationary sail as against a moving one. Smeaton remarks on the ideas of Mr Rouse, "an ingenious gentleman of Harborough", and he acknowledges the machine that his friend Ellicott had "contrived for the use of the late celebrated Mr B. Robins, for trying the resistance of plain surfaces moving through the air". Seeing no practical way of projecting an airflow against a stationary model, Smeaton settled for an "artificial wind" generated by moving the model against the air but not in a straight line. With disarming practicality he

41

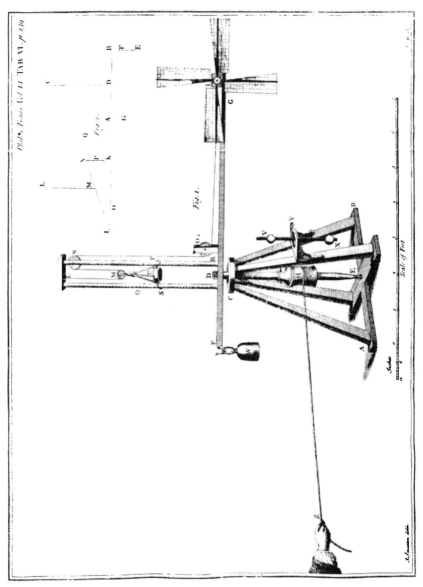

*Fig. 4. Windmill model tests, 1759 (Phil. Trans., **51**)*

remarks that "to carry the machine forward in a right line against the air would require a larger room than I could conveniently meet with". His solution therefore was the rotating model, hand driven, shown in Fig. 4. No explanation of its mode of operation is needed other than to point out that VX is a simple pendulum device, adjustable as to period by sliding the two lead weights, and used as a metronome to pace the rotation of the model. Smeaton specifies that one complete rotation of the model should correspond to two beats of the pendulum. The range of air velocities he used was 4 ft 4 in./s up to 8 ft 9 in./s. The effects of mechanical friction were cancelled by exactly the same routine as was used in the waterwheel experiments.

Smeaton set out to test the influence of four different parameters: the structure and shape of the sail; the angle of the sail relative to its plane of motion, otherwise known as the angle of weather; the "quantity of surface"; and the velocity of the wind. A number of traditional and recommended practices were compared. Smeaton tested "plain sails weathered according to the common practice" and those "weathered in the Dutch manner". Sails set according to Antoine Parent's specifications were tried and so were those whose angle of weather decreased with radius, an arrangement recommended by Maclaurin.

The results dealt summarily with Parent; he was wrong. His recommended angle of weather, 35°, was too large, at least double what proved to be best. Nor did Parent realise that it was necessary for the angle to vary with the radius of the whip (the arm to which the sail is attached). Maclaurin's formula did acknowledge this need but failed, according to Smeaton, to indicate how the variation in angle might be determined for a particular windmill in a given wind. In fact it proved to be experience which had evolved the answer, because the best settings Smeaton could find for his model were based on traditional Dutch practice.

The next stage of the experiment (the sails being set at the best angle) investigated variations in sail area and shape. It emerged that increasing the sail area was beneficial up to a point. Beyond that point it seemed that further increase in sail area was counter-productive because "when the whole cylinder of wind is intercepted, it does not then produce the greatest effect, for want of proper interstices to escape".

Smeaton next proceeds to examine the effect on performance of all manner of combinations of wind velocity and sail speed. He concludes, to put his results as comprehensively as possible, that:

(1) The peripheral speed of a sail is proportional (nearly) to wind velocity (V).
(2) The maximum load lifted is proportional (nearly) to V^2.
(3) The maximum effect (work done) is proportional (nearly) to V^3.
(4) Because peripheral speed is proportional (nearly) to wind speed, windmills, as they get larger, turn more slowly in a wind of given speed.
(5) The force exerted by the wind is proportional to the square of the radius of the sails.

Smeaton's investigation of windmills is nothing like so conclusive as the work on waterwheels. There are two reasons for this. In the first place there was, with waterwheels, a clear-cut issue to be addressed: which form of waterwheel was best? Smeaton answered the question. No such basic issue could be identified with windmills and one feels that in the wind-power experiments Smeaton himself was never entirely clear as to precisely what he was attempting to show. In the event he analysed and compared rather few sets of data in as many ways as he could but the results, ingeniously and exhaustively presented, lack really firm conclusions. In the second place, with waterwheels Smeaton could deal quantitatively with potential and actual performance. He computes the energy potentially available, compares the performance actually produced and deduces efficiencies in real terms. For windmills no such quantitative results are achieved. Indeed far from solving the problem of quantifying the energy of the wind Smeaton never so much as identifies it.

Nevertheless Smeaton produced some useful guidelines for practising millwrights endeavouring to harness wind power. He showed that there was an optimum area of sail to be carried on a mill of a particular size and rotational speed, and that the angle of weather should progressively be reduced from axle to tip.

The watermill and windmill experiments are revealing of Smeaton's methodology as a young experimenter approaching 30 years of age. Given a specifically posed problem his command of appropriate experimental techniques is manifest. His powers of abstraction, however, and the extension of the enquiry into areas of fresh insight, are limited. He dealt rather feebly, for instance, with the merits of increasing the number of blades on a waterwheel or sails on a windmill; and he failed to realise that as the size of a windmill increases then, so far as performance is concerned, a law of diminishing returns must operate. By contrast, with water power, the potential for sustained improvement is immense simply by increasing the head and flow used to drive a wheel of given size.

However, perhaps this is expecting too much. For the 1750s Smeaton's experiments were remarkable and gained for their author the Copley Medal, the highest award given by the Royal Society for original research and a distinction won by very few engineers since 1759.

Mechanic power

In his prime-mover experiments Smeaton had been touching on problems of momentum and energy and the concept of work. Indeed he had determined the performance of the model engines by measuring the "work done". In the waterwheel experiments he had, in effect, computed efficiencies by calculating the total work done by the falling water (weight of water × distance fallen in 1 min.) and comparing this with the product of load multiplied by the distance it was raised at the same time. Smeaton had no doubt that "The raising of the weight, relative to the height to which it can be raised in a given time, is the most proper measure of power." There remained, however, a critical and vexed question: what was the relationship of this "mechanic power" to the weight of a body and the velocity at which it was moving.

In the paper he read to the Royal Society on 25th April, 1776, Smeaton addressed himself, in an elementary way, to what was at the time a very obscure issue.[9] He remarks of his purpose:

"I resolved to try a set of experiments, from whence it might be inferred what proportion or quantity of mechanical power is expended in giving the same body different degrees of velocity."

He says incidentally that:

"This scheme was put into execution in the year 1759, and the experiments were then shewn to several friends, particularly my worthy and ingenious friend, Mr William Russell."

All of this indicates two things: the research developed immediately and directly out of the watermill and windmill experiments, published in 1759, and it took Smeaton no less than 17 years, admittedly over an intensely busy period, to reach his conclusions.

Smeaton begins by stating the essence of a dispute which had absorbed the energies of two factions sincethe seventeenth century. Was the quantity of motion, or "momentum", of a moving body to be defined as the product of mass and velocity (MV) which was the Newtonian view; or was Leibniz's "living force" (*vis viva*), the product MV^2, the correct measure? In retrospect it seems extraordinary that there was any need to reconcile the concepts of momentum and energy and the mathematical expression of each. The fact that one measures a force acting for a given time ($Ft=MV$) and the other measures a force acting over a given distance ($Fs=\frac{1}{2}MV^2$) is easily demonstrated. In Smeaton's day, however, so long as it was held that either MV or MV^2 must itself be a measure of force, then the significance of time or distance for which or through which a force (in our modern sense) acted was necessarily obscure.

Smeaton regarded the MV–MV^2 dispute as something more than a problem in theoretical mechanics (and for many that was all it appeared to be). That his view was broader is evident from the remark that

> "Some of these errors [due to confusion over MV and MV^2] are not only very considerable in themselves, but also of great consequence to the public, as they tend greatly to mislead the practical artist in works that occur daily, and which often require great sums of money in their execution."

No other comment in Smeaton's writing so adequately sums up his attitude to theoretical mechanics and its relationship to practical engineering. Thus Smeaton declared an interest in the problem not only because there was one, and not merely because his prime-mover experiments were at odds with "commonly received doctrine", but because he recognised the value to practical engineering of sound theory properly applied. In taking this position Smeaton was equalled by few and excelled by none.

The experiments on "the Quantity and Proportion of Mechanic Power" were conducted on the apparatus shown in Fig. 5. Its mode of operation is self-evident and the details are neatly worked out as always. The driving weight in the vertically falling scale pan could be changed; the cord could drive the vertical spindle via either of the "cylindrical barrels" N and M, one having twice the diameter of the other; and the cylindrical lead weights K and L could be moved to any position on the arm HI.

Smeaton conducted the tests at nine different settings, "each of which was repeated so many times as to be satisfactory". Driving weights of either 8 oz. or 32 oz. were applied to each "barrel" in turn and the revolving masses were placed at either their maximum

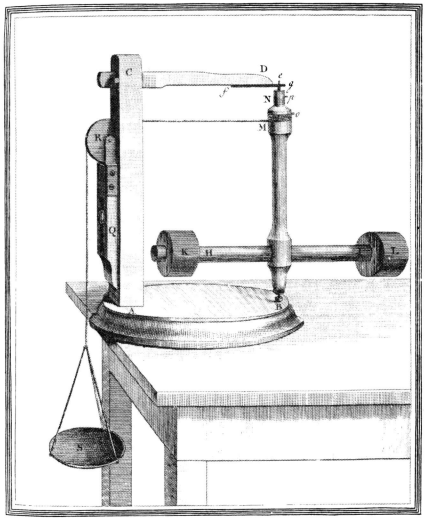

*Fig. 5.   Apparatus for studying "mechanic power", 1776 (*Phil. Trans.*, **66***)*

radius—8¼ in.—or half of it. Smeaton's conclusions are exactly what we would expect from this straightforward experiment, although his way of expressing them is somewhat laborious:

"I say, from these agreements under the very different mechanical powers applied, which were varied in the proportion of 1 to 16, we may safely conclude, that this is the universal law of nature respecting the capacities of bodies in motion to produce mechanical effects, and the quantity of mechanic power necessary to be employed to produce or generate different velocities (the bodies being supposed equal in their quantity of

47

matter); that the mechanic powers to be expended, are as the squares of the velocities to be generated, and *vice versa*; and that the simple velocities generated are as the impelling power compounded with, or multiplied by, the time of its action, and *vice versa*."

To put it simply, what Smeaton is saying is:

If P is the work done ("mechanic power"), W the weight applied, d the distance fallen, V the velocity given to the masses M, and t the time of the action, then

$$P = W.d$$

and P is proportional to MV^2 while V is proportional to $W.t$.

This is as far as he goes; but the conclusions which Smeaton reached by observing proportional relationships are not to be underestimated. He made this comment:

"that while those, that have adhered to the definition of Sir Isaac Newton, have complained of their adversaries, in not considering the time in which effects are produced, they themselves have not always taken into account the space that the impelling power is obliged to travel through in producing the different degrees of velocity. It seems, therefore, that, without taking in the collateral circumstances, both of time and space, the terms, quantity of motion, *momentum*, and the force of bodies in motion, are absolutely indefinite; and that they cannot be so easily, distinctly, and fundamentally compared, as by having recourse to the common measure, viz. mechanic power."

Finally Smeaton cannot resist expressing his position in strictly practical terms. He returns to the waterwheel problem and points out that "having treasured up 1000 tuns of water" at a certain head it will be possible to grind just so much corn in a watermill. The flow rate may be great or small, and the time to perform the task will vary accordingly, but the work which can be done is fixed.

The concepts of power, work and energy were finally clarified, defined, and placed on a sound mathematical basis by men such as Wollaston (1806) and Peter Ewart (1813) in England, and chiefly by N. L. M. Carnot (1783 and 1803), Lagrange (1813), Borgnis (1821) and Prony (1826) in France.[10] Smeaton can be seen as making an important early contribution to this development and it is significant that his papers on mills and mechanic power, having been reprinted in 1794 and 1796, were translated into French in 1810 and reprinted in 1827 (see Chapter XI) when interest in these subjects was at its height. Thus in 1829 Coriolis effectively paraphrased Smeaton's statement, quoted above, by saying that the errors in the past had arisen from not paying attention to *work*... "All practioners today mean by living force the work which can produce the velocity acquired by a body." The advance was that the equation

$$W.d = \frac{1}{2}MV^2$$

had now emerged.

Impact

Smeaton had been interested in problems of impact since the early days of his waterwheel experiments, and had made some investigations on the subject before writing the 1776 paper. However, it was not until April 1782 that he presented "New Fundamental Experiments upon the Collision of Bodies" to the Royal Society. The apparatus (he says):

> "I had not leisure to complete to my satisfaction till lately; which I mention to apologise for the length of time that these speculations have taken in bringing forward."[11]

The apparatus (Fig. 6) displays to the full Smeaton's extraordinary skill in devising experiments. The general view shows two pendula pivoting on knife-edges at the top, moving across the faces of a pair of graduated segmental scales and carrying lead weights of equal mass at their lower ends. The detailed view illustrates a lead weight BD and a curious spring device controlled by a ratchet. In order to test the elementary problem of impact between hard, elastic bodies the ratchet was disconnected and the curved springs, leather-covered, moved freely. The arm on the right was raised to the end of its scale, at N, and released. On impact its motion was totally arrested and the left-hand weight, C, flew off and reached a height virtually the same as that of D at the outset.

This of course was the result expected: with almost perfectly elastic bodies there is practically no loss of energy on impact. Smeaton now moves quickly to the question of soft, non-elastic collision, and the function of the ratchet is revealed.

The toothed bars were attached to, and pivoted on, the springs at k. Where the ratchet passed through the stud mn it could be made to engage a tooth through the pressure of the wire spring opq. On impact, each spring would bend and run the ratchet over the tooth until the compression of impact was complete. Their elasticity thus arrested the springs could exert no force of rebound upon one another and therefore behaved as if they were soft and non-elastic.

49

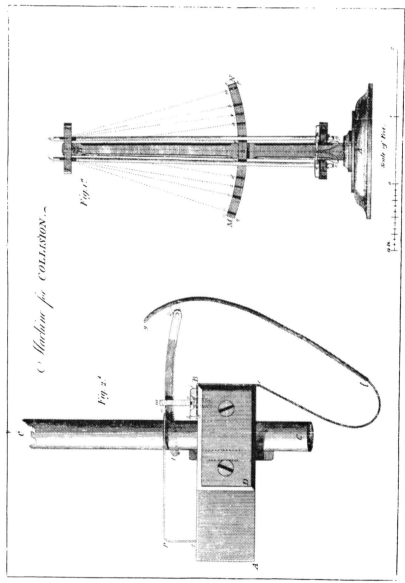

*Fig. 6. Apparatus for studying impact, 1782 (Phil. Trans., **72**)*

After impact the two weights moved together and reached a height nearly equal to half that from which the first weight C had been released. Again, the result conformed to expectation. Now comes the truly ingenious part of the experiment. The oscillations having died away and the two weights, ratchets still engaged, resting at the lowest point, the two arms were lashed together with thread, the ratchets released, and the thread cut. The two weights then sprang apart and each ascended to almost one-quarter of the original height of D. Thus Smeaton actually released, and measured, the energy which had been "lost" (or, rather, transformed) during impact. He found, within experimental error, that it equalled one-half of the work done by the weight D at the moment of impact.

By any standards this was a remarkable piece of experimentation, demonstrating quantitatively the nature of non-elastic impact and, indirectly, providing proof of that puzzling but fundamental principle in dynamics—the conservation of linear momentum.

However, Smeaton immediately turns to the practical consequences and translates his conclusion, "that in the collision of non-elastic soft bodies, one half of the mechanic power residing in the striking body is lost in the stroke", to explain the low efficiency of the undershot waterwheel. Here he makes a mistake in supposing that such impact and its attendant losses are of the same type as occur when work is done—and energy expended—in compressing and deforming a lump of Plasticine for example. Whereas such a soft and non-elastic material does experience a permanent "change of figure" on impact, water does not.

The truth is that Smeaton never did understand why undershot wheels are so inefficient. In principle at least he comprehended overshot wheels. He sensed that in the perfect case they might be 100 per cent efficient and that energy losses were not inherent in their mode of operation; but while he also realised (correctly, but for the wrong reason) that 50 per cent efficiency was the upper limit for undershot wheels, he did not see that even in this ideal situation the 50 per cent loss was accounted for solely by the kinetic energy of the tail-race. Instead he is preoccupied with "change of figure" and "resistance of the air" never suspecting—as no-one else did at the time—that the energy "lost" in turbulent impact is actually being wasted in the form of heat. How strange that in 1851 James Prescott Joule should establish a figure for the mechanical equivalent of heat by churning water with a paddle wheel.

Before leaving the impact paper we briefly note that Smeaton also considered the problem of collision between "hard and non-elastic bodies", as imagined by the mathematicians. Needless to say, he dismissed the concept of such hypothetical material as a "repugnant idea containing in itself a contradiction" which he puts tersely and with clear insight.

The essence of Smeaton's work in mechanics can be summarised as follows. His classic work on waterwheels demonstrated the validity of quantitative model experiments and effectively initiated this branch of experimental hydraulics; the results were of great practical importance. He strongly emphasised the concept of mechanical work, showed experimentally that work done was proportional to kinetic energy, not momentum, and demonstrated that work done was a proper measure of performance of prime-movers. He argued strongly, and convincingly, the case against those who imagined there was a species of material which was hard and non-elastic, and he determined by direct measurement the energy "lost" in impact between soft non-elastic bodies.

Pipe flow experiments

Smeaton made notable contributions to another branch of hydraulics; the friction loss in pipes. His original manuscripts on this subject are now lost (see Chapter XI) but John Farey presented a summary in Rees' *Cyclopaedia* in 1818.[12]

Early in the eighteenth century Pierre Couplet had investigated the nature of the head loss in five long lengths of iron pipe, of various diameters, at Versailles. Published by the Académie des Sciences in 1732 and again by Belidor in Vol. 2 of *Architecture Hydraulique* (1739), these were the earliest, and for many years the only, full-scale tests of their kind. Couplet's tests indicated two things: that in long water-pipes of small bore, friction losses were very considerable and that the relationship between V (velocity of flow) and h (head) in such cases was not of the then accepted form, $V^2 = 2gh$. Precisely what form the relationship *did* take was not elucidated at the time, and the conventional view is that the first satisfactory pipe-friction formula which properly expressed Couplet's results was established by Du Buat in his *Principes d'Hydraulique* of 1786.[13]

In fact it transpires that earlier Smeaton had discovered that the required equation was of the form

$$\frac{h}{L} = \frac{aV + bV^2}{D}$$

where D is the pipe diameter and L its length; and he assigned numerical values (in English units) to the parameters a and b. This expression is identical in form with the equation first published by Riche de Prony in 1804 and elaborated by Thomas Young in 1808.[14]

Smeaton had found that his own observations in practice did not agree very well with those of Couplet, and in consequence he made experiments with a pipe 1¼ in. bore, 100 ft in length. Exactly when he did so is not recorded by Farey, but it may have been in the 1760s and certainly before Smeaton reported in 1780 on improvements to the water supply systems at Edinburgh.[15]

The results of his experiments are shown in Fig. 7. He drew a "best fit" curve through the results and then extrapolated a table giving the head loss, per 100 ft length, for pipes of various diameters (assuming h to be inversely proportional to D) with given velocities of flow. The table is set out fully in the article by Farey, and in 1818 it was still regarded as a reliable design guide for the flow of water in pipes. Indeed a modern analysis shows that the test results are entirely

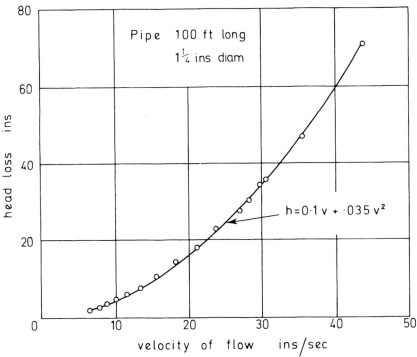

Fig. 7. Smeaton's experiments on pipe flow

acceptable for the practical conditions of turbulent flow at relatively low Reynolds' numbers in moderately smooth pipes.[16]

It is interesting to note that Smeaton was very probably instrumental in deducing another empirical equation of hydraulic flow, namely the formula $v = C\sqrt{gd}$ for a broad-crested weir. When William Jessop used this formula, with $C = 0.95$, to design a weir on the Avon at Bristol it is likely he was applying an equation originally deduced by Smeaton himself from field observations.[17] See also Chapters VI and VII.

Practical measure of horse power
It is remarkable that so late as the mid-eighteenth century few if any trustworthy data were available on power developed by horses, or by men, in pumping water, raising coals and so on. Smeaton naturally turned his attention to this subject and, during the years following 1760, made several careful observations on the rate of work achieved over various periods of time. The results are given briefly by Farey, in the article just mentioned, and more fully in a paper communicated to the Institution of Civil Engineers in 1839.[18]

Four examples will suffice to indicate the nature of Smeaton's observations. While the lock-pit excavations were in progress on the Calder & Hebble Navigation he noted that four men working a full day's shift pumped at the rate of 39 cu. ft raised 1 ft/min per man; i.e. 2400 ft.lb/min. By contrast, using a pump of his own design, installed at Ackworth Hospital in 1764, he found that one man in an hour worked at the rate of 4140 ft.lb/min. Similarly, four horses operating a scoop wheel and working 8 h/day raised water at 20,400 ft.lb/min per horse, while two horses working 4½ h shifts raised coals at 27,000 ft.lb/min per horse.

By 1765 Smeaton had fixed on 22,000 ft.lb/min, or its equivalent in other units, as a standard for the power developed by a horse in an 8 h working day; though he might reduce this by 20 per cent to be on the safe side in design. Reviewing the data available in 1818, Farey concluded that no better figure could be given. When James Watt in 1783 settled on 33,000 ft.lb/min as the basis for expressing the "horse power" of his steam engines he seems to have chosen on purpose a maximum for the strongest horses working in a short period of time.[19]

Hydraulic limes
Other examples of Smeaton's scientific approach to engineering problems could be given and one of these, the experimental work on

steam engines, is considered in Chapter VIII. A classic case is the investigation of hydraulic limes which he fully describes in his book on the Eddystone Lighthouse, published in 1791.[20]

In executing the lighthouse Smeaton was concerned above all to ensure the structure's strength and permanence and was obliged, among other priorities, to consider the problem of mortars: their manufacture, preparation and application. He knew from traditional practice that "two measures of quenched or slaked lime, in the dry powder, mixed with one measure of Dutch Tarras, and both very well beat together to the consistence of a paste, using as little water as possible", was the mix normally used to achieve permanence in hydraulic structures. Indeed he says "that it would in time grow hard even under water". He was aware too that masons generally reckoned that mortars made with salt water would never harden so well and were prone to remain, and/or attract, damp. Smeaton was not convinced that in tarras mortar[21] hardening and drying were necessarily dependent on one another and this was one issue he proposed to investigate. The other was the problem of identifying the best sources of raw materials for mortars and how best to prepare and use them.

Smeaton's test specimens were quite small, a ball of mortar 2 in. in diameter which was made by mixing lime with a minimum quantity of water to which was added, by degrees, various amounts of tarras and sand. Smeaton immediately discovered that specimens made of "common lime and sand" when immersed in a pot of water rapidly disintegrated. Similarly mortars comprising two parts of slaked lime and one part of tarras were generally no better. However, by using equal measures of lime and tarras (and minimum water) Smeaton was able to manufacture a mortar that would set under water.

A less than thorough engineer might have left it at that and proceeded to build, but Smeaton had recognised too many interesting and relevant parameters not to conceive of an exhaustive programme of research. He posed four questions:

Question 1   What difference in the effect results from lime burnt from stones of different qualities, in point of hardness?

Question 2   What difference results in the strength of the mortar when made up with fresh, or with Sea Water; the compositions being immersed in the same water?

Question 3   What difference results from different *Qualities* of limestone, so far as I could procure the specimens?

Question 4   Whether *Tarras Mortar*, after having been once well beaten, becomes better by being repeatedly beaten over again?

The first two questions were quickly answered. There were no differences; the hardness of the raw stone was immaterial and sea water would make just as good a mortar as fresh water. Out on the Eddystone Rock the latter was to be of no small advantage.

The third question was more difficult. Smeaton knew that Aberthaw lias limestone was well regarded as a source of lime and was, like tarras, capable of setting under water. The Aberthaw product was compared with eight other limestones, from sources as far apart as Sussex, Lincolnshire, Lancashire and Somerset, and in addition Smeaton took the trouble to conduct a simple *chemical* analysis. This was an inspired move because it revealed that the very pure limestones, of the type that "would best answer the purposes of Agriculture" but would not make an under-water cement, differed from those that would in so far as the latter were characterised by a very marked clay component in their composition. This fact intrigued Smeaton considerably, and rightly so.

The answers to the fourth question were inconclusive but they did lead Smeaton on to consider whether tarras was really the best material available to him for rendering his cements hydraulic. He found a classical alternative—pozzolana—and he acknowledges both Belidor and Vitruvius as his sources of information. Amazingly Smeaton was able to pick up a "job-lot" of Civita Vecchia pozzolana in Plymouth, imported by a merchant who had hoped, vainly as it turned out, to sell it to the builders of Westminster Bridge.

Civita Vecchia pozzolana was as good as tarras in every respect and even better in one. When made up with Aberthaw lime "it exceeded in hardness any of the compositions commonly used in dry work; and in *wet* and *dry*, or wholly wet, was far superior to any I had seen or experienced". Smeaton's remark that it would "make a cement that would equal the best *merchantable Portland Stone*" was no mean prophecy.

Smeaton tried diligently to locate, or make, an alternative to trass and pozzolana but failed. He chose a 1 to 1 mixture of Aberthaw lime and Civita Vecchia pozzolana to build the Eddystone Lighthouse; and to ensure the maximum possible strength and durability no sand was used. However in his experiments the role and proportions of sand in mortars were examined. Smeaton was able to show that a perfectly good hydraulic mortar could be made with as much, and even more, sand than the lime and pozzolana content combined. His tabulation of twenty lime/pozzolana/sand ratios drew attention to the considerable reduction in cost per cubic foot of mortar if sand was used.

As noted already Smeaton was intrigued by the differences between "common lime" and hydraulic lime and the influence on the latter of its clay content. He remarks:

> "It remains a curious question, which being myself unable to resolve, I must leave to the learned *Naturalist* and *Chemist*, why an intimate mixture of clay in the composition of limestone of any kind, either hard or soft, should render it capable of setting in water, in a manner that no *pure* lime I have yet seen from any kind of stone whatever, has been capable of doing. It is easy to add *Clay* in any proportion to a pure lime; but it produces no such effect."

He concludes:

> "In short, I have as yet found no treatment of pure calcareous lime, that rendered it more fit to set in *water* than it is by nature, except what is to be derived from the admixture of *Tarras, Puzzolana,* or some *ferruginous* substance of a similar nature."

Smeaton was within an ace of reaching a singularly important conclusion and yet he never did. Considering that 37 years elapsed between the experiments and their publication the fact is the more amazing. Materials such as pozzolana, trass and Santorin earth[22] will impart hydraulic properties to lime because of their volcanic origin and the intense heat by which they were produced. Similarly the reason why Aberthaw limestone will make a hydraulic lime is because the calcinating process converts the clay content of the rock into the necessary compounds of aluminium and silicon.

As Smeaton observed, "It is easy to add *Clay* in any proportion to a pure lime"; and so it is, but to have a hydraulic effect it has to be roasted as well.

Before John Smeaton's time, before the first decades of the industrial revolution that is, it would have been impossible for a scientist, no matter how practical his bent, to have worked as a civil engineer of any stature. After Smeaton's time civil engineering began to develop apace and every practitioner was so busy building canals and railways and a host of other works that the opportunity to pursue scientific enquiries scarcely existed. Smeaton flourished at a period, the only period perhaps, when one could do both. The fact that he did both so well is testimony to a combination of intellectual powers and practical genius that was unique.

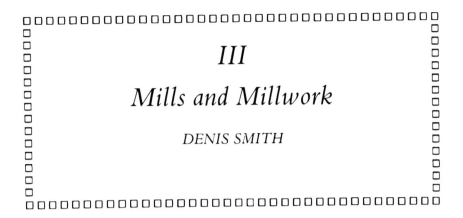

III

Mills and Millwork

DENIS SMITH

Throughout Smeaton's long engineering practice, millwork was one of the most regular of his many activities and is therefore an important aspect of his work. His earliest mill design was made in 1753, the last in 1791, and during this period nearly 60 new works were constructed to his designs (see Appendix III).[1] He was also involved in planning and supervising modifications to existing mills, and from time to time he was professionally retained to arbitrate in disputes between rival millowners and between millers and other parties.

It is not possible here, or indeed necessary, to consider each of Smeaton's mill designs in detail.[2] From his various drawings, reports, and letters it is, however, possible to establish something of his design philosophy and identify characteristic features of his millwork. Unlike many of his contemporaries, Smeaton did not emerge from the ranks of artisan millwrights and it is interesting to speculate on how he acquired his undoubted expertise in such matters. We know that from childhood he had keenly observed the work of millwrights and mechanics and at an early age enjoyed making mechanical devices. It is perhaps sufficient to say that innate ability allied to keen observation and intelligence is a potent teacher. The tour of the Low Countries in 1755 gave him first-hand knowledge of continental millwright practice and this was obviously an important influence on his work. Typically, he was also conversant with the published works of Parent, Maclaurin, and Desaguliers, amongst others, and we know from his Diary that he was acquainted with the Dutch mill books even before his 1755 journey.[3]

Although his model experiments on windmill performance were widely known, he designed relatively few windmills and will here be considered principally as a designer of water-powered millwork. Smeaton leaves us in no doubt that there was a rational, numerical, basis for his design work. Writing to a client in 1786 he said his objective was "to get the most Power possible out of a given quantity of water in dry seasons" and that "The construction of Mills, as to their Power, is not with me a Matter of *Opinion* it is a Matter of *Calculation*".[4]

Preliminary site investigation

Two principal facts have to be established in order to assess a prospective mill site; namely, the fall and quantity of the available water. A site survey was often necessary to determine level differences, and rivers and springs might need to be gauged. It was also necessary to estimate the effect that the new work might have on adjacent mills. A typical feasibility study is Smeaton's report on a proposed mill to be supplied from a farm pond at Worksop:

> "The fall from the surface of the farm-yard pond . . . is 9 feet 6 inches, which is a sufficient fall for the erection of a mill; the principal difficulty, therefore, attending this affair, is to supply the said pond with water, sufficient to answer the intended purpose.
>
> "The quantity of water necessary depends upon the quantity of corn to be ground, which was stated to me as 10 loads per week, that is, 30 Winchester bushels.
>
> "The quantity of water necessary to grind one bushel of wheat into flour, will grind five quarters of malt, so that supposing 10 quarters of malt to be brewed per week, the quantity of water that is necessary to grind 32 bushels of wheat per week will despatch the whole business.
>
> "Now 3600 cube feet of water will, in this situation, be required to grind one bushel of wheat; and, therefore, 115,200 cube feet will be necessary to grind 32 bushels; and this quantity, at least, must be supplied to the farmyard pond in a week."[5]

He goes on to show that the quantity of water presently available is not sufficient; but more than enough to supply the deficiency could be obtained from a spring. This rises 6 ft above the pond level and its flow, which he gauged, can be taken into the pond along a 2-mile feeder channel. All this gives a good idea of the data to be gathered before estimates of costs and work in the drawing office could begin.

In discussing the design of water-powered machinery it is convenient to separate the details of the waterwheel and its control gear from that of the power transmission machinery applied to a variety of industrial purposes.

Waterwheel design

The typical waterwheel of eighteenth-century Britain was the Vitruvian wheel; that is, a vertical wheel carried on a horizontal axle. Smeaton's many workmanlike designs for these include wheels of the undershot, breast, and overshot types. In all these cases the water delivers its energy at the perimeter of the wheel whilst the power take-off is from the central axle. To transmit this energy a strong and stiff connection is required between the rim and axle. Two systems were used: compass arm and clasp arm (Fig. 8). The compass arm system comprised radial spokes. In a typical Smeaton design there were six timber spokes, or arms, each about 5 in. square in cross-section. They would be mortised into the wheel rings and into the timber axle. The axle mortices were a source of structural weakness and provided an entry for water into the heartwood of the shaft. Smeaton was certainly aware of these problems. Two remedies were available; one was the "clasp arm" form of construction and the other, pioneered by Smeaton, was the use of cast iron for the axle. In the clasp arm form, two pairs of parallel arms crossed each other at right angles forming a square opening in the centre which "clasped" the axle which was therefore left intact. Obviously the arms were no longer radial and Smeaton sometimes suggested a curved clasp arm to ensure a radial mortice in the ring. His use of cast iron will be considered later.

With a few exceptions, Smeaton's waterwheels were so proportioned that their diameter/width ratio lay between 3 and 4. In his undershot and breast wheels he invariably made the flat float boards radial and usually stipulated a clearance of $\frac{1}{4}$ in. between the tip of the float and the masonry breastwork. This small clearance on a timber wheel 20 ft in diameter required accurate work from the millwright, and is what Smeaton described as making the breastwork "to a true sweep, answerable to the wheel".[6] With wheels of the normal diameter/width proportions Smeaton used just two shroud rings with either compass or clasp arms. But in wider wheels as, for example, those at Knouch Bridge Mill where the diameter was 11 ft 6 in. and the width 8 ft, Smeaton said:

> "The construction I commonly use in wheels of this sort, is three pairs of clasp arms with three rings, and then to put on the boarding of the soal parallel to the axis, so that the boards are nailed down upon the rings like a floor upon joists."[6]

In his report on this job Smeaton stated his method of proportioning waterwheel buckets. The radial width of the shroud was 9 in. and

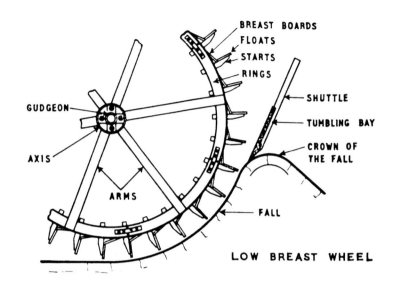

BREAST BOARDS
FLOATS
STARTS
RINGS

GUDGEON

SHUTTLE

TUMBLING BAY

CROWN OF
THE FALL

AXIS

ARMS

FALL

LOW BREAST WHEEL

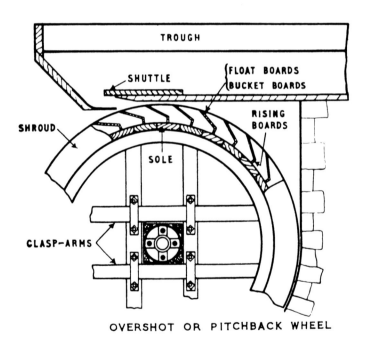

TROUGH

SHUTTLE

FLOAT BOARDS
BUCKET BOARDS

RISING
BOARDS

SHROUD

SOLE

CLASP-ARMS

OVERSHOT OR PITCHBACK WHEEL

Fig. 8.   *Smeaton's typical waterwheels (drawing by P.N. Wilson, Trans. New-comen Soc., 30)*

there were to be 36 buckets. Smeaton required "the rising boards to be 4½ inches broad, and the breadth of the bucket board such, that the point of one bucket may advance to the centre line of the heel of the next bucket, and the cutting edge to be thrown to the outside".

A decision would also have to be made about the number of buckets or float boards on a given wheel. Early in his career Smeaton stated that with breast wheels the minimum criterion was to ensure that "one float entered the curve before the preceding one quitted it".[7] Analysis of his designs reveals that he regarded a circular pitch of about 1 ft as satisfactory—that is there would be one float, or bucket, per foot of perimeter circumference, though for wheels exceeding about 20 ft this pitch was increased somewhat. The diameter of a wheel relates, of course, the rotational speed in revolutions per minute to the peripheral velocity in feet per second. Smeaton appears to have used the latter as a fundamental parameter, saying in 1759 that:

> "Experience confirms that a velocity of 3 feet in a second is applicable to the highest overshot wheels, as well as the lowest . . . however . . . I have seen a wheel of 33 feet high, that has moved very steadily and well with a velocity but little exceeding 2 feet."[7]

In a letter to Mr Whatman about his papermill in Kent, written in 1787, however, he says:

> "I have now gone thro' the Calculation for your mill at Loose, and have settled the sketch for the wheel, the water trough, and the shuttle . . . I propose the wheel to be 19 feet diameter or height, to be 5 feet out and out and 4 ft. 8 in. within the shrouds and to make 4⁸⁄₁₀ turns a minute."[8]

This would give a peripheral velocity of 4.7 ft/s, and indeed his later practice appears to have been to use somewhat greater speeds of this order.

Power transmission
Smeaton designed mill machinery for a variety of purposes. Shafts and gearing transmitted rotary motion to the common face stones for grinding corn, edge-runner stones for oil-mills and gunpowder manufacture, and for driving rolling, slitting, and boring-mills in ironworks. Reciprocating power take-off was required for water pumping, furnace blowing engines, and sawmills. Stamp mills, fulling stocks and forge hammers were tripped by rotating cam drums.

In his corn-mill designs Smeaton followed common practice in having a vertical "pit-wheel" fixed to the waterwheel axle which drove a "wallower" on a vertical shaft. His typical pit-wheel had horizontal teeth projecting from the wheel face which meshed with the staves of a lantern wheel wallower. At this stage the speed stepped up at between 2.5 and 3.5 to 1. Mounted on the vertical wallower shaft was the main "spur wheel" which drove the "lanthorn" connected directly to the runner stone. At this final stage the speed was again stepped up. In a typical Smeaton corn-mill the runner stones turned at speeds at between 10 and 15 times that of the waterwheel. Millwrights had a rule-of-thumb method of determining the optimum speed of flour grindstones.[9] This was to divide 5,000 by the stone diameter in inches to give the speed in revolutions per minute. If this rule is applied to those designs of Smeaton where the rotational speed of the waterwheel is given, then his gearing provides stone speeds within 4 per cent of the accepted rule. As an example Smeaton's design for a Scottish mill in 1771 gave the following details:[10]

"FOR THE WHEAT MILL

Water-wheel, in diameter,	11 feet
The main cog-wheel,	54 cogs, at 5-inch pitch
The great lanthorn,	19 do at do.
The spur-wheel,	62 at 3½ inch pitch
The lanthorn on the spindles,	13 at ditto.
The diameter of the French stones,	4 feet.

N.B. The water-wheel is intended to go eight turns per minute."

Using the millwright's rule the speed should be $(5,000/48) = 104 \cdot 16$ rev/min, and the actual speed $= 8 \times (54/19) \times (62/13) = 108 \cdot 4$ rev/min. We note that here again the peripheral velocity of the wheel is 4.6 ft/s.

Cast iron in millwork

Smeaton is widely credited with being a pioneer in the introduction of cast iron in millwork. The best evidence for his early use of the material is given in a letter he wrote to the Carron Company in February 1782. He was discussing the validity of hammer blows to test the relative merits of cast and wrought iron ship's anchors and said:

"of the windmill axis and oil-press that you cast for me the year before the last, the former has withstood the fury of all the storms that have happened since, without the least liklihood of injury; . . . The oil-press is in constant work, and every five or six minutes is subject to an alternate pressure and release from it equivalent to 300 tons of dead weight, tending directly to rend it in two; and yet I believe a single well-directed blow of a sledge hammer would break it. If the length of time of the use of these utensils is not thought sufficient, I must add, that in the year 1755, that is 27 years ago, for the first time, I applied them as totally new subjects, and the cry then was, that if the strongest timbers are not able for any great length of time to resist the action of powers, what must happen from the brittleness of cast iron? It is sufficient to say, that not only those very pieces of cast work are still in work, but that the good effect has . . . drawn them to common use, and I never heard of any one failing."[11]

Smeaton specified cast iron in millwork for various reasons. In power transmission, for example, he said:

"As the main geer will be often wet, it will make it wear much longer to have cast-iron rounds in the great lanthorns, particularly in the wheat mill, which will come to the greatest pressure."[10]

On another occasion he said:

"If the staves of the great lanterns are made of cast iron, as will be advisable, they may be made of a flattish or oval figure, and thinner than if made of wood, so as to give room for a stronger cog."[6]

The consequent reduction in size of iron parts was also a factor in waterwheel design. Smeaton noted on a drawing of 1780:

"The float boards of the water wheel are proposed to be of iron plates which compared with those shown of wood will allow the Bucketts to be more capacious, & a better entry for the water."[12]

The greater weight of cast iron could also be advantageous. For his water-powered boring machine at Carron Ironworks he said:

"The rings of the two water-wheels I have designed to be of cast iron, in order that they may act as loaded flies, and thereby preserve the motion more steady."[13]

During a period of 20 years, from 1769 to 1789, Smeaton designed cast iron axles for eight waterwheels.[14] Figure 9 shows a typical design, made in 1780 for Carshalton mills. The 10 ft long iron axle carried a breast wheel 18 ft in diameter and 3 ft wide. The shaft is generally octagonal in section with two circular sections 7 in. diameter, for the wheel bearings. At one end a 2 ft 6 in. square box formed the centre for the clasp arms of the pit wheel. The waterwheel itself comprised six timber compass arms, and a note on the drawing explains:

"All the arms mitre together upon the axis in the centre; they are fixed by being bolted between the flanches cast upon the axis & a couple of iron rings to each flanch."[15]

65

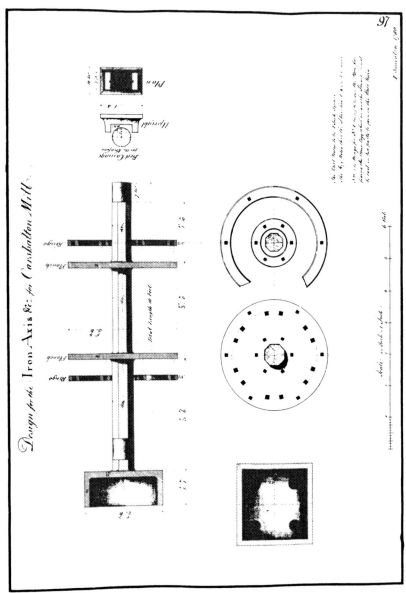

Fig. 9. Carshalton mill, iron axle, 1780 (Designs, 1, f. 97)

Having made wooden patterns for gear wheels Smeaton would try and persuade his clients to use them. For example, writing to Mr Whatman in 1782 he said:

"In our mill at Deptford we have two iron nutts of 17 coggs, one of 5 inches pitch for the pit wheel, and the other of 3²⁄₁₆ pitch upon the spindle of the stones: they both go very sweetly, and the latter I think beyond any thing I ever saw: if you find that you can adopt these numbers and pitches, as the patterns were taken a good deal of pain with, if you chuse it we can get you a cast taken from each."[8]

However, Smeaton was prepared to put the case before his clients and allow them to make up their own minds. One extract from a report will illustrate the point:

"Iron rings will not be needed for this wheel; wooden ones, of the common scantlings, viz. about six inches square, will be sufficient.

"As the same patterns for the wheels and nuts as in the gun-mill are proposed here to be made use of, I aprehend they will be done cheaper than of wood, but if otherwise, wooden wheels of equivalent numbers will do; also, if the practice of making iron axes for the water-wheels, be found to recommend itself so far as to be equally cheap with wood, they may also be used here."[16]

So much then for the general principles of Smeaton's common mill-work design practice. We shall now consider some examples of his specific designs for water-powered machinery.

Waterwheels and returning engines
Smeaton designed many Newcomen-type atmospheric or "fire engines" (Chapter VIII). This single-acting, essentially reciprocating, machine was well suited to pumping, but its application to mill-work was limited by the difficulty of obtaining rotary motion. Smeaton therefore strongly recommended its use in conjunction with a waterwheel where the tail water was pumped back to the top of an overshot wheel. He had good, practical, reasons for preferring this system to that of a fire engine with a crank. Although he saw no material differences in fuel costs between the two systems he nevertheless felt that:

"no motion communicated from the reciprocating beam of a fire engine can ever act perfectly equal and steady in producing a circular motion, like the regular efflux of water in turning a water-wheel, and much of the good effect of a water mill is well known to depend upon the motion communicated to the mill-stones being perfectly equal and smooth as the least tremor or agitation takes off from the complete performance."[17]

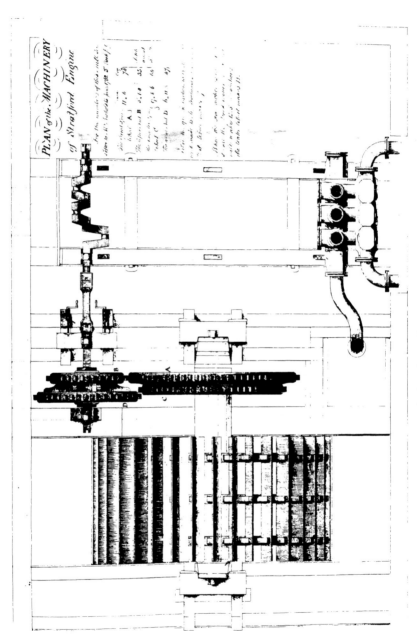

Fig. 10. Stratford mill, machinery, 1762 (Designs 2, f. 146)

He went on to note that a fire engine often stopped suddenly in mid-stroke, whereas, "when a water-mill stops for want of water, the motion is lost by degrees", and concluded, with characteristic clarity:

"By the intervention of water, these uncertanties and difficulties are avoided, for the work, in fact, is a water mill...

"For these reasons, were I to establish a work of this kind at my own cost, I should certainly execute it by the intervention of water, and therefore must greatly prefer it."

In breweries the combination had even greater benefits. Here the engine condensate provided hot water for the mash tuns, the beam engine lifted water from wells, and, as Smeaton told a client in 1788—when the Boulton and Watt engine was gaining ground:

"A rotary motion for grinding the malt is necessary; but for my own part I would as soon do this by a water wheel (to preclude which there is no patent) as by the rotative motion of a heavy fly...

"The pumping of worts I would suppose to depend upon the water wheel: for as I conceive those businesses taken singly are *light* matters in proportion to the grinding of the malt, or pumping of the water (which I would always suppose to be separately done by the full power of the engine) then the water wheel cistern, though of a very moderate size, will retain a treasury of water whereby the worts may be pumped when the fire engine is at rest."[18]

Water pumping engines
Smeaton designed several waterwheel-powered engines for raising water for waterworks and other purposes. His typical design comprised a waterwheel driving a three-throw crankshaft. From each crank a rod transmitted the drive to one end of each of three beams pivoted in what Smeaton called a "regulator frame". The other end of the oscillating beams operated three reciprocating pumps. We shall now consider some particular installations.

The Stratford engine. This was his first of such pumping engines, designed in 1762 and built at Stratford in east London where, as Smeaton said:

"I was employed to make a design for converting an Old Corn Mill, opposite the Fire Engine there into a Water Engine for raising Water... and also for building a new Corn Mill to grind with the Spare Water."[19]

Each plant had its own waterwheel under a common roof. A unique feature of this machine was the two-speed gear drive to the pump crankshaft (see Fig. 10). A large spur wheel on the waterwheel axle drove a pinion on the crank axle. Two drive ratios were possible, either 78 to 35 or 66 to 47, and on his drawing Smeaton noted that:

> "When the quick motion is in, the Crank will make 15·6 Revolutions while the Water Wheel makes 7.
>
> "When the slow motion is in, which I call the Flood motion, the Crank will make 15·5 Revolutions while the Water Wheel makes 11."[20]

It is clear that Smeaton wished to maintain a reasonably constant pumping rate under variations in river flow. Whether this variable gear drive was successful we do not know but no evidence has been found to suggest that he ever used it again. The Stratford engine was constructed by Joseph Nickalls of Blackfriars, who had worked previously for Smeaton on the Calder & Hebble Navigation.

London Bridge waterworks. The tidal mill-race effect under the arches of old London Bridge had been used for waterwheel-driven pumps since the sixteenth century. The first arch from the north end was let in 1581, the second in 1583, the fourth in 1701, the third in 1761, and the fifth in 1767. It was for this fifth arch that Smeaton designed an undershot wheel 32 ft diameter and 15½ ft wide to drive three pumps on each side, the pump barrels being 10 in. in diameter with a 4½ ft stroke. The wheel and the regulating frame on the starling of the fifth bridge pier, but not the frame on the fourth pier, are shown in Fig. 11.[21] The 14 ft dia. spur wheels, of clasp arm construction, drove lantern pinions on the crank axles at a fixed ratio of 80 to 23. Pump rods were connected to the arch heads at the ends of the 18 ft rocking beams by an ingenious double-chain device (already used on the Stratford engine) which ensured that, for both the upward and downward motion of the rods, one pair of chains worked in tension leaving the other slack. The wheel and engine construction was massive and it is not surprising that Smeaton referred to it as "the Great Engine". This too was built by Nickalls and completed in 1768. It developed up to 50 or 60 hp.[22]

The Ravensbourne engine. This was designed in 1778–79 for the Deptford waterworks where Smeaton and his friend John Holmes were joint proprietors. Three regulator beams, 19 ft long, worked three pumps of 10 in. bore. The engine is similar to those previously described but an interesting feature here is the addition of weights at the crank end of the regulator beams. Smeaton says these "are intended to over-haul the forcers and fill the barrels" and that as a consequence:

> "the crank-rods will, together with the crank, be always bearing down-

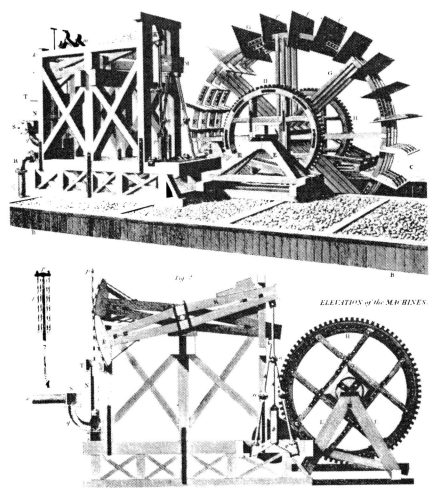

ELEVATION of the MACHINES.

Fig. 11. London Bridge waterwheel and pumps, 1768 (engraving by Wilson Lowry (1820) from a drawing by John Farey—Rees' Cyclopaedia)

wards; there will, therefore, be no use for under-brasses for the crank rods, or upper-brasses for the crank, otherwise than for safety; they may, therefore, be made of yew or hard oak."[23]

He gives explicit instructions about the connection of the pump forcer rods to the regulator beams and with characteristic care says: "I propose that every part of the engine may be put together, and in working condition in the yard, before any part of it is removed to the engine house."

71

In all Smeaton designed five such pumping installations between 1762 and 1778. In addition he designed, in 1775, a temporary water-powered contractor's pump for draining a bridge cofferdam.[24] His drawing shows an undershot wheel 14 ft in diameter, with a crank on the wheel axis driving oscillating link-work to the remote cofferdam. This timber linkage, of 3½ in. square section, was in two lengths, 150 and 115 ft, angled in plan. At the cofferdam its horizontal reciprocating motion gave vertical motion, by means of a rocking T beam, to a pair of pump rods. This would appear to be the only occasion on which Smeaton used such a device.

Ironworks machinery
The expansion of the iron-making industry, and consequently of the metal-working trades, in the second half of the eighteenth century required the design of water-powered machinery somewhat outside the scope of the average millwright. Smeaton was consulted about the design of blast furnace blowing engines, forge hammers, rolling and slitting mills, edge-tool grinders, and cylinder-boring machines. The distinctive problem with this type of work was the unpredictable and intermittent nature of the load. Whereas corn-mill design experience had been reduced to a set of rules, and forge hammers had similar load characteristics to fulling stocks, other ironworks machinery proved more difficult. The design of blowing engines was complicated and, as Smeaton said:

> "The power required for boring depends so much upon the circumstances of the thing to be bored, that it is a matter that cannot be reduced to any exact calculation."[25]

His ironworks machinery designs span a 20-year period from 1764. His earliest extant drawings are those for Kilnhurst hammer mill forge in Yorkshire, and show various stages in the evolution of the final design.[26] It was an extensive works comprising four water-wheels driving bellows 6 ft 6 in. long for Finery and Chafery forges. In addition, two 15 ft diameter wheels operated drome hammers and an 18 ft dia. wheel, 4 ft 4 in. wide, powered a slit mill. Two years later, in 1766, Smeaton designed an improved blade mill at Winlaton on Tyneside. Here an overshot wheel, 13 ft diameter, 8 ft wide, drove pulleys 5 ft in diameter, which in turn drove grindstones through leather belts. Smeaton claimed that: "This mill will go with at least half, if not one-third, of the water now used to do the same business."[27]

Smeaton's most extensive connection with ironworks, however, was with the Carron Company near Falkirk. His reports and drawings cover the period from 1769 to 1785 and include dams, furnace blowing engines, boring mills for guns and engine cylinders, tilt hammers, stamps and rolls. In 1769 there were four blast furnaces at the works when Smeaton was consulted about the best distribution of the available water between them—a complicated problem. Smeaton requested current performance figures and was told: "When No. 1 blows 25 cylinders per minute, she will make 28 baskets per day. When No. 2 blows 34 bellows per minute, she will make 20 baskets per day."[28] Smeaton described the problem thus:

"As the several blast furnaces at Carron are of different dimensions, work upon different kinds of ore, and take different quantities thereof at a charge, the wheels take their water at different heights ... it seems impossible to fix upon any absolute criterion or common measure to which they can all be reduced.

"It remains, therefore, that the number of charges ... which each furnace can work off in a given time, relative to a given quantity of water, is the only handle we can at present lay hold of, and is, as I perceive, the same by which the managers and workmen reckon."[29]

Having measured the river flow, in "cube feet per minute", he designed overshot waterwheels driving cranks and oscillating beams in a timber structure resembling his "regulator frame" in water-pumping engines. Instead of pumps, cast iron cylinders containing pistons were connected by rods to the beam. The blowing cylinders were connected by pipework terminating in a nozzle, or "nose-piece". His published drawings for No. 1 furnace engine show a spur gear of 64 teeth on the waterwheel axle driving a pinion of 31 teeth on the crank axle. Two timber rocking beams, pivoted in the centre, each drove a blower cylinder attached at each end. The four cylinders were each 4 ft in diameter.[30] On the No. 2 furnace engine a four-throw crank was on the waterwheel axle and connecting rods were attached at one end of the rocking beams. The four blowing cylinders were 4 ft 6 in. in diameter (see Fig. 12).[31]

In 1770 Smeaton designed a boring mill for the works. The building straddled a divided watercourse which powered two 18 ft dia. breast wheels, one driving a cylinder-boring mill and the other a mill for boring cannon. Smeaton's drawings show excellent details of the cast iron gearing, shafting, and ingenious arrangements for feeding the cutters into the bore.[32] One of his last jobs for the Carron Company was the design of a tilt hammer at the Clay Mill forge in

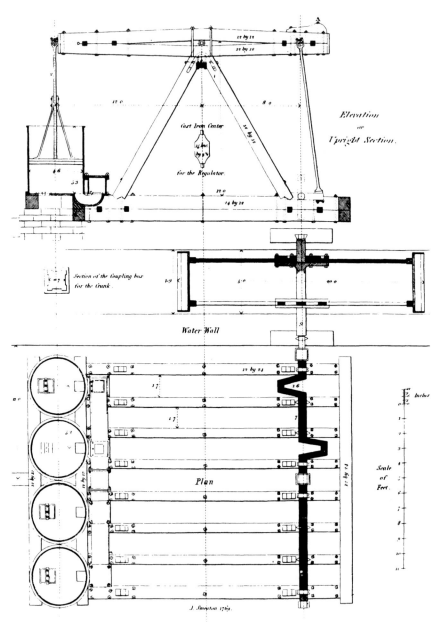

Fig. 12. Blowing engine for Carron ironworks No. 2 furnace, 1769 (Reports, 1)

1785. An 18 ft diameter waterwheel drove, through gearing, a hammer beam camshaft which powered three tilt hammers. The large, middle, and small hammers were tripped by rotating drums having 8, 12, and 16 tappets. When the shaft rotated at $18\frac{3}{4}$ rev/min the hammers made 150, 225, and 300 blows per minute respectively.[33]

Whilst undertaking this work for the Carron Company Smeaton also designed machinery for an ironworks on the River Coquet in Northumberland in 1776,[34] an iron hoop mill in Wandsworth in 1779, and a stamp mill in 1780 for Wanlockhead lead mines in Lanarkshire.[35]

Mill dams

Largely in connection with his ironworks millwork Smeaton designed some six dams in the 1770s. The first, in 1772, was an arched dam on the River Carron, 140 ft wide and 8 ft high.[36] The Carron Company impounded the large quantity of water required to power their machinery and at Dunipace, further upstream, Smeaton also designed a straight dam 7 ft high in 1773. This had sloping air and water faces with a rubble fill protected by flat stones laid on edge,[37] similar to his river navigation weirs (Chapter V). In 1776 he designed another rubble dam, 8 ft high, for the Swalwell ironworks in County Durham.[38] In the same year he tackled his largest dam, for the Coquet ironworks in Northumberland. It was an arched structure, 162 ft wide, with a vertical air face 8 ft high, built to a radius of 170 ft.[39] The curved wall had an outer skin of bonded, and cramped, masonry with a rubble core laid in sloping courses (see Fig. 13). Referring to this Smeaton said:

> "There is not a more difficult or hazardous piece of work within the compass of civil engineery than the establishment of a high dam upon a rapid river that is liable to great and sudden floods, and such I esteem the river Coquett, and such the dam here proposed."[40]

However, his dam survives today very much as originally constructed (Fig. 14).

Horse millwork

Smeaton's earliest design for animal-powered machinery appears to be his drawing of 1761 for a horse-driven screw pumping engine at Kew, in Surrey.[41] An octagonal timber-framed building housed the horse gear. A two-horse tackle and track of 25 ft diameter drove the main gear wheel of 144 teeth. This drove a pinion of 23 teeth turning,

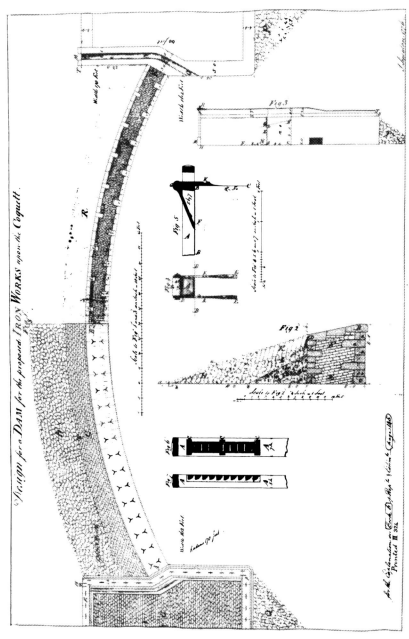

Fig. 13. Dam on River Coquet, 1776 (Designs, 2, f. 56)

through a form of Hooke's joint, an inclined Archimedian screw. This was 24 ft long, 2 ft 6 in. inside diameter, and lifted 13½ gal. at each turn. The lift was 11 ft and Smeaton notes that the horses caused the screw to make 20 turns per minute, which he describes as "light work for 2 light horses".

In 1779 Smeaton devised a substantial horse-driven water-pumping engine for His Majesty's Victualling Office as part of his report on the water supply to the brewery at Weevil, near Gosport. In addition he was concerned with watering the occasionally large fleet moored at Spithead and he said:

> "I expect that two horses at the New Well engine will perform the ordinary service I see going on; but, if the full quantity of 200 tons be required to be daily delivered, then, to keep the service going during twenty-four hours, will require three sets and one spare horse in case of accidents to the rest, that is, in the whole seven horses."[42]

In this case the pinion drove an iron axle carrying a flywheel and a crank. A connecting rod attached at one end of a rocking beam drove the pump. The pump had a 3 ft stroke in a 6 in. barrel and when worked at "sixteen to eighteen strokes per minute . . . and, if worked 24 hours, will amount to 400 tons per day". At 18 strokes per minute the horses have to make 2.125 circuits per minute, at 2·27 miles/h, of their 30 ft dia. track. Smeaton ended his report by adding:

> "If thought necessary, by way of easing the horses, a wind engine might be raised upon the same building, of sufficient power to perform the whole service, whenever the wind amounts to a fresh breeze."

Windmills
Unlike his extensive watermill practice, Smeaton designed relatively few windmills. Of the 47 mills in his own list of those executed, compiled in 1780, only four are windmills. Nevertheless, he had a great influence on wind millwright practice. His model experiments on sail performance, details of which were published in 1759 (see Chapter II), guided his own design work and, moreover, his results were still being quoted in pocket-books and other technical works a century and a half later.

The gearing to drive the stones in wind-powered corn-mills is similar to that in watermills and need not be re-considered here. The special problems of harnessing wind-power relate to the design of the sails themselves as efficient collectors and to the characteristic variability of the energy source, both in strength and direction. Smeaton's windmill sails were always of the common type; that is a timber framework to be covered with sail-cloth to produce an aerodynamic surface. In designing sails the principal decisions to be made are: the overall size, the form and proportions, and the system of producing the warped surface, or "weathering", of the sail. Of the overall size of sail Smeaton said, in his 1759 paper: "Supposing the radius to be 30 feet, which is the most usual length in this country", and he followed this tradition very closely. He also favoured sails with enlarged extremities and said:

> "The figure and proportion of the enlarged sails, which I have found to answer in large, are . . . where the extreme bar is ⅓d of the radius (or whip as it is called by the workmen) and is divided by the whip in the proportion of 3 to 5."

A triangular section was on the leading side of the whip and the trailing edge was parallel with the whip. By the mid-1770s this triangular leading section was much reduced in area and comprised a solid board, "made to fix with slotts & take out, which is needful in storms, & hard gales of wind".[43] The warped sail surface was achieved by mortising the various sail bars through the whip at varying angles.

On his windmill sail drawings Smeaton included a scale from which the millwright could measure the amount of "weather", by off-sets, of a particular sail bar. A good example of his later weathering practice is given on a drawing of 1774.[44] In this case the sail has 25 equally spaced sail bars. There is a near linear increase of weather up to number 12 (measured from the tip of the sail), then the rate of increase diminishes up to the maximum angle at bar number 20. Thus the maximum obliquity is four-fifths in from the outer end and, continuing inwards, he says that bar 21 is the same as 20; 22 as 19; 23 as 18; 24 as 17; and the 25th as the 16th. Smeaton cautioned his clients saying:

> "It will be necessary to attend minutely to these directions for the weathering of the sails and boards; the effect depends upon it, and however uncommon they may appear, the success will follow."[45]

His earlier mills had the conventional four sails but his last three each had five sail arms with the consequent disadvantage that if one sail should be damaged you were left with an unbalanced, unworkable, mill. A four-sail mill could always be worked using only two, opposite, sails.

A characteristic of Smeaton's windmills was his method of preventing excessive deflection of the sails. The windshaft was extended

Fig. 14. Coquet dam (photo by Norman Smith)

in front of the sails and, from its end, ropes with tensioning turn-buckles or pulley blocks were attached to points about two-thirds down the whip (see Fig. 15).[46] He specified cast iron windshafts for some mills, and they usually had square boxes cast on the shaft forming the centres for clasp arm brakewheels. The longest of these windshafts was about 14 ft from the tail bearing to the sail centre with a 7 ft extension for the rope stays. Using the millwright's rule for the speed of corn-mill stones (quoted earlier) it would appear from Smeaton's gear ratios that he expected the sails to turn at speeds between 12 and 18 rev/min. Although Smeaton was aware of Andrew Meikle's introduction of the spring-sail with multiple hinged shutters in 1772[47] he never adopted it in his designs even though it was not pro-tected by a patent. Smeaton's common sails made it tediously difficult to accommodate variations in wind speed.

His mills were better adapted to accommodate variation in wind direction. He never designed a post-mill—most of his mills com-prised a square masonry base surmounted by a timber smock struc-ture carrying a geared cap. For a mill at Wakefield, designed in 1755, the cap was turned by gearing driven by an endless chain descending

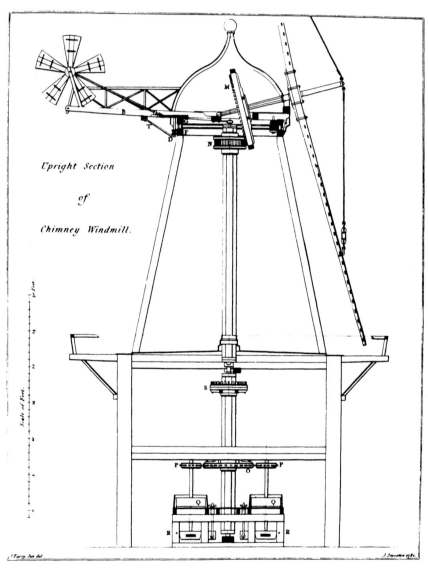

Fig. 15.   Windmill at Newcastle-upon-Tyne, 1782 (Reports, **2**)

to a balcony.[48] For one of his later windmills at Newcastle, designed in 1782, the cap was driven by a five-bladed fantail (see Fig. 15). A large gear reduction was required to convert the relatively high speed/low torque of the fantail to the high torque/low speed of the pinion meshing with the rack around the curb of the cap. In this case Smeaton made the ratio 3,308 to 1. In addition, he provided a crank in the middle of the oblique spindle connecting the fantail to the curb pinion so that, "the mill may be turned in a calm by hand".[49]

Although Smeaton proved himself an able practitioner in all his millwork designs he nevertheless regarded himself as being in a form of partnership with the men who would carry out the work. In a report to a client he would say: "in regard to the thickness and strength of the parts, your millwright will, I doubt not, judge properly"[50] and, on another occasion: "The rest of the machinery, being the framing or harness for the hammer, is supposed to be subject to the corrections of the forge carpenter."[51] That Smeaton had an enormous influence on mill construction may be judged from the remarks of an eminent engineer writing in 1853 when he said:

> "Parent, Euler, and other geometricians have written much upon the nature and construction of windmills; but as we consider the experiments and researches made by our own countryman Smeaton to be far superior in point of practical utility, we shall content ourselves with giving his opinion."[52]

This they were still doing, well into this century.[53]

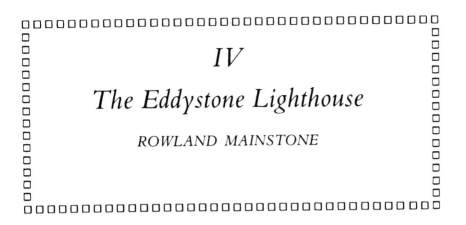

IV

The Eddystone Lighthouse

ROWLAND MAINSTONE

Smeaton's memorial on the wall of the old parish church of Whitkirk is appropriately surmounted by a relief of the Eddystone Lighthouse. The memorial inscription refers to it as his principal work "erected on a rock in the open sea (where one had been washed away by the violence of a storm, and another had been consumed by the rage of fire) secure in its own stability and the wise precautions for its safety, seeming not unlikely to convey to distant ages, as it does to every Nation of the Globe, the name of its constructor".[1]

The invitation to rebuild it, after the destructive fire, came in January 1756 from Robert Weston, and was the turning point in Smeaton's fortunes. Weston was the principal shareholder of the small group of proprietors who held the remainder of a 99-year lease from Trinity House that enabled them to collect dues from shipping in return for maintaining a light on the Rock.[2] He was acting on behalf of them all and had first sought the advice of the Earl of Macclesfield, President of the Royal Society. Smeaton had only 3 years ago turned from making scientific instruments towards the practice of civil engineering, so he was not widely known in the field, yet the President felt able to recommend him in warm terms (see Chapter I).

The task was a daunting one, hardly to be compared with more usual civil engineering works of the time—roads and bridges, canals and fen drainage, or even dock and harbour works. The main problems stemmed from the site and its extreme exposure to the fury of the sea.

The Eddystone Rocks, as well as being a great hazard to shipping passing up and down the Channel or entering or leaving Plymouth, present one of the most difficult sites imaginable for the construction of a lighthouse. They lie 14 miles south of Plymouth and almost midway between the Lizard and Start Point, fully exposed to gales from any direction between west and east and to the ground swells that persist for days after storms in the Bay of Biscay. At high tide they are largely covered. At low tide when the sea around them is calm, they are exposed in several roughly parallel reefs that are nowhere much above 40 ft wide. Their surfaces have a sharp dip towards the west which continues for a considerable distance below the water and leads to a massive build-up of any seas coming from this direction. The jagged rocks below water for some distance around also add greatly to the difficulty of mooring supply vessels in the vicinity. The rock itself is a hard gneiss, difficult to cut, partly on account of its tendency to split along the grain if a cut is attempted in any other direction.

As well as having to face these difficulties, Smeaton was heavily dependent on wind, tide and sea conditions in getting to and from the Rocks, and had to contend with the further hazards arising from war with France. With only sails and oars as means of propulsion the journey from Plymouth was always lengthy and sea conditions sometimes made landings impossible for weeks at a time even in the best seasons of summer and autumn. The war presented the double hazard of French privateers and the English press gang, the latter being in fact the more troublesome in taking away sailors at crucial moments. Local fishermen interfered more than once with essential moorings.

On the other hand, Smeaton was extremely fortunate in having the complete confidence and unswerving backing of the proprietors, chiefly in the person of Weston. He discussed his plans fully with them and reported regularly on progress, but was given complete authority to proceed as he saw fit.[3] In particular they sanctioned the adoption of a design completely in stone instead of a less costly one partly in timber as the previous structures had been. This certainly promised a saving in maintenance to offset partly the greater cost; but it was still a notable decision since the structure burnt down had served for almost half the term of the lease so that there was a good chance that a slightly modified one of the same type would last for the remaining term.

The successful completion of the lighthouse in 1759 in this more durable form fully vindicated the proprietors' confidence and the recommendation from which it initially stemmed. Smeaton's achievement aroused widespread interest—so much interest, indeed, that visitors wishing to see his models and talk about what had been done threatened, for a while, to take up all his time. Many years later, at the request of friends and of Trinity House, and to satisfy the continuing curiosity, he wrote his *Narrative of the Building*, which became one of the classics of the literature of civil engineering.[4] Any subsequent writer must start by acknowledging his great debt to that work.

Design

At the outset Smeaton had no first-hand knowledge of the site and the conditions he would encounter there, and he knew little of the previous lighthouses. Since a visit to Plymouth was unlikely to be profitable so early in the year, he attempted first to learn what he could about the previous structures. Apart from demonstrating that it was possible to build on the Rocks, they could provide valuable indications of the types of structure that would not, and would, survive the action of the sea. The first house, built by Winstanley between 1696 and 1698 and considerably strengthened in 1699, had been completely washed away in a storm only 4 years later. Its successor, built by Rudyerd between 1706 and 1709, had, on the other hand, survived many storms until burnt down in December 1755.

Weston was able, at his first meeting with Smeaton on 14th February, 1756, to provide a number of drawings and models, chiefly of Rudyerd's structure.[5] They left important details open to doubt, but nevertheless gave useful leads. Winstanley's house, as finally completed, had a whimsical elaboration of form and architectural detail that seemed almost to invite the sea to do its worst.[6] It appeared also to have been anchored to the sloping surface of the Rock only by twelve irons. Rudyerd simplified the form to a simple frustum of a cone devoid of projections apart from a cornice just below the lantern to throw off water rising up to this level, and an open iron stair to give access from the Rock.[7] This cone had a base diameter about one-third of the height up to the lantern, and a diameter at that level about one-fifth of the height. To anchor the structure to the Rock he first cut the sloping surface into steps and then inserted a larger number of ingeniously designed iron keys. The other most notable feature was the way in which timber and stone were combined. Externally the whole structure might easily have been taken for a purely timber one. It consisted here of 71 tapered uprights butted side by side. These were secured at intervals throughout their height to timbers running circumferentially inside. Internally the construction was entirely of timber in the upper half, where a store-room and living quarters were provided. In the lower half, which was solid apart from the necessary provisions for access, it was also mostly of timber, here in the form of superimposed horizontal beds of squared oak logs laid parallel to the steps in the rock and at right angles to them in alternate beds. Four or five courses of large blocks of Cornish moorstone were, however, interposed at intervals. A timber mast rose vertically in the centre and continued through the first two rooms above. Structural integrity was ensured largely by bolting the timbers together and otherwise interconnecting them, and by tying down the horizontal logs at the base to the Rock by means of the upward projections of the inset iron keys. In Smeaton's words the structure was "a piece of ship-wrightry", merely ballasted by the courses of moorstone.[8]

In considering why Rudyerd's house had stood so much longer than Winstanley's, Smeaton concluded that it had done so partly because of its simpler overall form and partly because, by ballasting it, Rudyerd had prevented the layers of timber from being lifted if water seeped between them. Rudyerd had here "laid hold of the great principle of Engineery that WEIGHT is the most naturally and effectually resisted by WEIGHT".[9] Smeaton was less impressed by the widely held view that the "elasticity" of the timber structure was its chief merit, enabling it to give way to the sea without being overthrown. Of its considerable movement in a storm there seemed to be no doubt; but Smeaton attributed this chiefly to a want of sufficient diameter at the base, so that it was able to rock slightly. He preferred to place his trust in adequate weight, adequate strength, and a broader base.[10]

Rudyerd's use of timber also had two clear drawbacks. It had not only permitted the final destruction by fire; it had also been the cause of repeated trouble from rot and worm attack. These necessitated difficult piecemeal renewals, few of which were completely satisfactory, so that there was a gradual weakening of the whole structure that might soon have led to its collapse even without the fire.[11] A house made completely of stone would undoubtedly last longer with less maintenance if it could be given a similar strength. Against this it would cost more and take longer to build unless time could be saved by careful planning of all the operations.

Reflecting along these lines, Smeaton produced his first schematic design for a structure entirely of stone.[12] He kept essentially to the simple form and internal planning of Rudyerd's house; but, to obtain a broader base without a proportionate increase in diameter throughout the height, he adopted a curved profile suggested by the trunk of a growing oak firmly rooted in the ground. Bearing in mind the sloping surface of the Rock, he tested this profile by turning a piece of wood to it and then fitting this to the sloping surface of another block.

Without an enclosing timber structure, completely new means were devised to hold the masonry together. No mortar could be relied upon to do this during the crucial construction period; it would always be liable to be washed out before it had gained strength. The common expedient of using iron cramps—both vertically and horizontally between blocks—was ruled out chiefly because of the great number that would be needed and the great expenditure of time in fixing them, out on the Rock. This left only the alternative of shaping the blocks themselves so that they interlocked, like dovetail joints in timber. With some further cutting back of the steps in the rock surface to form dovetail recesses, the lowest courses of stone could similarly be engrafted into the rock.

This dovetailing could not be worked out in detail until the Rock surface had been examined and precisely surveyed, and other details of the design had been considered further. Smeaton drew an idealised plan of two typical successive courses showing, in each, six outer rings of dovetailed blocks around a single central block, with all joints breaking from course to course.[13] He also considered means of preventing whole courses above the level of the Rock from sliding on one another if hit by a heavy sea before the mortar was set between them, and of temporarily securing individual blocks of an incomplete course. Final choice could again be made later.

At this point he presented his proposals to the proprietors. They agreed, in principle, that the house should be rebuilt in stone.[14] He therefore felt free to travel to Plymouth, inspect the Rock, develop his ideas further, and make other necessary plans and arrangements. To assist in making an accurate survey of the Rock surface, he made an instrument with a long horizontal arm swinging about the centre of the plate of a large theodolite mounted on a tripod.[15]

Smeaton was in Plymouth from 27th March to 15th May, 1756. Soon after his arrival he was visited by Josias Jessop, a foreman shipwright in the dockyard, who had been in charge of repairs to Rudyerd's lighthouse for some time before the fire.[16] Though he found Jessop wanting in powers of invention, he formed a high opinion of his judgement and executive skills. Jessop also knew a great deal about the Eddystone Rocks, about conditions there, and about possibilities of approach and landing. During Smeaton's stay the two men set sail for the Rocks whenever the weather seemed suitable. There were only ten such occasions and only on four of them could a landing be made. With perseverance, however, it was possible eventually to make the necessary survey as well as to test the rock itself to see how it could be cut or drilled and how long these operations were likely to take.

The remaining time was not wasted. When forced to lie off the Rocks, Smeaton observed the action of the sea around them and considered means whereby the approach to them and the landing of materials could be facilitated, including the possible mooring of a supply vessel in the vicinity. When unable even to approach closely, he twice changed course for other harbours to see how they might serve as refuges in case of need, and to enable him to visit nearby quarries. While waiting on shore for better weather, and not engaged in setting his observations on paper, he inspected other sources of stone nearer Plymouth and looked for a suitable site for a shore base and work-yard. He was also shown a piece of Portland stone from one of the docks that had been badly holed by a small shellfish, and subsequently saw marble rocks on the shore similarly eaten away.

He concluded from the last observations that the more easily worked Portland stone should not be used in positions exposed to the sea if the new structure were to be made as permanent as possible. He now saw no real obstacle to the carrying out of his initial plan for a stone structure if one of the Cornish granites were used everywhere externally. To proceed in this way would require much more work than a simple rebuilding to a slightly improved version of Rudyerd's design. In particular there would be a far greater quantity of stone to be taken to the Rock and set in place. He nevertheless thought that, with proper planning, he should be able to complete the construction in no more than four seasons. To achieve this it would be necessary to limit the initial cutting of the rock surface to the essential minimum, to do everything possible on shore to reduce what had to be done on the Rock, and to plan the whole operation so that progress was dependent as little as possible on the weather. He regarded the last two as fundamental. What he had already seen convinced him that it would be worth doing a week's work on shore to save an hour on the Rock.

Immediately on his return to London (having visited the Portland quarries on the way) Smeaton again met the proprietors, who confirmed their previous agreement to the use of stone.[17] The most important aspect of the design still to be considered was the precise way of fitting the structure to the Rock. The actual work here—both in cutting the rock and setting the first courses of stone—would be the most difficult that had to be done. It was therefore essential to plan it

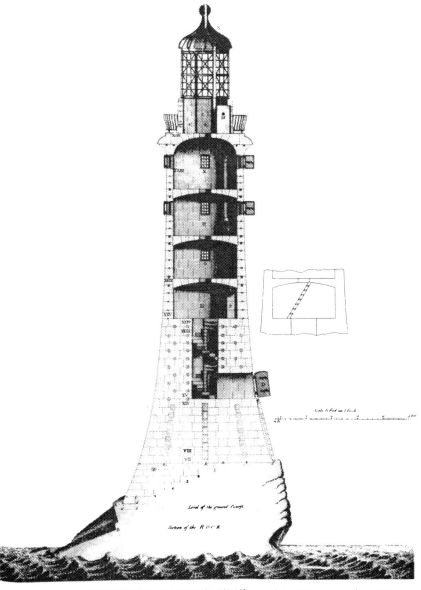

SECTION *of the* EDYSTONE LIGHTHOUSE *upon the* E & W. Line, *as relative to* N° 8.
on Supposition of its being LOW WATER *of a* SPRING TIDE.
Engraved in the Year 1763 by W. E. & J. Rooker

*Fig. 16. Eddystone Lighthouse, 1759 (engraving by Edward Rooker from a
drawing by Smeaton—Narrative, pl. 9)*

with the greatest care and to leave nothing to chance. To assist in planning, and to take full advantage of the measurements he had taken, he first made with his own hands a precise three-dimensional model of the rock surface as he had found it. He then made a second model showing how he intended to cut the level steps and dovetail recesses for those courses that were to be engrafted into the Rock. These models were supplemented by further models of the lower courses themselves and of the whole house and by a paper cross-section of this to show the internal arrangements proposed. Some details were still tentative, but the design was now essentially complete, so it will be convenient at this point to describe the structure as built (Fig. 16), before turning to its construction.

The structure as built

Six steps were cut into the Rock, each with two dovetail recesses and with its top surface slightly below the lowest adjacent rock surface so that the blocks laid on it would be further prevented from sliding. These steps were filled in with dovetail blocks breaking joint in successive courses—granite blocks on the outside and Portland stone on the inside (Fig. 17). In line with the objective of reducing work on the Rock to a minimum, the size of the blocks was as large as it was judged could be safely landed and placed in position with suitable tackle. A reasonable limit for most blocks was considered to be about 1 ton, with a few of up to 2 tons. To secure each block as it was set in place, and before a course was complete or the mortar hardened, it was wedged in place on each side of the engaged dovetail and treenailed down to the rock or blocks beneath to prevent lifting.

Course VI provided the first complete circular level platform. Above it the anchorage directly to the Rock was lost but it became possible to adopt the simple symmetrical arrangement of blocks in concentric rings envisaged in the first idealised plan. To prevent sliding of whole courses on one another an additional means of interconnection was introduced in the form of marble joggles. These were cubes set in matching recesses on the top and bottom faces of successive courses, shown shaded in the cross-sectional elevation, up to course XIV. From course XV to course XXIV, some further modification was needed on account of the entrance passage and central stairway. There was no longer a single central block. To give cohesion to the course, the four blocks of the inside ring were now designed to interlock with hook-scarf joints. The number of marble joggles was also increased and their size reduced. The use of treenails

90

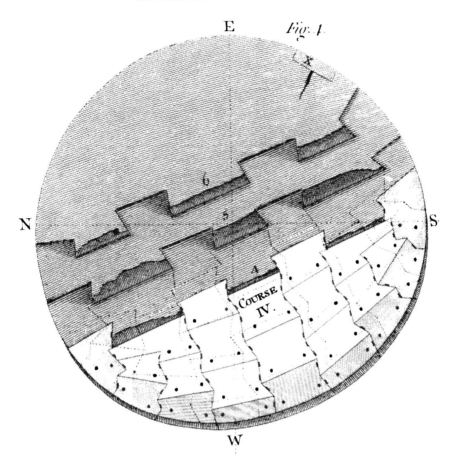

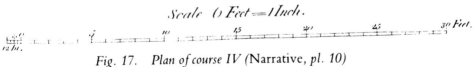

Fig. 17. Plan of course IV (Narrative, pl. 10)

and wedges continued; so did the use of Portland stone for the interior masonry.

Above course XXIV the structure changed to a circular wall, one block of granite thick, spanned at intervals by vaulted floors each with a central opening for a removable ladder. Dovetailing of the blocks was now abandoned, except in the vaulted floors. Iron cramps on the tops of the blocks were substituted, or pairs of continuous chains level with each floor. Smeaton felt that the weight of the masonry above would keep the horizontal joints watertight in the finished structure;

but he feared possible leaks through the vertical joints. Each vertical edge was therefore grooved and a flat lath-like piece of marble was inserted and mortared into the adjoining grooves of each pair of blocks as a water bar.

Though he still kept essentially to the same internal arrangements as had been previously adopted by Rudyerd, his careful consideration of every aspect of design led him to interchange the uses of the two habitable rooms just below the lantern. Rudyerd had made the upper room the kitchen/living room to minimise the necessary length of flue from the stove. Smeaton made the bedroom the upper room, so that it would be warmed by the rising warm air from below and the heat radiated by the flue pipe passing through it, and so that it would be free from the dampness from which Rudyerd's bedroom had suffered.

The lantern was framed in iron, with iron ties extended down to the main masonry wall at the level of the cornice. The copper flue pipe rose through it into a copper ball at the top. Warned by the damage he had observed early in 1757 to the steeple of the church at Lostwithiel, Smeaton also decided to provide a lightning conductor and considered that this flue could serve as its upper part.[18] It was continued downward, via the lead kitchen sink and drain pipe and an external strip of lead, to an iron chain bolted to the rock and long enough to have its foot at all times in the sea. The light was provided by two concentric rings of candles, suspended over pulleys so that they counterbalanced one another.

Construction

Smeaton fully realised the crucial importance of proper planning of the whole construction process. This was not merely a matter of planning the necessary operations with respect for the conditions under which they would have to be carried out. Success would also depend on ensuring that those working on the rock, or responsible for getting them to it and supplying them with what they needed, were able to take full advantage of all opportunities that the weather offered, and given sufficient incentive to do so. Planning of the operations was closely linked with the detailed design of the structure, and we have already seen instances of ways in which the design was influenced. It also entailed the design of suitable lifting shears and the design or selection of much more besides, from boats to mooring arrangements. Obtaining the best output from the workforce was partly a matter of choice and disposition of men, partly a matter of conditions

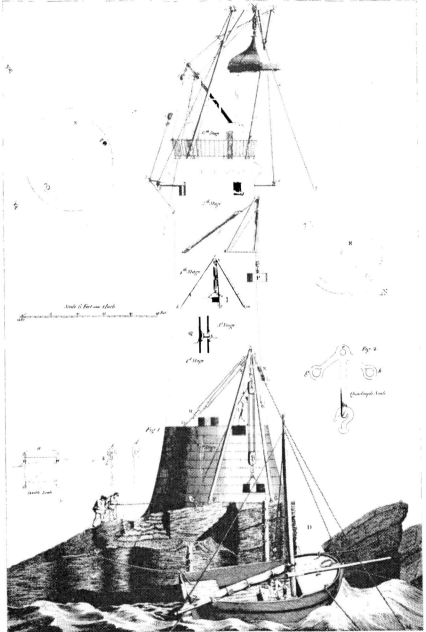

Fig. 18. Construction of Eddystone Lighthouse (engraving by James Record from a
drawing by Smeaton—Narrative, pl. 14)

of pay and engagement, and partly a matter of supervision and encouragement.

For the shore base and work-yard a site was secured on Mill Bay, just to the west of Plymouth Hoe. Here there was provision not only for handling shipments of stone and cutting the blocks exactly to size but also for their trial pre-assembly and marking.[19] At about ½ mile north-east of the Rock a vessel was moored to serve as a store and provide accommodation for those working on the Rock. To facilitate construction there, several different lifting devices were used, each appropriate to a particular phase of the work. These are well illustrated in one plate of Smeaton's *Narrative* (see Fig. 18).

In addition to the necessary seamen, two companies of masons were established. It was arranged that they should work alternate weekly turns on shore and on the Rock. Terms of engagement and rates of pay were devised to encourage both seamen and masons to play their full part in achieving the maximum hours of work on the Rock that weather and tides permitted.[20] They were both fair and, in relation to other available employment at the time, generous. Smeaton therefore felt fully justified in dismissing anyone who did not readily accept them.

In reading the *Narrative* one is, however, struck most forcibly by the part that Smeaton himself played throughout the construction. At the outset he appointed Jessop his "general Assistant" or, as we should now say, his resident engineer.[21] This did allow him, from time to time, to attend to other business. The Eddystone Lighthouse, however, remained his main interest—even his consuming passion—until it had been completed and lit. He personally set out work on the Rock, made moulds for cutting the stones, supervised every new or critical operation, stepped in when men fell sick, shared all hazards, and even took the "post of honour" when this entailed a risk that others were reluctant to take.[22] Once, when the work was nearing an end, his zeal led to his collapse, probably from carbon monoxide poisoning, as he watched too attentively the heating of iron bars for the lantern in a charcoal fire inside one of the rooms of the lighthouse.[23] Much earlier he almost suffered shipwreck, which was averted by the presence of mind of one of the sailors.[24] It was perhaps partly this that, shortly afterwards, drew from Weston the admonition "venture not too rashly", to which Smeaton replied:

"With respect to any rashness that may be in my constitution, I hope it is counterbalanced by Mr Jessop's calmness, whom I think Providence has put along with me to keep me out of dangers that I might sometimes run into."[25]

Though he confessed, in connection with his having to dismiss one of the two foremen first appointed, that he found the management of men even more difficult than control of the elements, his sustained personal involvement must have contributed greatly to the successful completion of construction within the estimated four seasons.

The remainder of the first season, after the design had been completed and approved, was devoted to the necessary cutting of the rock surface and other preparation for the start of building.[26] The first landing was made on 3rd August, 1756, and the setting out of the steps was soon completed. Cutting and levelling then commenced, the first step for the base course being at a height of about 7 ft above LWST and therefore 9 ft below high water springs. With some interruptions from bad weather, this work was nearly finished in mid-September. Yet it took until early November to do what remained, and the store vessel was not finally brought back to Plymouth for the winter until 26th November, having been almost wrecked and then blown nearly to the Scilly Islands on the way.

There was much to be done on shore during the winter if everything was to be in readiness for building to start early next summer—from the cutting of stone to the building of additional vessels to carry it out and the selection of a suitable mortar for the very testing conditions to which it would be exposed. Smeaton therefore decided not to return to London. He remained in Plymouth, usually visiting the work-yard twice a day and devoting his evenings and other free time to the experiments on hydraulic limes that have already been described in Chapter II.

It was also in the winter of 1756–57 that Jessop, under Smeaton's direction, made drawings of the masonry courses and several models for Mr Weston. Most of these have survived and are now in the Royal Scottish Museum, Edinburgh (see Chapter XI). They include a model of the lighthouse itself, to the scale of 1 in. to 4 ft, and of Course VII (Fig. 19). The latter we know was sent to London in March 1757.[27]

The first stone, weighing 2½ tons, was landed and set on 12th June, 1757, and the remaining three stones of this course were set the next day. They were bedded in the lime/pozzolana mortar selected as a result of the experiments, wedged and treenailed down as described above, and then grouted with a more liquid mortar to fill the vertical

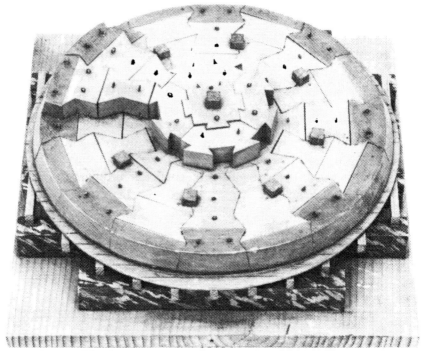

Fig. 19. Model of course VII made by Josias Jessop, 1757 (Royal Scottish Museum)

joints. Finally all the exposed ends of the joints were given a temporary protection of plaster of Paris to prevent the mortar from being immediately washed out by the next high tide.

The first course represents the beginning of a careful and often difficult series of operations in which 1,493 pieces of stone weighing nearly 1,000 tons were cut to shape, transported to the Rock, placed in position, and fixed together into a practically monolithic whole. Setting of the second course, consisting of thirteen stones, proceeded less smoothly. It was twice interrupted by gales and, on the second occasion, five stones that had not been fully set and fixed were washed away. Smeaton himself immediately returned to Mill Bay to obtain replacements when this was discovered, satisfied, however, that all his permanent fixings had held. The course was completed on 30th June. After this, work proceeded without major incident until the worst storm yet experienced interrupted the completion of course VII—the first full circular one rising above the top of the Rock. This storm washed away the lifting shears and two stones that were awaiting setting, and it badly damaged the windlass. Work resumed on 3rd

September after an enforced break of 15 days, and rapid progress was made until 20th September. There was then a further interruption which delayed the completion of course IX until 30th September. In view of the length of time that this course had taken, and the poor progress at the end of the first season, Smeaton decided to leave course X until next year.

He was pleased, on making a first inspection on 12th May, 1758, to find that all this masonry had become a single solid mass, the mortar having now become as hard as the Portland stone itself. A long series of delays nevertheless ensued, due to trouble with the moorings—including the loss of the buoy. Thus it was not until 2nd July that construction could be resumed. However, as the height above the water increased, there was less interruption from bad weather, and by 2nd October the centring was erected for the vaulted floor over the lowest room. Smeaton's hope was to complete this floor, so as to make the room habitable and make it possible to exhibit a temporary light from the house during the winter—much as Winstanley and Rudyerd had each done at the end of their third seasons. He was disappointed, however, by the onset of bad weather before the floor was complete and by the refusal of Trinity House to allow a light to be exhibited in this way. No more was done after 7th October.

Work on the Rock was resumed on 5th July, 1759. It was now becoming more akin to normal building construction on shore, apart from occasional difficulties in getting to the Rock or landing materials, and the much greater inconvenience in finding anything missing or having a man fall ill. Smeaton records one instance of improvisation when a quantity of block tin that had been ordered to harden the lead for setting door hooks was forgotten. He wished to see the hooks set before returning to Plymouth and accordingly melted down all the pewter plates and dishes that could be found on the store vessel. The main structure up to the cornice was completed on 17th August. It then rose about 50 ft above the bottom of the well hole and was found to lean eastward a mere 1/8 in. at this height. Since it was not now likely to be wet internally by the sea, the seamen were directed to wet the insides of all rooms to prevent the mortar from drying out too rapidly and assist its proper curing. The cupola of the lantern was lifted in one piece and fixed in place on 17th September, and on the following day Smeaton personally screwed in place the gilt ball on its summit. Glazing and all other preparations for exhibiting a light were completed by 9th October, when Smeaton and all others apart from the light-keepers left.

Smeaton's achievement

The light was first exhibited, as previously arranged with Trinity House, on the evening of 16th October. Stormy weather prevented Smeaton from being present, as he had hoped to be; but he went out again as soon as possible and was told that all was well in spite of the sea having washed up to the cornice and, being broken up there, had cast spray over the top of the lantern. Some motion had been felt, but not enough to cause any fear or surprise. Smeaton had, indeed, observed a similar motion on 5th October and had concluded, from observing that it was almost as sensible when the sea rolled over the Rock without touching the house, that it was essentially a motion of the rock imparted to the house.[28]

This weakness of the rock itself, coupled with a desire that the light should have a greater range and should not be obscured periodically in bad weather by being enveloped in a column of water or spray, led to the construction of a new lighthouse in a slightly more sheltered position on the parallel reef to the south-east between 1878 and 1882. After more than 120 years the upper part of Smeaton's tower was then dismantled and re-erected on a new base on Plymouth Hoe, the original base being left to stand on the Rock. The only weakness of the tower had proved to be in the upper horizontal joints of the masonry. These had opened under the action of the upward force exerted by waves hitting the underside of the cornice, necessitating the addition of internal vertical ties and, in 1865, a slight reduction in the projection of the cornice. Dismantling showed the mortar to be still in excellent condition.[29]

The best tribute to Smeaton's achievement was the extent to which his ideas inspired the designs of all later masonry lighthouses built in similarly difficult situations. The next, that of John Rennie and Robert Stevenson on the Bell Rock, built between 1806 and 1811, followed Smeaton's design in almost every respect.[30] In later structures the manner of interlocking was usually simplified, and advantage was taken of the availability of new cements and of new sources of power to expedite construction. The Fastnet Rock lighthouse, completed in 1904, still closely followed Smeaton's profile and general arrangement.

The most revealing comparison is with the new Eddystone structure—for this might be regarded as a direct constructive criticism of Smeaton's tower, just as his was of Rudyerd's.[31] The different choice of site was necessitated by the two new factors of the old site being still occupied and the now proven weakness of the rock itself at this point. But it involved founding the new structure below low-water level and, hence, the construction of a cofferdam and repeated pumping to allow work to commence. With the only means at his disposal this would probably have taken Smeaton another year. Sir James Douglass's simplification of the manner of interlocking the blocks of stone allowed the elimination of Smeaton's marble joggles by introducing interlocking bed joints as well as interlocking vertical joints. An increased wall thickness in the upper part of the structure (necessitated by the increased height) allowed the same manner of interlocking to be adopted throughout. There was therefore no need either for Smeaton's separate water bars in the vertical joints of the wall. Finally a vertical-sided cylindrical base was introduced below the inward curving profile of the upper part of the tower. Construction was very greatly facilitated and speeded by mooring a steam tender about 120 ft away to the south-east and transferring all stone and other materials directly from the tender to the place where they were needed on the structure. Each transfer, powered by a steam winch in the stern of the vessel, was completed in about 3 min.

The cylindrical base of the new structure was wide enough, in relation to the foot of the tower rising from it, to leave a narrow platform all round on which it was possible to land in the same way as it had been possible to land on the Rock itself in the case of the earlier structures. But its primary purpose was to divide an approaching wave and divert it to each side rather than, as Smeaton's sloping base had done, diverting much of it upwards.

Smeaton did foresee that, in a heavy sea, waves would rise towards the lantern, and he provided the cornice to protect it. However, he was unable to foresee the extent to which his choice of a continuously curved profile would lead to large quantities of water being thrown up vertically in some conditions of the sea. His choice of this profile was governed only by considerations of stability and strength under the assumed horizontal pressure of an advancing wave. It was guided by the analogy of the oak tree, already referred to. This, he assumed, was loaded horizontally by the wind and, stripped of its branches and foliage, should be just as well fitted to resist the pressure of a rapid current of water.[32] In adopting the simplest appropriate form that he could conceive for the purpose, he was also following that "first principle of taste, *Judgement*" that he had recognised in Rudyerd's eschewal of all the architectural elaborations of Winstanley's design.[33]

Arguing more generally he wrote:

"That the building should be a column of *equal strength*, proportionate in every part to the stress it was likely to bear, . . . was a view of the subject I was naturally and forcibly led to. . . . I therefore endeavoured to form it, and put it together so, that . . . no man should be able to tell me at *what* joint it would overset; for, if at any height the uppermost course was, when compleated, safe, it became more safe by another course being laid upon it; and that upper course, though somewhat less in weight, and in the total cohesion of its parts, than the former; yet every course, from the first foundation, was less and less subject to the heavy stroke of the sea."

At the same time he candidly admitted that he had followed his "*feelings*, rather than *calculations*".[34] He gave no mathematical construction for the profile, and seems to have drawn it by eye.

This recourse to his "feelings" was equally relevant to the choice of the other means for ensuring cohesion of the masonry. His approach here was a wisely cautious one: "yet, when we have to do with, and to endeavour to controul, those powers of nature that are subject to *no calculation*, I trust it will be deemed prudent not to omit . . . any thing that can without difficulty be applied, and that would be likely to add to the security."[35] Thus he used marble joggles as well as oak treenails to hold successive courses together in the circular solid above the Rock surface. He had originally considered using interlocking bed joints rather than joggles, but he decided against them because, in his view, they would introduce "unnecessary trouble and intricacy" as compared with "the much more plain, easy, and simple method of joggles".[36] He realised that, until the mortar hardened, everything would depend on the treenails, and the joggles would be of little value; also that, once it had hardened and there was more weight above, there should still be little need for them. Even in retrospect many years later, he felt that they contributed something to the consolidation of the whole mass, and that he could rely on them to continue to do so more confidently than he could rely on any wooden elements.

The dovetailed interlocking of the blocks that formed the vaulted floors in the upper part of the structure was more questionable. The intention was to unite the blocks so that each floor became, in effect, a non-thrusting monolith that would simply sit on the horizontal ledges cut to support it in the outer wall.[37] In fact these dovetails could never have achieved the necessary cohesion, though hook-scarf joints just might have done. The encircling chains—modelled on those that Wren placed around the dome of St Paul's and seen merely as a possibly redundant "extreme precaution"—were really the essential means for preventing the floors from pressing outwards.

In any critical assessment it should, however, be remembered that hardly any of the analytical tools we now have at our disposal were in existence in 1756.[38] Structural theory was very much in its infancy and, even today, it is still necessary to mount very costly research programmes to learn more about wave actions and wave loads on static structures in the open sea. Smeaton could, indeed, learn little of value from what he described as "*systematical* writings".[39] He was dependent on his own observations and experiments, the lessons he could learn from the available information about Winstanley's and Rudyerd's lighthouses, and the ideas he could pick up from accounts of other works, notably from those of Wren in the *Parentalia*, from Price's account of Salisbury Cathedral, and from Belidor's *Architecture Hydraulique* (the main source for the dovetail jointing of the masonry).[40] Simply by exercising "a turn for contrivance in the mechanical branches of science", he was required "to take into consideration the peculiarities, the advantages, and disadvantages of the situation, as well as other circumstances" and "solely from the nature of the thing ... find out the proper methods of executing" the new structure.[41]

His achievement was also at least as much one of organisation and practical execution as of design. Though successors like the Stevensons and Douglasses improved on it, they learnt much from Smeaton's approach and followed it in all essentials, merely taking advantage of new means that were not available to him. Perhaps Rudyerd's earlier achievement should be counted a partial precedent; but, since he never recorded what he did, its only value to Smeaton was as a demonstration that he was not attempting the impossible. Of earlier achievements of which more is known, there was only one that was of such far-reaching importance, and called for such radical innovations in design and such close and continued involvement in all aspects of execution by the designer. This was Brunelleschi's construction of the dome of Florence Cathedral in the early fifteenth century—an achievement without a similar prior assurance that it was not impossible but without the problems that arose from a tiny exposed site far at sea.[42]

Finally we give a few facts and figures relating to Smeaton's lighthouse taken, except where noted, from the text and drawings in the *Narrative*:

General Assistant   Josias Jessop
Foreman   Thomas Richardson

Clerk	John Harrison
Work on the rock began	5th August 1756
Light first exhibited	16th October 1759
Light last exhibited[43]	3rd February 1882
Volume of masonry[43]	13,340 cu. ft
Height of light above mean sea level	80 ft
Construction cost[44]	£16,000

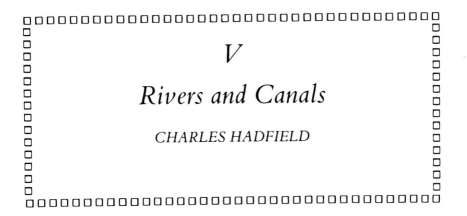

V

Rivers and Canals

CHARLES HADFIELD

Inland navigations engaged Smeaton's attention during practically the whole of his career and were a major preoccupation of the years 1760–73. The Calder & Hebble Navigation was his second big civil engineering job, following on from the Eddystone Lighthouse; three other navigations were constructed or improved in accordance with his designs and for 6 years he devoted much time to planning and building the Forth & Clyde Canal, the largest of all his works. In addition he reported on five other canal schemes and at least as many river navigations.

Calder & Hebble Navigation
When in the autumn of 1756 a group of men met at the "Talbot", Halifax, to revive the idea of making navigable the Upper Calder River[1] from Wakefield (where it would connect with the existing Aire & Calder Navigation) upwards to the neighbourhood of Halifax, their minds turned to Smeaton, the local man. Probably some present knew him, for his home at Austhorpe Lodge was not far away. He was then too busy upon the Eddystone, but when in June 1757 they asked again, he agreed to come, and made his survey in October and November.

By that time many English rivers had been improved by building locks, usually at situations where short side-cuts could carry the waterway past water-driven mills, and by cutting off the bigger meanders: among them the Wey, Warwickshire Avon and Welland in the seventeenth century, and in the eighteenth the Mersey & Irwell, Aire & Calder and Don. Thomas Steers had been concerned with the Mersey & Irwell, and when Smeaton arrived in the Calder Valley,

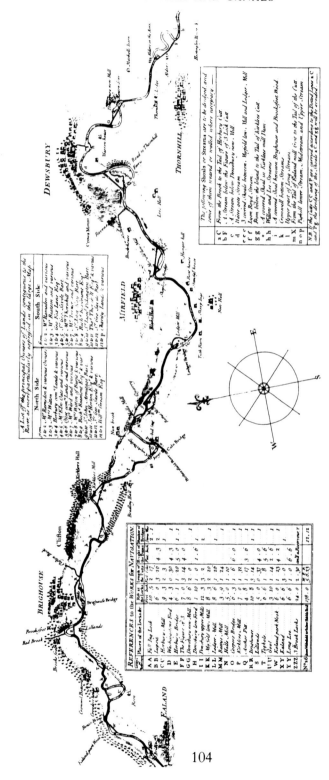

Fig. 20.   Part of Smeaton's plan for the Calder & Hebble Navigation, 1757 (engraving by R. W. Seale)

surveys by John Eyes and Steers in 1740 and 1741 were made available to him.

Smeaton faced a more difficult problem than had his predecessors. They had all, like him, to avoid or placate millowners whose livelihood depended upon the maintenance of a head of water while that of boatmen consisted in depleting it, but none before—or after—faced such a steep declivity (178 ft fall in 24 miles) or the threat of floodwater off the Pennine slopes.

His plan was to dredge shoals, construct 26 locks and make 5¾ miles of artificial cut between Wakefield and Brooksmouth (Fig. 20) and then for half a mile up the Hebble valley to Salterhebble near Halifax, where a reservoir would be built. Such a navigation would take 20–25 ton boats drawing up to 3 ft 6 in. (such as could navigate the Aire & Calder also in most seasons) and not harm the thirteen mills concerned "either by Back Water, or Loss of Water, or the Meadows adjoining by occasioning or continuing Floods thereon sensibly longer than usual...". The engineering cost would not be less than £30,000; construction time 7 years.[2]

An authorising Act, amended to extend the navigation beyond Brooksmouth to Sowerby Bridge, was obtained in June 1758. Smeaton gave evidence upon it,[3] saying he had seen locks in Flanders and Holland and that "he proposed to make the Locks better than most of the Locks he had seen on any River in England".

The Act passed, and £36,000 subscribed, Smeaton was appointed engineer at a salary of £250 a year from 25th November, 1759; this to be a part-time job but one demanding (and receiving) frequent attendance on site.[4] As an assistant or resident engineer he had Joseph Nickalls, paid 20 guineas to cover the cost of moving from London to Wakefield and an annual salary of £100 raised, in August 1760, to £120. Nickalls arrived at the end of December and work on the Wakefield–Dewsbury stretch probably began early in 1760. By the summer Smeaton had done many of the working drawings of locks, weirs (or "dams" as they were called) and bridges, of which examples still survive in the Royal Society collection,[5] see Figs 21 and 22.

Smeaton thought highly of Nickalls but for reasons that are not clear, and possibly without real justification, Nickalls was dismissed in November 1761. To take his place John Gwyn, already on site as a foreman, was appointed superintendent of carpentry, and Matthias Scott of masonry and digging; their appointments dating from March 1762, at annual salaries of £50 and £60 respectively, and they to work directly under Smeaton's direction.

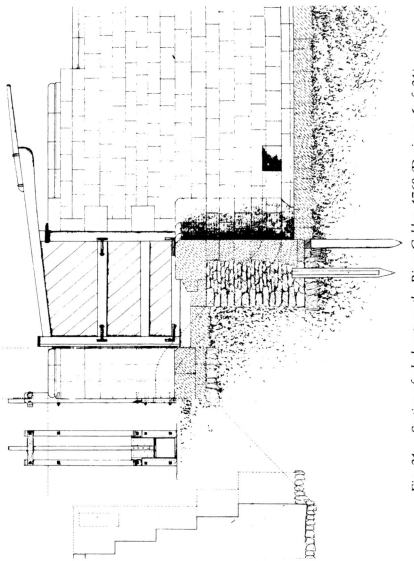

Fig. 21. Section of a lock gate on the River Calder, 1760 (Designs, 6, f. 21)

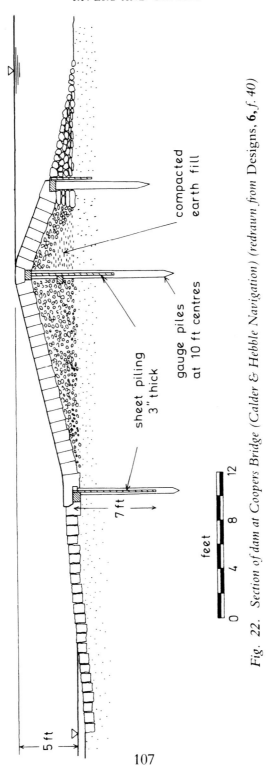

compacted
earth fill

gauge piles
at 10 ft centres

sheet piling
3" thick

7 ft

5 ft

feet

0   4   8   12

Fig. 22. Section of dam at Coopers Bridge (Calder & Hebble Navigation) (redrawn from Designs, **6**, f. 40)

By July 1764, after a total expenditure of £56,000, the navigation was open from Wakefield to Brighouse: a distance of 18 miles with seventeen locks, the locks having a length of 64 ft between gates, a width of 15 ft and an average fall of 8 ft. Not a great deal remained to be done and Smeaton hoped everything would be finished within the next year.

In September, writing to John Holmes, he remarked that:

"the works are going on very well but we are still subject to the same rubbs, that have ever tortured the undertaking from the beginning, and will continue to the End; that is, difference of opinion, partys and disputes amongst our Rulers."[6]

A month or so later a new committee, Rochdale- rather than Halifax-based was elected. In December they told their clerk to write to Brindley and offer him the job of finishing the navigation. He was appointed at a meeting on 31st January, 1765, to which he produced a plan, and Smeaton was discharged on the same day, along with Gwyn and Scott.

Smeaton had worked hard on the Calder; but he took his dismissal well, saying:

"I shall never envy any Man the praise for doing better than myself while I am conscious of having done as well as those that have trod the same (or perhaps less difficult) Steps before me."[7]

He was to come back.

Consulting jobs, 1758–63

Before we turn to the Forth & Clyde Canal, let us glance at other waterway work of Smeaton's in these earlier years.

John Grundy had in 1756 surveyed for a canal from Louth in Lincolnshire to Tetney Haven whereby keels from the Humber could reach the town.[8] Four years later enough support had shown itself for the town clerk to write to Smeaton, who agreed to go over Grundy's proposals. His own report of 14th July, 1761[9] broadly confirmed them, landowners' backing was forthcoming, and in 1763 Smeaton gave the Bill Parliamentary support.[10] It was passed and the canal, taking keels 72 × 15 ft, was opened in 1770. It was 11¾ miles long with eight locks, one a sea-lock having gates pointing in both directions.

In 1759 Smeaton was in Parliament to support another difficult proposed river improvement, that of the Upper Wear.[11] His scheme provided for twelve locks and several cuts between Biddick Ford near Washington and the city of Durham.[12] The Act passed, but without result. Also in about 1759 he was called to southern England to get the extension of the Wey Navigation upwards from Guildford to Godalming, surveyed by Richard Stedman, through Parliament.[13] It was authorised in 1760, but thereafter he excused himself on account of "a large affair in the North".

In Lincolnshire the Fossdyke left the Trent at Torksey and ran to Lincoln. There it joined the River Witham which, passing under the shallow-channel medieval High Bridge, ran to Boston and the Wash. Action by landowners between Lincoln and Boston produced a report in November 1761 by Grundy, Langley Edwards and Smeaton.[14] They were to cure a situation they described as follows:

> "This once so flourishing river and country have . . . been falling into decay, by the banks . . . being suffered to become ruinous . . . so that those flood waters which were necessary and used heretofore, by their velocity and weight, to cleanse out the sand and sediment brought up by the tides, have been, and now are, suffered to . . . expand over the adjoining fens and low grounds, whereby those sands . . . have now so much choaked up the haven from Boston to the sea, that for several years last past the navigation thereof has been lost to shipping, and it is now become even difficult for barges of about 30 tons burthen to get up to the town on neap tides."

Their solution was a sea-lock and sluice at Boston, a new cut thence to Anthony's (now Anton's) Gowt, another to rejoin the river at Chapel Hill, and thence to dredge the river up to Lincoln and build four locks. Their estimates were £37,850 on account of drainage and £7,370 of navigation.

Smeaton and Grundy appeared on the subsequent heavily contested Bill.[15] It was passed. Over the following years the lock at Boston (the Grand Sluice) and three of the four others were built, and the long new cuts were made, with Edwards as engineer in charge. As soon as the Act had passed, Smeaton and Grundy reported on the Fossdyke, proposing to improve both drainage and navigation, mainly by dredging and embanking, for £3,817.[16] The Fossdyke lessees seem to have done little about it. In 1782 he returned to make another report, whose main purport was to improve land drainage.[17]

Smeaton reported upon another river in 1762: the Chelmer.[18] He concluded that the river could be made navigable from Chelmsford to Maldon, "yet there is so small a proportion thereof that is at present adapted to navigation, that it will prove the least expence, to perform the same chiefly by canals...". The navigation was eventually authorised in 1793.[19] So much for rivers; in these years Smeaton was also concerned with two schemes that were to grow into major canals.

In 1758 James Brindley, not yet employed by the Duke of Bridgewater, had been commissioned to survey for a canal upwards from Wilden Ferry (Cavendish Bridge near Shardlow) on the Trent to Stoke. In the same year Henry Bradford had proposed to make the Trent and Tame navigable upwards from the present head of the Trent Navigation at Burton to Tamworth, and Smeaton had worked over it, estimating for eight locks and a staunch.[20]

Brindley's reply was a scheme for a canal from Wilden Ferry to King's Bromley Common near Lichfield (roughly, the present Fradley), whence he proposed branches to Longbridge near Burslem (an arm would run to Newcastle-under-Lyme), Lichfield, and Fazeley near Tamworth, in all over 71 miles of canal. Smeaton, called in on this scheme also, went over the lines in November 1760 with Hugh Henshall and Brindley, the latter now in the Duke's employment, and approved them with emendations:[21] all became the bases of later canal building. Brindley had also envisaged an extension past Longbridge to a junction with the Mersey. Of interest to us is Smeaton's comment, that the Longbridge branch could indeed be continued over the watershed by lockage and "a deep cut through the summit, which will be of moderate length". Water could be provided, he thought, by colliery drainage, a reservoir, and if necessary "the help of a fire engine, to return the waters from a low level...". He therefore did not consider a tunnel, such as Brindley afterwards built at Harecastle, necessary.

Early in January 1762 Smeaton met Brindley again, this time to measure water that could be made available from the colliery soughs at Worsley to supply the Duke of Bridgewater's proposed extension to Runcorn. Given the heavy opposition that was expected from the Mersey & Irwell Company, it was essential to prove that they would in no way be deprived. Later that month Smeaton appeared before the Commons Committee on the Bill, to prove adequacy of supply. Brindley's evidence followed, the Bill passed, and the canal extension was built.[22]

It may have been on one of these jobs that Smeaton and Brindley made their well-known calibration of a water gauge for measuring the flow of water in a stream. This took the form of a rectangular notch cut in a long board 1 in. thick placed on top of a temporary dam.

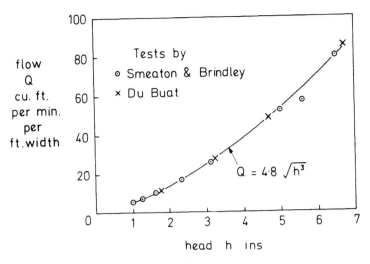

Fig. 23. Calibration of rectangular notch gauge

They measured the time required for 20 cu. ft of water to flow through the notch at various heads from 1 to 6½ in. The results (Fig. 23), together with some later tests by Du Buat, were still being quoted as providing the most reliable data available in the early nineteenth century.[23] It is also worth noting that in his 1762 evidence Smeaton gives a sensible figure for the loss by evaporation: 15 in. of water in the 5 months May–September.

Forth & Clyde Canal
And so to the "Great Canal" in Scotland. Earlier, Smeaton had been concerned with the navigation of the Clyde itself, reporting in 1755 and 1758; in the second report proposing dredging, and a river lock and dam below Whiteinch, downriver from Glasgow.[24] What he proposed resulted in the 1759 Clyde Act, to improve the navigation up to Glasgow, and build a bridge, for he appeared in Parliament upon the subject.[25] Eventually, deepening alone was decided upon, without a lock; the work was carried out successfully under John Golborne's direction.

When, in the early 1760s, interest revived in building a canal across the waist of Scotland, Smeaton was the obvious man to consult. Such a canal had been suggested earlier. Alexander Gordon did a survey in 1726 and later, in 1762, Robert Mackell and James Murray were commissioned to survey a line from the Carron River at Abbotshaugh to the Clyde at Yoker Burn below Glasgow.[26] Their report was favour-

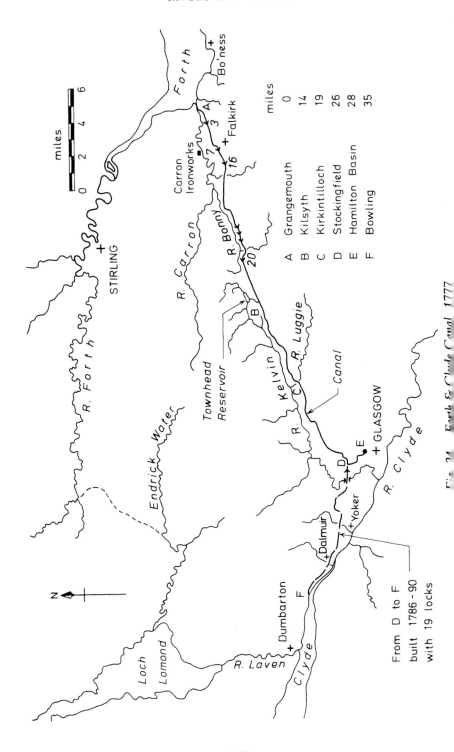

miles

		miles
A	Grangemouth	0
B	Kilsyth	14
C	Kirkintilloch	19
D	Stockingfield	26
E	Hamilton Basin	28
F	Bowling	35

From D to F
built 1786 - 90
with 19 locks

Fig. 24. Forth & Clyde Canal, 1777

able, whereupon in 1763 the Board of Trustees for the Encouragement of Fisheries, Manufacturers and Improvements in Scotland asked Smeaton to do another study. He said later[27] that the request was verbal, "to give them a design for the sort of canal, that in my judgement would best suit the country, when taken in every point of view". His long and careful report was dated 1st March, 1764, with a postscript of 22nd December.[28]

There were then many canalised rivers in the British Isles, some incorporating considerable lengths of artificial cut, but few canals. In Devon, the 4-mile long Exeter Canal with one pound-lock, which Smeaton had seen[29]; in Lancashire, the 10 miles (with branches) of the Sankey Brook from the Mersey to St Helens, with ten locks, and the lockless 7¾ miles of the Bridgewater Canal from Worsley to Longford Bridge, which the Duke was beginning to extend for another 25¾ miles to the Mersey; its ten locks at Runcorn would not be begun for some years yet. In Ireland the Newry Canal with fourteen locks had been completed in 1742 from Newry to the Upper Bann, and the complementary Lagan Navigation had been begun from Belfast towards Lough Neagh. None of these was a watershed canal, i.e., one climbing up a river valley to pass a summit and run down another, with the attendant problem of supplying the summit with water. One such canal had, however, been begun in 1756: the Grand from Dublin to the Shannon; by 1764 none of it had been opened, though much money had been spent on scattered work by the engineer Thomas Omer. Later, Smeaton was to be called to advise upon its future.

There was no precedent, therefore, within the British Isles for what Smeaton was to propose. However, in the south of France ran Riquet's great seventeenth-century achievement, the Grand Canal of Languedoc, now the Midi Canal. This was a true and very impressive watershed canal, complete with an elaborate reservoir and feeder system to supply the summit level, and at Malpas the only canal tunnel in Europe.[30] It had not been a financial success, however, so as an appendix to his report Smeaton set out the differences, ending his comparison with: " . . . the inference is very plain, that the same tolls which will hardly keep the French canal in repair, will make this a very beneficial undertaking to the British adventurers".

What, then, did Smeaton propose? There were two possible routes. The first ran up to the Forth to beyond Stirling, cut overland past the Bog of Bollat to the Endrick River, and thence by Loch Lomond and the Leven River to the Clyde at Dumbarton: a circuitous line involving difficult land cutting and rivers awkward to make navigable. The second, which he chose, used the Carron River and then the valley of the Bonny to Dullatur Bog, his summit level. Thence it ran down the Kelvin Valley to the Clyde at Yoker Burn below Glasgow (Fig. 24).

Such a canal would be 28¼ miles long, 40 ft 8 in. at surface and wider where possible to allow passing places, and 5 ft deep, with 77 (amended to 72) locks to surmount a rise and fall of about 147 ft, a short tunnel, two considerable and one smaller aqueducts, some sizeable embanking, and a towpath throughout. It would take existing Clyde river craft, 17½ ft wide, 56 ft long, drawing 4ft and carrying 40 tons or more. The cost he estimated at some £74,000. If, however, it were to be of reduced dimensions to take boats 9½ ft wide, the cost would fall to about £51,000.

Smeaton paid particular attention to the problem of supplying the summit with water, for his supplies had to provide lockage in both directions. He satisfied himself that there was ample water, by diverting streams near Kilsyth into the canal, for a much greater trade than was envisaged, without affecting local mills, but safeguarded supplies further by providing that locks should not exceed 4 ft fall, and that the summit level pound should be cut 1 ft deeper than the rest to provide a water reserve. He noted that should water supplies turn out to be more abundant, or traffic less than he had estimated, the falls of the locks could be increased and their number reduced, or even halved.

Mine adits, and indeed, at Worsley, small-bore canals tunnelled into mines, had been built, but Smeaton's was to be the first large-bore tunnel after Malpas. His paragraph, proposing to make it by cut and cover, is worth quoting:

> "Where the depth exceeds fifteen feet, which will not be above two hundred yards, I would propose the passage to be by a vault under ground; and though the matter of the hill seems to be a loose gravel, yet I apprehend the means are not very difficult by which it might be perforated. I would begin at an end and open the ground from the top, the same width I intended it at bottom, that is, eighteen feet, like the locks, with an allowance for the thickness of the walls; and cutting down the sides perpendicular, would shore the same from side to side with boards, beams, and braces, of ordinary Scotch fir, these keeping up the matter till the arch is built, the shores that are above the arch may be taken away, and replaced as the work advances, and the cross braces that interfere with the walls of the arch may be walled in, and afterwards cut out when the whole is completed."

Here, then, was a comprehensive plan for Britain's first watershed canal.

Smeaton's report caused years of argument as competing interests supported or criticised it. Chief among these were the Glasgow merchants, who wanted the canal nearer their city, and the Carron Company, who wanted the other end near their ironworks.

After a new survey by Mackell and James Watt on behalf of the Glaswegians and Carron Company, which brought the canal out by the Broomielaw, close to Glasgow, and near the ironworks at the other end, a Bill was introduced in March 1767 for a small boat canal 24 ft wide and 4 ft deep, a branch from Carronshore to Bo'ness being then incorporated. At that point interests based on the Forth area and Midlothian began a powerful opposition which was supported up and down Scotland's east coast. A rival subscription for "the great Canal, planned by Mr Smeaton",[31] that would take seagoing ships, was begun in London. Petitions in its favour poured in to Parliament. On 29th April the small canal's supporters fought off an attempt to kill the Bill by 201 votes to 141, but the great canal's supporters then stated they had raised £100,000 and promised that "the Canal shall be at least as deep and as wide as that proposed by Mr Smeaton" with cuts to Glasgow and Bo'ness. The Bill was thereupon defeated on third reading and withdrawn. The subscribers, with the Duke of Queensberry in the chair, then commissioned Smeaton in May 1767 to replan for a canal able to take craft 60 ft long and 20 ft wide, with enough water to carry 100,000 tons of traffic, two-thirds of which would pass from west to east. The Clyde junction was now to be further down river, near Dalmuir Burn-foot, the eastern end near the mouth of the Carron and below the works, and there would be a branch to Glasgow.

Smeaton now plans, in his second report,[32] a canal some 37 miles long having 42 locks, 70 ft long and 20½ ft wide. He reckons upon needing nearly three times as much water for the enlarged canal as before; therefore he lists the available streams and their annual supply, but says also that two reservoirs could be created: one at Townhead and the other by widening the canal where it crosses Dullatur Bog (west of lock No. 20). He concludes that there will be ample water to protect the supplies of mills and works.

Careful also to be informed of what difficulties lay ahead, he says:

> "the ground has been carefully examined by boring, by Mr Mackell ... who has delivered to me an account of the qualities of the soil for twelve feet deep, in no less than fifty-eight different divisions; together with many other measures of the hills and hollows through which it has been designed to pass ...".

The result is largely to confirm his 1764 route, except at the two ends.

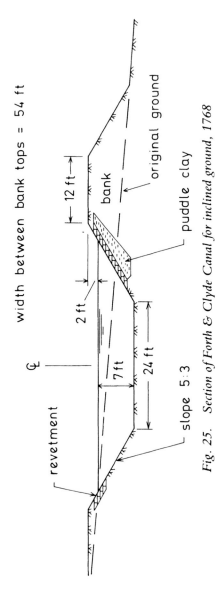

Fig. 25. Section of Forth & Clyde Canal for inclined ground, 1768

There he accepts the terminations suggested to him, but adds a second at the eastern end, at Grange Burn-foot (later Grangemouth). He now needs an extra aqueduct, but the tunnel has gone. His engineering estimate is £147,340 for a canal 7 ft deep, exclusive of parliamentary, legal and other charges.

So, as he proposed, it was enacted on 8th March, 1768, Smeaton giving evidence on the Bill.[33] It was the world's first sea-to-sea canal. On 14th March he submitted to the General Meeting of the Proprietors, at which Queensberry was elected chairman,[34] a scheme of management of the engineering work (see Chapter X). This was adopted so far as circumstances permitted and, it is interesting to note, introduced the term "resident engineer". At the same meeting Smeaton was appointed "Head Engineer" or "Engineer in Chief" at £500 a year, a most generous salary though it had to include his not inconsiderable travelling expenses. Mackell became "Sub-Engineer" or resident engineer (Smeaton's terminology rapidly came into use) at £315 a year, and on the administrative side Alexander Hart was made agent in Scotland at £200 a year. Shortly afterwards Alexander Stephen joined the team as "Clerk & Overseer", under Mackell, at £1 a week (raised in 1771 to £70 a year). In addition the land surveyor John Laurie was employed on an *ad hoc* basis, and in November 1770, with work well under way, Archibald Hope came in as "Comptroller & Auditor" at £60 a year. These men, with the active and intelligent support of a small management committee, were to direct a major part of one of the largest civil engineering projects in the eighteenth century.

Mackell and Laurie began detailed surveying in April. By the end of May Smeaton had staked out the eastern end of the canal line. He also submitted nine typical cross-sections of the canal for level and sloping ground (Fig. 25). In June the first excavation contract was let to John Clegg; the second, to Edward Smith, followed in July. William Charnley, a mason from the Calder sent to Scotland by Smeaton, began opening and working quarries; materials, including timber and pozzolana, were arriving. On site again in September and early October, Smeaton staked out a further length and found "every thing going on as well as can possibly be expected, in the infant state of the works". Four contractors were now engaged on spadework.

On the day before leaving Edinburgh, at a committee meeting, Smeaton was handed copies of reports by Brindley, Yeoman and Golborne.[35] Seemingly at the instance of the Carron Company, who considered themselves bypassed, those three engineers were commissioned to re-survey for a small canal; Brindley was probably there because Samuel Garbett and Charles Gascoigne of Carron Company and the Carron Shipping Co were also committeemen of the Birmingham Canal, whose Act had been passed a few days before that for the Forth & Clyde, and whose engineer Brindley was. Their reports, which *inter alia* proposed a narrow-boat, 4 ft deep canal and a re-routing nearer Glasgow, annoyed the canal company, who regarded the matter as settled by their Act, and were answered by Smeaton in a review on 28th October.[36] We need merely note one or two points. First, his own position, independent of any special interest:

> "whatever character my brethren may be ambitious of acting, I leave that to them; for my own part, I shall take this opportunity . . . to declare, that I do not act in consequence of any public authority or commission, to enquire, determine, and declare what is best for the Public, or what in its consequences will assuredly promote its good . . . I consider myself in no other light than as a private artist who works for hire, for those who are pleased to employ me, and those whom I can conveniently and consistently serve."

Therefore, he says, he could not have objected if the triumvirate had been sent for to examine his 1767 report; but: "to send for engineers to determine, whether the law itself be rightly founded . . . is . . . a sort of proceeding which, I think, every well-wisher to the success of the scheme should set his face against."

Smeaton respects Yeoman and Golborne, but by now he has had enough of Brindley, maybe for having said that he could build his proposed canal in four years:

> "As no difficulty is too great for Mr Brindley, I should be glad to see how he would stow a fire engine cylinder cast at Carron, of 6½ ft diameter, in one of his seven feet boats, so as to prevent its breaking the back of the boat, or oversetting . . . Mr Brindley recommends to begin at the point of partition (the watershed) because, he says, 'it is his constant prectice to do so . . .' but pray, Mr Brindley, is there no way to do a thing right but the way you do? . . . do you usually begin at the most difficult part of a work first, with raw hands, before they are trained to business? I have sometimes done so, and repented it."

Though we may agree with Smeaton that a narrow-boat canal was nonsense, and that 4 years was a foolish boast, Brindley was in fact right on two points: first, in suggesting that the River Carron should be straightened between the mouth of the Grange Burn and the Forth (this was done in 1783–85); and second, in recommending a change of route to take the line nearer Glasgow. Smeaton had rejected this, for it involved difficult ground, a substantial cutting, and a very large aqueduct over the Kelvin. Smeaton suspects that Brindley has only suggested the route in order to build the aqueduct:

"That my brother Brindley should prefer the Printfield passage, I can readily comprehend ... every man, how great soever his genius, has a certain hobby-horse he likes to ride; a large aqueduct bridge over a large river does not happen to be mine."

This was probably a reference to Brindley's proposed aqueduct over the Mersey. However, in 1770 Mackell was to suggest a similar diversion which, after re-appraisal, Smeaton approved.

For the time being this affair caused only a minor interruption. By the end of 1768 Smeaton had prepared drawings for swing and drawbridges, inverted syphons, etc. and for three typical locks. Work started in March 1769 on the first "land" lock (No. 3) using direct labour, not contractors. John Gwyn came down from Perth to superintend the carpentry and Charnley supervised the masonry. On site again in July, Smeaton reported in detail on water supply to the summit. By November work was in hand on Lock No. 5 and the first of the small aqueducts had been built; also, Smeaton decided on the layout of the flight of ten locks (Nos. 7–16) at Camelon just to the west of Falkirk. The contract for the first two of these went in February 1770 to William Gibb, the founder of the famous civil engineering family. In the previous month Charnley contracted for locks 17–19. A little later that year John Laurie surveyed for the reservoir at Townhead; by May rather more than 1,000 men were employed, including those in the quarries, and the first 9 miles of the canal had been cut.

It was in June 1770 that Mackell submitted his report on a new line for the canal west of the summit at Kirkintilloch, Laurie having taken the levels. This, as realised by Brindley, had the advantage of passing a good deal nearer to Glasgow than in Smeaton's plan and, moreover, would go on a constant level from the east summit lock No. 20 to Stockingfield. On the other hand an aqueduct of unprecedented dimensions would be necessary to take the canal over the Kelvin on its way to the Clyde. Partially to offset this, however, the 15-mile summit level would itself act as a reservoir and thereby simplify the water supply problems; Townhead reservoir alone probably being a sufficient supplement. Mackell considered that, on balance, there might be a saving in cost.

119

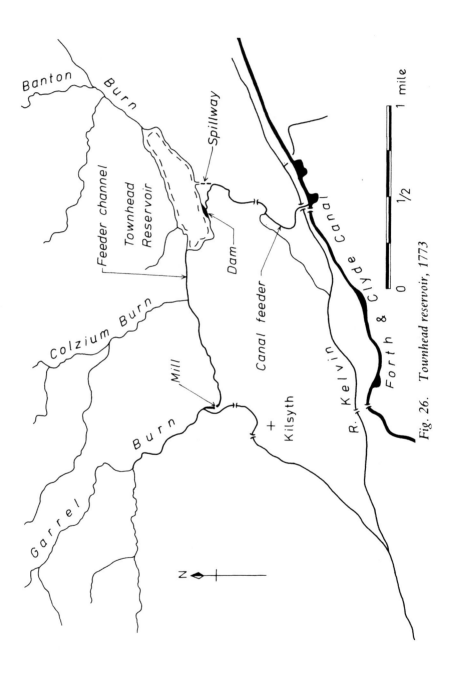

Fig. 26. Townhead reservoir, 1773

During his visit in July and August Smeaton gave careful consideration to this proposal. As to the cost, he showed that Mackell had been too optimistic, the new line would in fact be appreciably more expensive than the original plan; but the undoubted advantages outweighed the extra cost, and he gave the scheme his support, both in committee and, next year, in Parliament[37] where the necessary bill for re-alignment was passed in March 1771. Concluding his long report, dated 6th August, 1770, Smeaton says:

> "In the whole of this Business Mr Mackell has shown a great deal of Judgement & attention to the Interest of the Company. And I have the further pleasure to acquaint the Company that having carefully inspected the Works now going on, that they are in general, and in things the most material, exceedingly well executed and much to my satisfaction."[38]

Clearly, in Robert Mackell, Smeaton had a treasure of a resident engineer, and Mackell could scarcely have had a better or more understanding chief.

We may now consider in some detail the Townhead reservoir, that vital point of the scheme later described as the "sheet anchor of the navigation". An exceptionally favourable topographic situation had been found (see Smeaton's 1767 report) where the construction of an earth-fill dam, with a maximum height of about 25 ft and a crest length of less than 100 yd, would impound a reservoir covering 54 acres and containing 26 million cu. ft of water equivalent to 2,245 lockfulls (Fig. 26). From the sluice in the dam, water would be taken to the canal partly in an existing stream bed and partly in a new channel passing over the Kelvin in a small aqueduct. There was also a convenient place for the spillway. Banton Burn fed directly into the reservoir, but was not by itself sufficient. Colzium Burn, in its natural state, turned west and fell into Garrel Burn just below the tailrace of Kilsyth mill. To increase the supply of water to the reservoir, therefore, the gradient of this part of Colzium Burn was reversed, the tailrace was diverted into it, and a new feeder channel cut to the reservoir. By this ingenious system use was made of the entire flow of two streams and a good part of a third, without in any way reducing the power of the mill.

Cutting the channel to the reservoir began in May 1770; by August 1772 the dam was finished and the canal feeder in "great forwardness", and in March 1773 the reservoir had nearly been filled. A slip in the feeder embankment caused some delay, but all was ready by the summer of that year.

121

Meanwhile, in 1770 and 1772, Smeaton designed the aqueducts over the road at Camelon and over Luggie Water; and, after borings some 27 or 28 ft deep had been made, submitted plans for the two sea locks (Nos. 1 and 2) at Grangemouth. The contract for these went to John Easton in February 1771. William Gibb finished the Camelon aqueduct—one of Smeaton's more "architectural" designs—later that year. By Christmas 1771 the engineering expenditure amounted to £72,000 and, reporting this fact in July 1772, Smeaton could record that very good progress had been made along the whole line to Kilsyth. Finally, on 3rd September, 1773, the canal was opened from the Forth right through to Kirkintilloch, Gibb having completed the Luggie aqueduct there.

In this distance of 19 miles there were twenty locks accommodating a rise of 155 ft to the summit, the locks having a length of 74 ft between gates and a clear width of 20 ft; there were two sizeable aqueducts, numerous small ones, and draw and swing-bridges, as well as Townhead reservoir.

On several occasions Smeaton had suggested to the Company that his salary might be reduced, or even that he might resign, to reduce expenditure and as he had full confidence in Mackell. Each time his offer was very politely refused. However, in February 1773 he wrote again, saying that now the canal had been virtually completed to the summit level, and Townhead reservoir would shortly come into operation:

"and being very desirous of relieving the Company from all unnecessary Expenses, I beg leave to aquaint the Committee that the 14th of March coming will compleat 5 Years since I had the Honour of entering this Service and that I am ready and desirous of laying down my Salary at that time, and shall be ready to give my attendance so far as it shall be wanted ... upon my usual terms."[38]

The Committee decided, however, to continue his salary to September, and so in that month Smeaton finally left his great canal, with the warmest thanks from the Company for the very masterly manner in which he had planned and conducted his works. He kept in touch by letter for several years. His letter books of letters sent and received (which probably include his site and progress reports), running from March 1768 to April 1779, covered 770 pages (see Chapter XI). He had during the course of the work submitted at least 50 plans and working drawings,[39] and attended more than 20 committee meetings in London and Edinburgh, as well as giving evidence in Parliament on two Bills. It only remains to add that Mackell finished the canal to Stockingfield in November 1775 and to Hamilton Basin at Glasgow exactly 2 years later.[40] By that time the total expenditure had reached £164,000 and the Company could do no more for the present.

Mackell died in 1779. Asked in 1785 to resume operations, Smeaton replied: "it will be better to make a fresh beginning with a fresh engineer".[41] Robert Whitworth was accordingly appointed, and it was he who completed the line from Stockingfield to the Firth of Clyde, with the Kelvin aqueduct as his masterpiece, during the years 1786 to 1790. The canal then had a length of 37 miles, including the Glasgow branch, and the total expenditure came to £305,000.

River navigations 1766–74

Let us now return to the Upper Calder, where Brindley had taken over early in 1765, by the end of which year the navigation was probably open to Brooksmouth near Halifax. By June 1766 he seems to have left—his departure is unrecorded—for then he was engineer to the newly authorised Trent & Mersey and Staffs & Worcs Canals. The company's clerk, Thomas Simpson, became superintendent, and took the navigation to Salterhebble, probably during 1767.

Then disaster came. Early in October 1767 a flood damaged the works. The subscribers asked Smeaton to return and, generously, he did, reporting on 30th November.[42] The flood, he assured subscribers, was "higher than any flood in man's memory", higher than an extraordinary one of 40 years before. "These facts", he said, being considered, "it seems more marvelous that the works have not been wholly swept away, rather than that they have been broken in particular places." However, he allows himself to observe that, had he not been dismissed, he had intended (and had said so) to build flood-gates at the head of three cuts, and also to reinforce certain banks: "had this been put in execution, I cannot help saying, that the damages on the present occasion had laid in much less compass, though probably not entirely prevented". However, the damage has been from flooding, not from burst banks or collapsed locks: indeed only one lock had fallen, and that by external erosion. Therefore he proposes to build flood-gates (at more places than previously intended) and to raise and strengthen banks. Preventive work should be begun forthwith, the rest as soon as possible.

Emergency work did begin, but before much had been accomplished, another flood followed in February 1768, doing more damage, and yet a third in June. The concern now found itself with a

123

badly damaged navigation, a debt of £63,000, and unable to raise more money. In 1769, therefore, an Act incorporated the Calder & Hebble Company to take over the works, convert loan stock to shares, raise more funds, and increase tolls. With Simpson back as superintendent, and Luke Holt and Robert Carr as resident engineers, work began again along the lines Smeaton had recommended, and with his flood-gates; it was completed to Sowerby Bridge, in September 1770. He does another survey in December 1770,[43] telling shareholders in January that he "finds the river now put into as good a state of security as could possibly be expected at this time, and is, indeed, in a very defensible condition", and goes on to make a number of recommendations for improvement and bank strengthening.

Thereafter, the company more than once consulted Smeaton upon further improvements to meet their quickly growing trade. One such was Smeaton's suggestion to a meeting in July 1781, when he put forward a plan[44] to replace Brindley's staircase pair of locks near Salterhebble by two single locks to save "half the lockage water". They were so replaced in 1783 with Jessop as engineer in charge.

In early 1776 N. I. Korsakov, a Russian engineer officer, was sent abroad to study canal works. The Russian Consul General, Alexander Baxter, wrote to Smeaton to ask what Korsakov and his companion should see. Smeaton replied interestingly:

> "I would advise their beginning with the Forth & Clyde Canal, for though it is a Canal of the largest dimensions, yet as everything is done in the strongest and simplest manner, without any Pedantry or affectation, my belief is that they will get more real knowledge by considering the Construction of this Canal than all the rest putt together ... it might not be amiss to cast their Eye upon Upper Calder Navigation, which is a specimen of the making a River Navigable according to its own Course, and this is upon one of the most rapid Rivers in the Kingdom, of its Size, and quantity of water that comes down its Valley in time of Floods...."[45]

In the 1760s Smeaton was also concerned with another important river navigation, the Lee.[46] The commissioners of this thoroughly old-fashioned navigation that ran from the Thames tideway for some 31 miles to Hertford (with a fall of 111 ft) had, in August 1765, asked him to "settle the navigation on a new plan as will be most conducive to the good of the public". They tried again in July 1766, this time offering Thomas Yeoman to help him. He agreed, and reported in September 1766.[47] The Lee was indeed old-fashioned:

> "The present navigation ... above the tides way, being in all probability

formed upon such expedients as occurred before the invention of locks . . . its present principle . . . is that of pens and flashes from eighteen weirs and turnpikes."

He proposed, as he told the Commons committee, to convert the river to a 28-mile long navigation "which is extremely practicable, will be of much greater Certainty, not liable to Obstruction . . .". It would give 3 ft navigable depth, with 2 ft 6 in. in the driest seasons. This could be done without affecting adjacent lands by building cuts to shorten the river, a towpath, and 21 pound locks at an engineering cost of £23,023, excluding land and other costs,[48] and also the Limehouse Cut, from the Lower Lee to the Thames at Limehouse, which Yeoman had separately estimated at £5,310, including land.

> "The navigation will be not only improved by being rendered certain at all times, except in frosts and extraordinary floods, and by the shortening the distance, but by navigating in more still water, and in the straighter courses much labour in towing will be saved, and will be rendered so expeditious, that a vessel at moderate work will make her way upwards at the rate of two miles per hour, passing the locks included; that is . . . in about thirteen hours. Hence the ruin of horses, straining of barges, and great wear and tear of the tackle will be saved, as well as greater expedition be secured."[47]

The report formed the basis of the 1767 Act, upon which he appeared in Parliament.[49] Yeoman became engineer in charge. The Limehouse Cut was opened in 1770, and by 1771 about 11 miles of cuts and at least twelve locks had been built: a major modernisation. Smeaton returned to the Lee to advise on special points of difficulty in 1771, 1779 and 1782.[50]

Back in Yorkshire Smeaton was involved at about the same time in schemes for making navigable the upper Ouse and the River Ure with a canal branch to Ripon. He surveyed in 1766[51] and gave evidence to Parliament in March 1767.[52] The Acts passed, work began with John Smith as resident engineer and Joshua Wilson, another of the Calder-trained masons, as contractor for the locks.[53] By the end of 1769 the two big river locks at Linton and Milby (near Boroughbridge), both having a fall of about 10 ft and correspondingly large weirs, were completed. The whole 18-mile navigation was opened early in 1773 at a total cost of £16,400, with six locks, three weirs and a basin and warehouse (designed by Smeaton in 1771[54]) at Ripon. Jessop, as Smeaton's assistant, certainly did some of the levelling, and soundings in the rivers, and may have been deputised to take charge of the work; but Smeaton himself made several site visits and five of his reports are available.[55]

His last river job involved improvements of the Aire & Calder. This navigation, from the lower Aire above its junction with the Yorkshire Ouse to Castleford, and then along the Aire to Leeds and the Calder to Wakefield (where it joined Smeaton's Calder & Hebble), had been made navigable under an Act of 1699. It became most successful, and by the late 1760s was leased to the efficient but unpopular Peter Birt. From 1766 the idea of a trans-Pennine canal had been canvassed, to run from the Aire at Leeds to the Mersey at Liverpool, and in 1770 was authorised. Opposition to Birt, and enthusiasm for canals, combined in a plan to continue the Leeds & Liverpool Canal by another, the Leeds & Selby, to the Yorkshire Ouse, so bypassing the Aire & Calder for Leeds and canal traffic.[56]

Birt first, and then the company, in 1771, sought Smeaton's help upon improving the navigation in order to fight off the canal threat. His report of 28th December[57] was crucial to the future of this, one of Britain's most long-lived and important navigations. He begins:

> "it appears to me, that the original projectors of the navigation, not having had any notion of the extensive trade that was likely to be carried on by means thereof, have formed their plan upon too diminutive a scale, and particularly with respect to depth or draft of water [some locks having only 2 ft 6 in. over their sills] and also not being aware that it would become the practice of millers to draw and keep down their ponds, in order to levy contributions on the navigation."

In other words, to extract dues from boatmen for providing water that should have been available to them anyway. To these impediments shoals were added, and water shortages caused by giving the flashes necessary to get boats over them. Constant delays to craft resulted. Therefore he says:

> "I shall not take upon me to consider this matter in so extensive a light, as if the necessary navigation had never been made; but keeping to the present tract and works wherever it can be properly done, I shall content myself with such alterations as appear necessary to procure the essentials of a navigation, viz. the means of keeping vessels always afloat, so as to move freely in either direction when in the proper channel of navigation, and when not loaded beyond a proper draft of water."

He therefore plans for a minimum depth in dry seasons of 3 ft 6 in. This would involve extensive dredging, and also new locks and cuts, together with a long bypass cut to the lower Aire below Haddlesey. The company then petitioned for leave to bring in a Bill for improvements along Smeaton's lines; but by now opposition was widespread, and other canal schemes were being talked of that would completely avoid the rivers. So they withdrew from Parliament, and went back to Smeaton on the bypass canal. He, being too busy, put his assistant William Jessop on the job; the latter proposed a substitute cut nearly twice as long, from above Haddlesey to a point about 3 miles from the Aire's confluence with the Ouse. Smeaton approved it in December 1772,[58] and back to Parliament the company went, simultaneously with the Leeds & Selby Canal Bill, and battled well enough to postpone a decision to the following session.

By then the Aire & Calder had taken over part of its opponents' plan, itself proposing a canal from Haddlesey on the Aire to the Ouse at Selby. Smeaton and Jessop supported the new Bill in 1774,[59] making clear that the Aire cuts had been surveyed under Smeaton's direction, but that the Selby Canal was Jessop's own. There the Leeds & Selby Canal Bill was lost, though the promoters had tried to disqualify Smeaton as a witness because he held shares in the Calder & Hebble. The Aire & Calder's was carried, authorising the main Aire cuts Smeaton had recommended,[60] and the Selby Canal, at a cost of some £40,000. Jessop then built these, working with the navigation's resident engineer, John Gott.[61]

Canals, 1773–91

After the Aire & Calder, Smeaton's remaining waterway concerns were to be with canals, not rivers.

In 1756 the Grand Canal of Ireland had been begun by the Commissioners of Inland Navigation. Fifteen years later much had been spent, but no part was open. A company being planned to take over the work, one of its promoters, Redmond Morres, in June 1771 wrote to ask Smeaton to come over. Too busy then, Morres tried again in September 1772. This time Smeaton agreed, taking young Jessop with him. Both crossed to Ireland in June 1773, where Smeaton did a report;[62] another followed in 1775.[63] Thereafter the Grand Canal became Jessop's responsibility.[64]

Five canal surveys followed, for the Greasbrough in 1775, and in 1778 the Bude, Kingston & Ewell, Tyne bypass and Cann quarry.[65] None need detain us.

Later, before the passing of the Thames & Severn Canal's 1783 Act, Smeaton had been asked by a local landowner, Lord Eliot, to advise on the effect of the canal on his estate's water supply. Smeaton discussed this with the canal's engineer, Whitworth, but his advice had only partially been taken. When, therefore, cutting reached Lord Eliot's estate, within which lay three of the canal's locks (Cerney Wick, Latton and Eisey) Eliot stopped the company digging a feeder from the Ampney Brook and again asked Smeaton's advice. The latter did not mince his words, criticising the unequal lock falls of Whitworth's layout and suggesting an alternative supply.[66]

Smeaton's remaining canal work was in the Birmingham area. In 1771 he had reported briefly on a problem concerning the Birmingham Canal,[67] but his main contributions were subsequent to 1776. By that year water was becoming increasingly scarce; Samuel Bull, the company's engineer, therefore ordered from Boulton & Watt a small (20 in. dia. cylinder) steam engine to pump into the canal's Smethwick summit level. This began work early in 1778 and in April Smeaton tested the engine, finding it very satisfactory (see Chapter VIII); whereupon, in June, another engine was ordered for summit pumping. In 1782 he was consulted again, on possible improvements and extensions. He wrote:

> "I can sett forward from hence for Birmingham on Monday the 7th October and stay there one week if necessary; but that my stay may not be protracted beyond what is necessary shall be glad that every thing preparatory be done in the way of common surveying and Levelling; and in case there is anything critical in the latter, will carry my own level along with me."[68]

The company's request arose partly from their own wish to expand their branch network, partly to prevent the building of a rival promotion, the Bilston Canal from near Wolverhampton past Wednesbury to near Birmingham and then to Fazeley on the Coventry Canal. Smeaton saw at once that availability of water supplies governed all expansion of an already big canal network, much of it lying upon a plateau. Natural streams were few; most supplies had to come from mine drainage pumping and spring-fed reservoirs.

His report is a fascinating analysis of an industrial canal's sources of water.[69] Its conclusion was that expansion must be limited, even after all additional sources of mine pumping had been utilised and as much leakage (heavy in a mining area) as possible stopped. In 1783, by intense lobbying, the Birmingham Company managed to get the Bilston Bill shelved and, with Smeaton's support,[70] authority for a new company with virtually the same shareholders as the old (and soon to be amalgamated with it) to build their extensions from Wednesbury and also a Birmingham & Fazeley Canal. Upon the latter, the shareholders' meeting of 26th September, 1783 resolved that "it might be right to consult Mr Smeaton again relative to some material points in the execution of the intended Canal...". Smeaton, however, refused on grounds of ill-health. He was consulted later, always with water in mind, in 1786 when the company decided to lower their 491 ft summit by 18 ft between Smethwick and Spon Lane, so eliminating three locks at each end, and in 1789–91 when he advised the Birmingham Company in connection with the proposed Worcester & Birmingham Canal.[71]

On this affair he seems to have been employed by them to survey and estimate the Worcester & Birmingham's likely cost, which he put at £285,000 against £186,000 from John Snape, the Worcester & Birmingham's surveyor.[72] The latter company went ahead on Snape's figure, but indeed Smeaton's itself turned out to be an underestimate. Then in June 1791, having devoted much time and trouble to the scheme,[73] he appeared for the Birmingham Company upon the Bill;[74] his last attendance in Parliament and the end of a long career on inland navigations. His great pupil and assistant, William Jessop, was the leading river and canal engineer of the next generation.

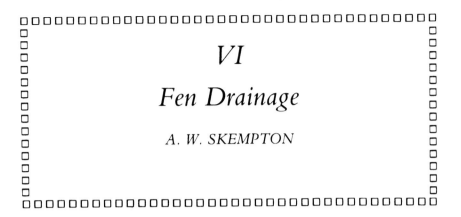

VI

Fen Drainage

A. W. SKEMPTON

Very little has been published hitherto on any of the fen drainage schemes with which Smeaton was concerned, but research in recent years now makes it possible to describe three of them in some detail. Summaries will also be given of two other reports, as well as comments on his ideas on flow in open channels and his method of calculating discharge through an outfall sluice for the River Torne in Hatfield Chase.

Lochar Moss

Although his proposals were not carried out, Smeaton's "Report on the Drainage of Lochar Moss, near Dumfries" is of interest as it refers to the first civil engineering job on which he was consulted.[1] He arrived at Dumfries in August 1754 and completed his report there on 21st September, submitting it to "The Duke of Queensberry and others concerned". There is an accompanying sketch map,[2] shown in a simplified form in Fig. 27.

The report is composed in four parts. First, the basic facts are set out: levels of the ground at various places and water levels along the River Lochar, depths of water on the riverside meadows after heavy rain had caused flooding, discharge of the river when in flood (300 cu. ft/s), and the observation that ordinary spring tides have a noticeable effect as far upstream as Bankend Bridge. Then come a few elementary remarks on the flow of water in rivers and channels. In the third section Smeaton explains his scheme. One essential feature is an outfall sluice, positioned at point A. This should have a clear waterway of 14 ft with a pair of self-acting mitre doors pointing to the sea. The sills of the sluice are to be laid at low-water mark. The sluice will allow "land water to flow out whenever it is higher than the water of the sea and prevent the sea water from flowing in whenever the tide without is higher than the land water within". Moreover, the greater the land flood the longer will the doors remain open. In addition it is necessary to shorten, and thereby increase the gradient of, the lower part of the river. This could be done by straightening the very circuitous course, but a better and more convenient method, probably involving no extra expense, is to cut a new channel 3 miles in length from the sluice up to point B, about ½ mile above Bankend. Further upstream, as the river has a nearly adequate fall (11 ft from Tinwald to point B) all that needs doing is to cut off the biggest loops and widen and deepen the bed where desirable.

These works, he says, should be sufficient to prevent summer flooding of the meadows; drains can then be cut into the slightly higher peat areas (known collectively as Lochar Moss). Once the flood levels in the river have been reduced, the tributaries need only be cleaned out.

Finally, assuming a hydraulic gradient of 1 ft/mile, Smeaton suggests suitable dimensions of the channel: 10 ft bottom width, side slopes of 1 to 1, and an average depth of 16 ft below ground level. He also gives estimates. The total comes to just under £3,000 without allowing for contingencies, legal charges, or the cost of land cut and covered.

The scheme was presumably considered to be too ambitious, and it also involved replacing a watermill at Bankend by another mill (allowed for in the estimates) near the mouth of Mouswald Burn. Smeaton must have made a favourable impression as his advice was sought in 1760 on some problems concerning the River Nith and its navigation downstream from Dumfries.[3]

Potteric Carr

This is the name given to about 4,250 acres of low ground south-east of Doncaster (Fig. 28). In the mid-eighteenth century the north-western part of the Carr had two drains running into a little lake, the Old Eaa, from which water flowed along a stream into the River Torne through a sluice at point f; the Torne was embanked from C to B; and a small area north of the embanked St Catherine's Well Stream drained via Huxterwell Drain also to the sluice at f. However, much of the land was subjected to flooding, and there was very obvious advantages in achieving a proper drainage for the whole Carr.

With this object in view the Corporation of Doncaster, jointly with

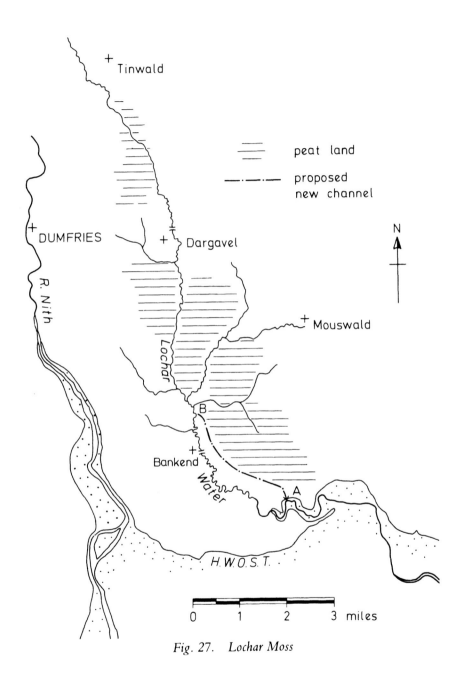

peat land

proposed
new channel

N

Fig. 27.   Lochar Moss

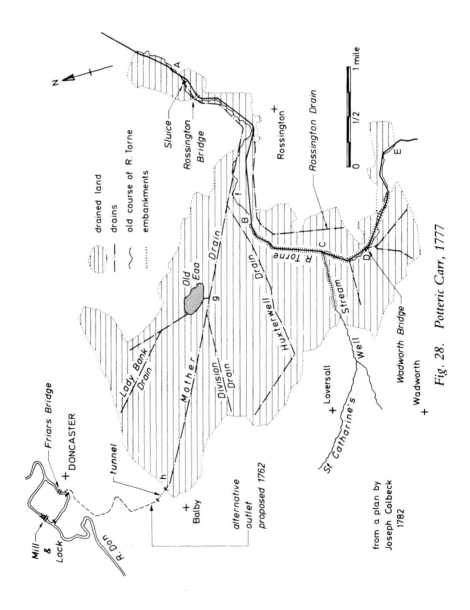

Fig. 28. Potteric Carr, 1777

William Dixon of Loversall, one of the principal landowners, decided to commission a report from Smeaton.[4] He visited the site in July 1762, took a series of levels, and reported in September on two alternative schemes.[5] First, to take the water from a new main drain in the Carr through a short tunnel beneath the ridge along which passes the Doncaster–Balby road, and thence in an open cut to the River Don just upstream of Friars Bridge. Second, to lead the main or "Mother Drain" to an outfall in the Torne, ¾ mile below Rossington Bridge, where a sluice should be built with doors pointing to the river and a draw door on the "land" side to maintain water level in the drains during dry seasons. In either case there would have to be a drain on the east side of the Torne.

The second scheme is simpler, but there may be objections from landowners further down the Torne even though it can be argued convincingly that any effect on their lands will be negligible.

Smeaton's levels showed that the lowest ground in the Carr lay almost 5 ft above river level in the Torne at the proposed outfall. With the usual requirement that water in the drains should be kept at least 2 ft below ground surface, there would be a fall of nearly 3 ft in a distance of about 3¼ miles from point g.

The levels in the Carr and along the Torne were correct; but very surprisingly something seems to have gone wrong with the levelling across to the River Don, for the river at Friars Bridge (so far as can now be ascertained) was probably at about the same elevation as the Carr itself,[6] whereas Smeaton thought he had found an ample fall.

Smeaton's fees of £26–5s–0d were ordered to be paid in November 1763 and in January 1764 he was asked to prepare estimates.[4] This he did in March after spending 6 days on site and charging a further £8–11s–0d at the rate of £1–8s–6d a day[7] (1 guinea plus 7s–6d expenses). The estimates relate to the first scheme,[8] which the clients evidently preferred. A petition went to Parliament in January 1765; Richard Sheppard, the Town Clerk, drew up the Bill, Smeaton submitted written evidence, and the Act was obtained in April.[9]

Towards the end of May, however, the Corporation sent for James Brindley "to take a Levell of Potterick Carr to find which will be the most effectual way and method to drain the same", and a month later they ordered payment of his fee of 8 guineas plus 1 guinea for travelling expenses from Barnsley.[4] The apparent explanation of Brindley's visit is that someone had spotted the possibility of an error in the levels to the Don and, if this is so, a likely person is Thomas Tofield (then living at Balby) one of the Commissioners named in the Act, a local landowner, an excellent botanist, and soon to become a respected consultant on fen drainage.[10]

Unfortunately Brindley's report cannot be found and the Commissioners' Minute Book is lost. There is a further complication, for a detailed report sent by Smeaton to Mr Sheppard, dealing entirely with the second scheme, is undated.[11] In it, Smeaton refers to having been on site "on the 20th of May last", and though this might be in 1766 a more probable date is May 1765; that is, before Brindley was asked to take levels.

At any rate this report to Mr Sheppard certainly forms the basis for the works which were carried out, and Smeaton redeemed himself (if this was necessary) by presenting a most logical set of proposals. These involved diverting the Torne in a long cut from B to A through a new bridge to be built adjacent to the existing Rossington Bridge, and using the latter to accommodate the Mother Drain. To avoid legal problems the outfall was now to be placed at point A, at the boundary of the Corporation's land, about ½ mile upstream of the position originally chosen. The hydraulic gradient consequently would be diminished to just under 5 in./mile, and this explains Smeaton's decision that the Mother Drain from A to g should have a generous bottom width of 18 ft and be carried on a horizontal plane at a depth of about 6 ft, or 2 ft below river level at the outfall. Upwards from g the drain dimensions would be reduced so as to be 4 ft deep with a 5 ft bottom at h. He also recommended that the new channel for the Torne should have a bottom width of at least 20 ft, with side slopes not steeper than 1 to 1, and though the area of "uplands" draining into the Carr was small, it might be desirable to lead this water into the river by catch-water drains along the edge of the Carr.

The rest of the story, if not known in all its details, seems to be quite straightforward. Work proceeded, almost exactly in accordance with Smeaton's report, in three stages.[12] In the first, completed by 1768,[13] the new Rossington Bridge was built and the new channel for the Torne cut from A to B; upstream from B to D the river was enlarged with raised and extended embankments; the Division and Lady Bank drains were enlarged, and the Mother Drain cut from h down to the old course of the Torne east of point f. Then came a pause while the northern parts of the Carr, belonging to Doncaster, were divided and inclosed; seemingly a long process.[14] The Commissioners' task now finished, they were succeeded by Trustees. Under the Trustees, whose Minute Books have survived,[12] work was resumed in 1772. Two years later, with completion of the second stage, the Mother

Drain had been extended under old Rossington Bridge to point A, where the outfall sluice was built (with a 12 ft waterway); Rossington drain had been cut and Huxterwell drain enlarged and extended northwards.

It is probable that Smeaton brought Matthias Scott from the Calder Navigation in 1765 as Surveyor or resident engineer. Certainly he was appointed (or re-appointed) to this post by the Trustees in 1772, though now as a part-time job. It was he who made the working drawings for the sluice. Tofield appears effectively to have been in charge from the beginning, and again this is known to be the case in 1772. Scott left 2 years later, when his place was taken by Henry Cooper, and, with Tofield still directing most of the operations, the third stage reached completion in 1777. By that time the Torne had been improved upstream from D to E, with an additional length of embankment, and downstream for a mile or so below the outfall sluice. Some small drains along the north and west boundaries (not shown in Fig. 28) had also been finished. Finally, the land surveyor Joseph Colbeck produced a fine map of the drainage in 1782.[15]

The total lengths of the cuts were: new River Torne 4.6 miles, Mother Drain 4.5 miles, branch drains 8 miles.

Potteric Carr neatly demonstrates several principles of fen drainage. First and foremost is the need to separate the "living waters" of the river and its tributary streams from the "land water" generated by rain falling within the area to be drained. This is achieved by embanking the river and streams where necessary, and improving their flow characteristics, in order to avoid flooding the land. The drains then have only to discharge the rain water plus the flow of any small streams from the higher land which cannot be led directly into the river. The drains must have an adequate capacity and an outfall as far downstream as possible. If there is any chance of the river backing up the drains when in flood, an outfall sluice is required. The agricultural need to keep water in the drains several feet below ground level means there is some temporary storage within the drainage system, and this "reservoir effect" is useful in smoothing out peak flows.

These principles were no doubt well understood, if not always followed, but they form the basis of Smeaton's practice and perhaps deserve to be stated explicitly here for readers not familiar with the subject.

Flow in open channels
It is natural to ask how Smeaton decided upon the dimensions of the

main drain at Potteric Carr and elsewhere; there is no simple answer. We note that Jessop in 1790, when making the first design for a steam pumped-drainage scheme for the Fens, assumed the pumps would rarely have to cope with a flow equivalent to more than 2 in. of rain in a week, or 12 cu. ft of water/s per 1,000 acres.[16] Smeaton may well have had some such sensible working rule which, incidentally, makes an allowance for the reservoir effect just mentioned, and applies to the winter months when evaporation is small.

That he also had a method of calculating the flow in open channels seems probable, though we have found no record of how the calculations were made. However, some indications are given in a letter, written in 1770, in reply to a query raised jointly by Tofield and Grundy on Deeping Fen.[17] In this Smeaton makes the following points:

(1) Flow occurs within the full cross-section of a channel even when the bottom of the channel lies below the level of the outlet; i.e. there is no "dead water".

(2) As an equal quantity of water must, in the same channel, pass in a given time through every section, the velocity will vary inversely as the area of the section.

(3) For a given flow the greater the velocity (under equal circumstances) the greater will be the gradient, and vice-versa.

(4) For a given cross-sectional area and gradient, the flow increases with the ratio (R) of area to wetted perimeter: that is, the hydraulic mean depth.

(5) This last fact justifies the extra expense of making drains with a horizontal bottom, rather than a sloping one, where gradients are small, and for digging the bottom below the level of water at the outfall, as at Potteric Carr.

All this is perfectly correct, in general terms. We are left wondering exactly what relationship he thought existed between velocity V and gradient S (a subject he is known to have studied for pipe flow, see Chapter I); but without indulging in too much speculation it seems possible to suggest that he had some kind of scaling law, involving S and R, from which the flow could be estimated in one channel from the observed flow in another of known dimensions and gradient. This was the method used by Antoine Chezy in 1769, in France, long before any reliable formulae had been published for direct calculations of the flow in open channels.[18] Smeaton would have no great difficulty in gauging flow or measuring gradients.

Holderness Drainage

Smeaton visited the east Yorkshire district of Holderness in November 1763 and reported in the following January,[19] as a consultant only. The scheme was designed and carried out by John Grundy. Essentially it improved the drainage of about 11,000 acres of low ground by cutting a new drain to the River Hull, where a large outfall sluice was built in the river bank just north of the bridge at Kingston-upon-Hull. Smeaton gave some useful advice, and received £20 in fees;[20] but of more interest is his second report, of December 1764, on the sluice.

The two engineers met the Trustees at Beverley in July when they were "desired to draw a plan and estimate for the Outfall Clough with Sections, Elevations, and in such manner as will enable the Work men to proceed upon".[20] Next month Smeaton visited Grundy at Spalding on other matters, though sluices were also under discussion and Smeaton learnt (and received a copy) of an early design by Grundy's father for a sluice at Deeping Fen.[21] Grundy himself then made drawings for the Holderness sluice[22] which went to Austhorpe for comment. Smeaton obviously enjoyed this job. He starts his report by saying: "The general design and idea of this sluice I much approve; but as I think it may be made stronger with the same expense, I therefore submit the following remarks to Mr Grundy's consideration." Then come fifteen practical comments, mostly to do with the foundations, which must have been highly beneficial; but Smeaton's enthusiasm is vividly expressed in the rest of his report, consisting of the most detailed bill of quantities and estimate yet found in the entire eighteenth-century engineering literature. It includes no less than 140 items, from the timber bearing piles and sheet piling to the masonry and brickwork, and every detail of the carpentry and ironwork in the "sea doors and land doors", down to the last bolt.[23]

Nothing reveals more clearly Smeaton's love for precise engineering design and his outstanding practical ability. It is also a tribute to the personal friendship and mutual respect of these engineers, so evident in their letters.

The sluice, with two 10 ft waterways, was built in 1765–66 and the principal drains were completed by 1768, under Grundy's direction with Joseph Page as resident engineer.[20]

Adlingfleet Level

Before the completion of a comprehensive drainage scheme in 1772 most of the 5,000 acres of low ground shown in Fig. 29 were often flooded and some parts lay almost permanently under water.

Smeaton first visited the area in 1755 by request of the owners of Haldenby manor. His report cannot be found but from comments in a later report, of 1764, it appears that he recommended enlarging the existing drains and rebuilding the inadequate outfall sluice at Ousefleet; "not supposing at that time", he says, "that the proprietors would be willing to be at the charge of getting an act of Parliament in order to enable them to make new drains in any more proper direction".[24]

Next, in 1759, John Grundy reported to Mr Marmaduke Constable and another owner of land in Eastoft.[25] A sufficient fall existed from Eastoft to Ousefleet, but the sluice had a width of only 6 ft and the drains were too narrow with too many sharp bends. Technically it would be feasible to improve the system, but many landowners were involved and the outfall came under the jurisdiction of the Court of Sewers, so the difficulties might be overwhelming without an Act. All that could be done immediately, he thought, was to erect an engine (i.e. a wind-driven scoop wheel) near point K to relieve the land in Eastoft.

Sensibly, the principal landowners got together and decided to obtain an Act. On their behalf Mr Constable wrote to Smeaton and Grundy. After a rather muddled episode, with letters crossing in the post,[26] it emerged that Smeaton would take the levels and draw up a report, based on a land survey to be made by Charles Tate, who had recently surveyed the Holderness scheme. Tate produced an excellent map. Smeaton visited the site in July 1764 and, with "more accurate instruments" than he had at his disposal in 1755, took levels at some two dozen points as well as determining high and low water at Ousefleet and Trent Falls.[27] His report is dated 3rd December, 1764.[24]

Again he points out that the existing system could be satisfactory if improved by enlarging and straightening the drains and rebuilding the sluice with its sill 3 ft lower: at low-water level. However, on a broader view of the situation it would be better to cut a new main drain from Green Bank in the south to an outfall sluice to be built in the bank of the River Trent, at point A, where low water is 1 ft 8 in. lower than at Ousefleet. This position offers the advantage that, with the same sill elevation as proposed at Ousefleet, the sluice doors at Trent Falls would remain open for a greater length of time at each tide.

Taking low-water mark in the Trent as datum, Smeaton finds that the lowest land, in Haldenby Common about 4 miles from the outfall, lies at +8 ft 10 in.; and in Eastoft Moor, about 5½ miles from

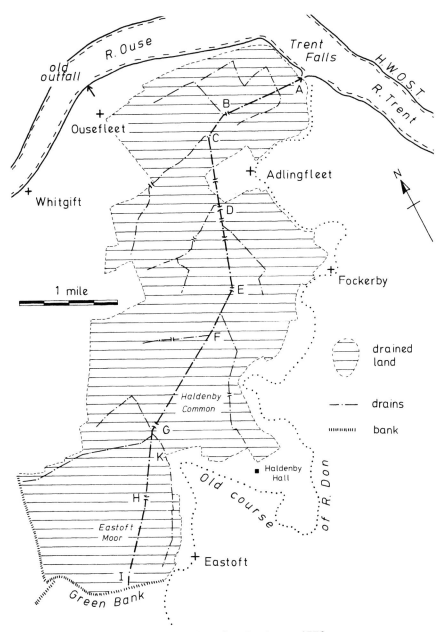

Fig. 29. Adlingfleet Drainage, 1772

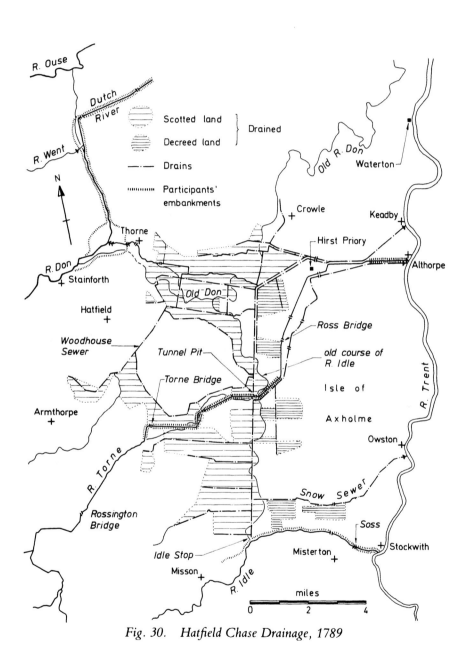

Fig. 30.   *Hatfield Chase Drainage, 1789*

142

the outfall, ground level is +10 ft 5 in. Thus with the sill of the sluice at +1 ft 8 in. and allowing 6 in. of water flowing on the sill, and with an "ample and sufficient" fall of 1 ft/mile, water in the drain will be comfortably more than the 2 ft below ground surface required for good drainage.

The outfall sluice, Smeaton says, should have a clear waterway of 10 ft. From the sluice to point E he plans to make the drain with a horizontal bed, at sill level, and a bottom width of 10 ft with side slopes of 1⅓ to 1. As the ground falls away from the Trent, the depth of cut will decrease from about 12 ft at a point 100 yd behind the sluice to 10 ft in the neighbourhood of B and to 8 ft at the lowest point along the line of the drain between E and F. Further south the ground rises very gently and the drain can be made progressively narrower and shallower, on a slope of 10 in./mile, with sides at 1 to 1.[28] The barrier banks along the south and south-west boundaries must in any case be raised, strengthened and extended to give full protection against floods outside the area.

Here it is necessary to explain that Adlingfleet differs from Potteric Carr, and indeed from most other drainages, in having no river or streams traversing its boundaries. Not only is the surrounding land exceedingly flat, but the River Don, the old course of which is mapped in Figs 29 and 30, was diverted by Vermuyden in the early seventeenth century as part of his work for draining Hatfield Chase, and ever since has run from Thorne through the Dutch River to Goole. Vermuyden was only partly successful with Hatfield Chase, and we shall see later in this chapter that Smeaton contributed to the improvement of this large tract of land, but almost nothing was done to drain parts of the area between Hatfield Chase and Adlingfleet level. Hence the need for barrier banks along the southern boundary of the latter. Once these were built, however, the level could be drained simply by carrying away the rainfall, as not a single stream of any significant size is involved. The natural levees of the old River Don form the eastern boundary and to the west there is the Whitgift drainage system.

Returning to Smeaton's report, he gives estimates for both schemes but recommends the new drain to Trent Falls, despite its higher cost. The landowners adopted his advice and obtained the necessary Act in March 1767.[29] His fees and expenses came to the modest total of £28–16s–4d, paid by Mr Constable who was later reimbursed by the Commissioners.[30]

The five Commissioners named in the Act held their first meeting in April and James Stovin, appointed Clerk, was ordered to have copies of Smeaton's report made for their use.[30] A letter went to Smeaton but evidently he suggested that Grundy should carry out the works, for at the next meeting, in June, Grundy was asked "to prepare proper Plans, Sections & Estimates for building the outfall Clough [i.e. sluice] at the place and as proposed by Mr Smeaton and the Mother Drain". At the same meeting Charles Tate was requested to stake out the drain from the sluice to point E and David Buffery became Surveyor of the Works, at £50 a year.

Construction proceeded efficiently. Grundy took full charge, making working drawings, certifying the contractor's bills, and so on. Buffery proved an able assistant, and Tate a skilled land surveyor. Most of the contracts were let between August and November 1767 and the main works reached completion in 1769. Then came the cutting of new side drains, enlarging such of the old ones as were to be incorporated, building sluices at the mouth of each side drain and numerous small bridges. Finally, after an exact survey, the Commissioners made their Award in June 1772.[30]

As usual this sets out the areas of drained land field by field in each parish, but it also gives details of the outfall sluice together with dimensions of the Mother Drain (at nine cross-sections), of all the side drains, and the barrier bank. From these we find that Grundy followed Smeaton's plans with only a few relatively minor modifications.

Some idea of the effort put in by Grundy and Tate can be deduced from their fees, which amounted to £302 and £348 respectively.[30] The engineering works cost about £5,000 but with legal, Parliamentary and land charges, and salaries, the Commissioners' fees etc., the total would have been something like £7,000: an economical figure for the vastly improved drainage of 5,000 acres of potentially very valuable farming land. In a report of December 1768 Grundy gives precise quantities and costs of the main drain: 170,000 cu. yd excavated at a unit cost varying with the depths of cut and averaging just under 3*d*/cu. yd.[31] The contractors were James Pinkerton and John Dyson, in partnership. Later they both established firms which became well known. Apart from the main drain, 5.8 miles in length, the side or branch drains totalled 12.3 miles; typically they had a bottom width of 5 ft, a depth of 6 or 7 ft, and side slopes of ⅔ to 1. Excavation of the sluice pit, about 20 ft deep, cost 4½*d*/cu. yd. As usual at this period the outfall sluice was built by separate contractors for masonry, brickwork and carpentry.

144

Hatfield Chase

The large tract of low ground known as Hatfield Chase had been drained, with partial success, by Sir Cornelius Vermuyden in the early seventeenth century.[32] For more than 100 years subsequently the taxes raised on the 14,000 acres allotted to Vermuyden and his fellow Participants in the undertaking (the "scotted land" in Fig. 30) and on the 3,000 acres of "decreed land" awarded to local landowners,[33] were absorbed in maintenance of the rivers, banks and drains, and in paying off the high initial capital expenditure. Only by the mid-eighteenth century was it possible to contemplate any major improvements of the system, and the first sign in this direction was a request to Smeaton to advise on two matters concerning the southern parts of the drainage. His report is dated 19th September, 1764.[34]

Misterton Soss Part of Vermuyden's work was the diversion of the River Idle into the eastern branch leading to the Trent at Stockwith. To do this he dammed the northern branch at Idle Stop, built a tidal sluice near Misterton with embankments between the sluice and the outfall, and a barrier bank along the north side of the Idle from the sluice to relatively high ground near Misson. The Trent itself was already embanked to protect the adjacent land from high tides which, with the river in flood, rise 14–16 ft above normal low-water level between Stockwith and Keadby.

By these means tidal water and floods in the Idle were kept off the low ground north of the barrier bank. In addition, the carrs south of the Idle (in Gringley and Misterton parishes) were converted to "summer grounds", that is pasture land subjected only to winter floods.

The sluice, originally a timber structure, had been rebuilt in the 1670s with masonry walls and two pairs of pointing gates to act also as a lock for navigation up the Idle to Bawtry. Its walls were 16 ft high, with a clear waterway 17½ ft in width, and normally a depth of about 4 ft of water in the sills. The barrier bank required frequent maintenance but even so was breached from time to time in exceptional floods, and had been so breached in the winter of 1763/64 at a point a short distance downstream from Idle Stop.

Smeaton realised that as the width of Misterton Soss was not more than one-half the width of the river it must act as a restriction to flow. He therefore suggested that additional sluice doors be built adjacent to the lock, in a locally widened cut. In this way the flood water would rise to a smaller height, increasing the safety of the bank, and would also run off more quickly with advantage to the pasture land on the southern carrs.

The wisdom of this advice was apparent, and the Commissioners of Sewers who had administrative responsibility for Hatfield Chase drainage ordered the work to be done in 1772, and again in 1782.[35] The Participants, however, were understandably reluctant to spend money on a scheme which would be of most benefit to the ground outside their own limits, and contented themselves with raising and strengthening the bank.[36] However, when eventually in the 1790s the complete drainage of Everton, Gringley and Misterton carrs was undertaken, with Jessop as engineer, additional sluices as proposed by Smeaton were incorporated in the design, providing an additional waterway of 30 ft width.[37] They remained in action well into the present century, and can still be seen; but a new sluice working in conjunction with flood water pumps has recently been installed at Stockwith.

Snow Sewer   This is the name of an old watercourse which was enlarged and extended as a main drain for the carrs south of the Isle of Axholme. It has a length of 6 miles and an outfall sluice on the Trent at Owston. During his site visit in August 1764 Smeaton noted that, with the sluice doors shut by the tide, water in the drain was just overflowing onto the lowest grounds and standing 2 ft 11 in. above the level of the sill. Measurements also showed the sill to be 4 in. above low water in the Trent, and at that stage the sluice was running with 6 in. of water on the sill.

To remedy this state of affairs Smeaton proposed building a new sluice with a 15 ft waterway, in place of the existing 12 ft width, and with a sill lower by1½ ft; that is 1 ft 2 in. below low water. The drain should then be enlarged to a 15 ft bottom width taken on a dead level for 2 miles from the sluice; further west it could be made progressively shallower and narrower. He explains in the simplest possible terms the advantage to be gained by deepening the sill, and the bottom of the drain, below low-water level. He also counters an anticipated argument that the sluice, being laid lower, will not run so long and will be more liable to silting up.

Smeaton's recommendations were carried out in due course as part of the programme of remedial works initiated in 1776, as we shall see.

River Torne   Though many of the drains were, like Snow Sewer, inadequate to cope with heavy rainfall, the worst features of the system arose from flooding of the River Torne. From the point where the river originally joined the north branch of the Idle, near Tunnel Pit (see Fig. 30), Vermuyden had made a new cut running north-east on a course with four right-angled bends to the neighbourhood of

Hirst Priory; here it received water from a short main drain and proceeded eastwards (as the "South River") to an outfall sluice on the Trent at Althorpe. Vermuyden also cut a main drain, known as the New Idle, running north from Idle Stop and passing under the Torne at Tunnel Pit to Dirtness Bridge. Thence, as the "North River", it turned north-east to Hirst Priory and then east to another, slightly larger, sluice at Althorpe. Four branch drains entered the North River as shown in Fig. 31. At some later period a communication was made between the North and South Rivers near Hirst Priory so that in times of flood the Torne could flow out through both sluices though, at the same time, the drains would also be carrying their maximum discharge. Equally serious causes of trouble were the insufficient depths of cut for the Torne where it passed through slightly higher grounds and the inadequate height of its banks elsewhere.

Some improvements could have been made had more funds been made available, but it seems that no very clear or comprehensive idea existed as to the best course of action. One good suggestion for a partial improvement, made in 1761,[38] probably by the Surveyor of the Works (i.e. the resident engineer) George Forster, was to divert the North River at Pilfrey Farm to a new outfall sluice at Keadby: see Fig. 31(c). This, however, required an Act of Parliament and capital expenditure too great to be considered at that date, so nothing was done. Ten years later renewed and serious complaints about the overflowing of the Torne led the Commissioners to call on Thomas Tofield for advice.[39] He came to the conclusion, in a report of September 1773,[40] that it would be best to divert the river outside the drainage area altogether in a new cut from the region of Torne Bridge northwards to the Don at Thorne; there being a fall of nearly 6 ft in this distance of about 7 miles. The engineering cost was estimated at less than £3,000 but again an Act would have to be obtained and much negotiation for the purchase of land would be necessary.

In 1773 Matthias Scott, who was now Surveyor of the Works,[41] began the first practical improvement by enlarging the North River from Crowle Bridge to Althorpe.[42] In 1774 the Participants sought advice from Thomas Yeoman. In a report dated December 1774 he suggested that the waters of both the North and South River should be taken in a new cut to an outfall on the Trent near Waterton where, by his estimation, river level was at least 4 ft lower than at Althorpe.[43] As soon as the low grounds in this region were clear of water, in June 1775, Scott made a survey of the route as pointed out by Yeoman, finding the length of cut to be just over 6 miles and a fall of 4 ft 5 in.

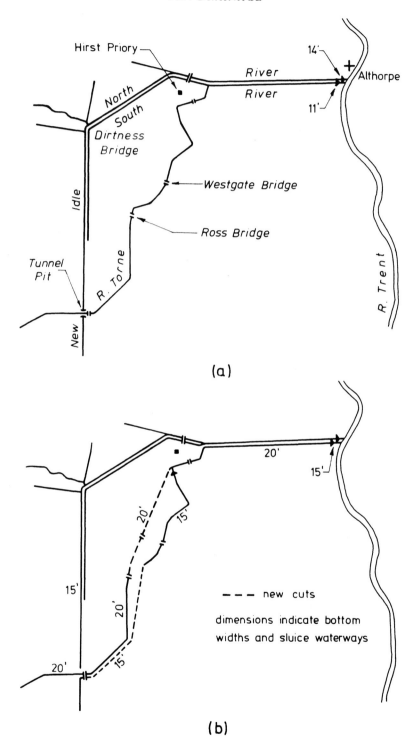

(a)

(b)

--- new cuts

dimensions indicate bottom
widths and sluice waterways

148

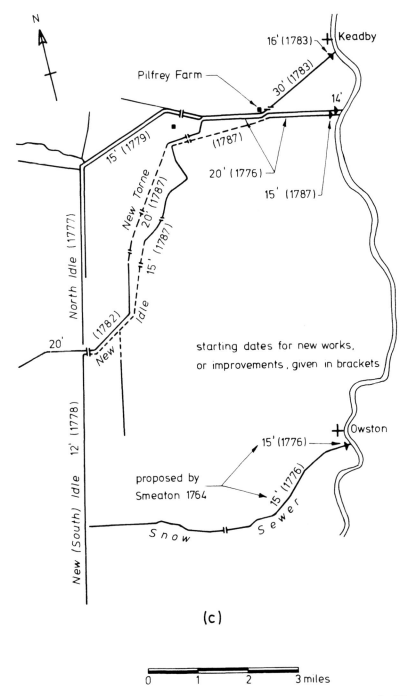

N

16' (1783) ✛ Keadby

Pilfrey Farm

30' (1783)

14'

15' (1779)

(1787)

New Torne

20' (1787)

20' (1776)

15' (1787)

15' (1787)

North Idle (1777)

(1782)

New Idle

20'

New

starting dates for new works,
or improvements, given in brackets

12' (1778)

✛ Owston

15' (1776)

proposed by
Smeaton 1764

15' (1776)

New (South) Idle

S n o w

S e w e r

(c)

0   1   2   3 miles

Fig. 31.   Hatfield Chase Drainage: (a) pre 1776; (b) Smeaton's proposals 1776;
(c) Improvement carried out by Scott (1776–82) and Foster (1783–89)

149

from the North and South River to low water in the Trent. Assuming a sluice 16 ft wide and a 30 ft bottom width for the new cut, Scott estimated the total cost at nearly £10,000 including land and Parliamentary charges, though he was careful to point out that substantial widening of the existing drains and improvements in the Torne would still be required before the full benefits of the new outfall were realised.[44]

By this time determined efforts to improve the drainage were becoming financially possible, even if such radical schemes as those suggested by Tofield and Yeoman could not be undertaken. In the summer of 1776 work began on Snow Sewer in exact accordance with Smeaton's report of 1764, and widening of the South River to a 20 ft bottom width for 2½ miles above the sluice.[45] An accurate survey was also made of the whole drainage.[46] Then in September of that year Smeaton investigated the problem of the River Torne in great detail, presenting a report in October.[47]

After a general introduction recognising the importance of the subject and outlining the chief problems, he gives technical support to Yeoman's scheme; but goes on to say:

> "as I understand that the whole Course of the proposed outfall Drain, lays thro' Parishes and Lordships wholly unconnected with the Participants Concern in Hatfield Chase; in case Difficulties should arise in reconciling these different Interests, it seems to me of consequence to that Body of Gentlemen, and the Country at present depending upon their Undertaking, to shew how these Levels of Hatfield Chase may be drained, in a very competent Manner, without going out of their own Boundary."

And this he proceeds to do.

First, from levels taken along the Torne when it was almost bank full at Tunnel Pit, he finds there is a fall of 11½ ft from Torne Bridge to low water in the Trent at Althorpe, in a distance of nearly 13 miles. Thus, given an improved channel and a proper outfall sluice, there should be no essential difficulty in carrying flood water safely to the Trent. This he proposes to achieve by the following measures:

(1) building a new sluice with a waterway of 15 ft (instead of the present 11 ft) and a sill 2 ft below low water;
(2) cutting a new channel from the bend below Ross Bridge to the bend south of Hirst Priory, see Fig. 31(b); this makes a straighter course and shortens the length by 0.6 mile;
(3) cutting the bed on a dead level, at sill elevation, from the sluice up

to Hirst Priory and thence deepening the bed wherever necessary, in places by as much as 4½ ft;

(4) maintaining a bottom width of 20 ft throughout; and

(5) raising the banks between Torne Bridge and Ross Bridge and along the last 1½ miles leading to the sluice; the latter banks to be at least at the level of high water neaps in the Trent at Althorpe.

In addition:

(6) the New Idle drain is to be divided at Tunnel Pit and the southern portion taken in a new cut to join the old channel of the Torne between Ross and Westgate bridges and thence to the new Torne near Hirst Priory; and

(7) the drains north of Tunnel Pit be led into the North River and kept separate from the Torne; those drains and the new cut for the south drain to have a bottom width of 15 ft.

Estimates given in the report show £8,660 for spadework, excluding widening of existing drains, £3,600 approximately for the new sluice, bridges, etc., and a total of £13,500 without land and legal charges, fees and salaries.

Of particular interest are Smeaton's calculations for the sluice. At the time of his site visit work was in hand on widening the South River, so the Torne was running in the North River to the larger of the Althorpe sluices. This had a clear waterway of 14 ft and a sill at the level of low water in the Trent. Observations made 1 h before low water, with the Trent standing 1 ft above the sill, showed a depth of 2 ft of water above sill level in the channel just upstream. In other words, there was a head loss (*h*) of 1 ft. Smeaton says this indicates a flow of 6,000 cu. ft/min, and then points out that if the sluice had been 15 ft with a sill 2 ft deeper it would run 21,000 cu. ft/min under the same head or, with the same flow, the head loss would be only 1 in. Moreover, if the banks are raised to allow water level to rise safely to a height of 9 ft above low water with the doors shut, they will open so soon as the Trent falls below normal high-water neaps and, shortly after opening, the sluice would run at 44,000 cu. ft/min under a head of 4 in.

Clearly Smeaton had a method of estimating discharge through sluices, and the simplest explanation consistent with this set of figures is that he was evaluating the velocity of flow across the sill by the formula

$$v = C \sqrt{2gh}$$

with C taken as 0.95, and rounding off the resulting flow to the nearest whole number in thousands of cubic feet per minute. We note that the coefficient C is equal to 1.0 in the idealised case of a very wide approach channel and no energy loss in the sluice. Allowing for the (partly self-compensating) effects of a finite velocity of approach and energy losses[48] the values of C in Smeaton's examples happen to average just over 0·95 and vary between about 0·85 and 1·1. Thus his calculations were not merely illustrative but had sufficient accuracy to be reliable in practice.

However, his scheme, though brilliant in many ways, did not go quite far enough, and two modifications were made before a really satisfactory solution could be obtained. In the first of these, which Smeaton had undoubtedly refrained from recommending on grounds of cost, Scott revived the earlier proposal for a new cut to Keadby, but now simply to deal with the northern drains: see Fig. 31(c). The necessary Act was obtained in 1783, with Scott giving evidence a few months before he retired.[49] The work, involving a 16 ft sluice and a 30 ft bottom width cut, was carried out by his successor Samuel Foster.[50] It was Foster who in 1787 began work, following Smeaton's plans for the most part, on the new Torne and South Idle drain, but with the

Table 1   Outfall sluices for Hatfield Chase

Sluice	Dimensions (ft)	
	1775	1789
Keadby		
Width	—	16
Depth	—	−0.5
Althorpe, North		
Width	14	14
Depth	0	0
Althorpe, South		
Width	11	15
Depth	0	−2.0
Owston		
Width	12	15
Depth	+0.3	−1.2
Total waterway	37	60

Depths of the sills are given relative to low-water levels in the Trent: Keadby −2.0 ft O.D. (Newlyn), Althorpe −1.4 ft and Owston +0.5 ft.

significant improvement of providing separate outfalls; using the new 15 ft sluice at Althorpe for the drain and the adjacent northern sluice for the Torne, now unencumbered by any land water.[51] All this reached completion in 1789,[52] and a measure of what had been achieved is given by a comparison of the outfall facilities, as set out in Table 1.

Apart from widening the existing drains, the new works included 10 miles of cut, a substantial amount of banking, three sluices and several bridges. Very roughly the cost, spread over the period 1776–89, amounted to some £20,000; paid out of annual income (about £2,400) plus a loan of £3,200 in 1788. Hatfield Chase had now been drained, to use Smeaton's phrase, in "a very competent Manner". Subsequently further improvements were made, but the work by Smeaton, Scott and Foster established the basic pattern for many years, and constitutes one of the most important schemes of its kind in the eighteenth century.

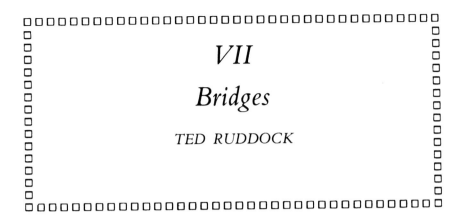

VII

Bridges

TED RUDDOCK

All the bridges and navigable aqueducts for which Smeaton made individual designs and which were actually built are listed in Table 2 excepting only one or two very small single-arch bridges and some swing and lifting bridges on his canal and river navigation works. Several single-arch aqueducts were also built on the Forth & Clyde Canal without specific drawings. Of the bridges in the table, Hexham Bridge was destroyed by a flood 2 years after its completion and Camelon aqueduct has been removed, but all the rest are standing and in use (though the "ornamental" bridge at Amesbury is now only a footbridge). Such long survival might suggest that they were built with more than necessary strength, and therefore at unnecessarily large expense; but the fact is otherwise. Smeaton's reports and estimates, and the minute books of his clients, reveal a constant and scrupulous care to avoid unnecessary expense. The masonry structures of his bridges were lighter than those of his best-known contemporaries (men such as Robert Mylne, James Paine and John Gwynn[1]) and the foundations were built with economy that hovered more than once on the brink of inadequacy. The longevity of the bridges should therefore be seen as a tribute to the knowledge and skill, both practical and scientific, which he applied in the search for economy.

Smeaton's study of bridges had matured to firm principles some years before he actually built a bridge, as a result of his presence in London during the building of Westminster Bridge in 1740–50 and his involvement in the planning for Blackfriars Bridge from 1753 to 1760.[2] It was in defence of his design for Blackfriars that he wrote a brief statement of his principles of bridge design in 1760,[3] and extracts from this pamphlet are used in the remainder of this chapter to

155

introduce discussion of various aspects of the bridges which were built. His Blackfriars design was actually rejected in favour of Robert Mylne's.

The years of his practice were a time of great advance in bridge-building. Masonry arches were built with longer spans, thus providing better clear waterways than was possible in previous centuries, and two completely new types of bridge began to be built—namely, cast iron arches and navigable aqueducts. Smeaton contributed to the improvement of dimensions and techniques of construction but took little part in the development of the new types of bridge. He neither designed nor built an iron bridge, and his aqueducts were relatively few and small. That he was willing to build a large aqueduct when it

Table 2. Bridges and aqueducts built to Smeaton's design

Construction and place	River	Date of design	Dates of construction	Number of main arches	References Designs	Reports
STONE						
Major public bridges						
Coldstream	Tweed	1763	1763–67	5	**4**, 150–157	**3**, 235–251
Perth	Tay	1764	1766–71	7	**4**, 122–128	**1**, 174–191
Banff	Deveron	1772	1772–79	7	**4**, 119–121	**3**, 349–352
Hexham	Tyne	1777	1777–80	9	**4**, 130–143	**3**, 267–344
Aqueducts						
Camelon (Falkirk)	(Road)	1770	1771	1	**5**, 28–35	
Kirkintilloch	Luggie	1772	1772–3	1	**5**, 25–27	
Minor bridges (public and private)						
Plymouth	Stonehouse Creek	1767	1773	1	**4**, 88–90	**1**, 306–309
Altgran	Altgran	1772	1777	1	**4**, 87	**3**, 359–361
Amesbury (Queensberry)	Avon	1775	1775	5	**4**, 100–103	–
Amesbury (Ornamental)	Avon	1776	1777	3	**4**, 95–98	–
BRICK						
Minor bridges (public and private)						
Newark	Flood plain of Trent	1768	1768–70	74	**4**, 105–109	**1**, 327–332
Cardington		1778	1778	5	**4**, 104	–

was really necessary is shown by his inclusion of £4,000 for a crossing of the River Kelvin in his 1767 estimates for the Forth & Clyde Canal; but he made it clear that he preferred to avoid the need for large aqueducts in his published answer to a proposal by James Brindley for an altered route involving an even larger structure.[4]

Arches and piers
The arches proposed in Smeaton's design for Blackfriars Bridge were circular segments of 120° arc. With regard to their stability and strength he wrote:

> "Having chose such a figure for them as having no tendency to vary their original form, either by their own gravity, or the incumbent load, they admit of being made of the least thickness possible with the strength required, which proves a double easement to the bases of the piers, not only by saving weight in the arch itself, but of a great load of rubble work necessary in the haunces, in order to preserve the form of the arch when unnatural.... An arch, that has a tendency to persevere in its original figure, is stronger than a much thicker arch, which, from its figure, tends to dissolution, and requires artificial helps for supporting thereof..."

Concerning the ability of a pier to support the arch on one side without the opposing thrust of the next arch—a condition which would occur during construction:

> "The question...is...whether the piers that Mr. Smeaton has proposed, are capable of resisting singly, the arches that he has proposed. In order to know this, as he does not know that the quantity of the lateral pressure of arches, under different circumstances, have ever been truly and clearly determined, he diligently applied him to this work, before he determined the thickness of his piers; and having succeeded herein equal to his wishes, he has given such a size and form to his middle piers as will resist several hundred tons more lateral pressure, than the middle arch will exert thereon.... The thickness of his arches are such, as... time has evinced to be right, many examples of which he can produce.... As Mr. Smeaton has observed very different dimensions having been used with equal success, he thought himself at liberty, rather to form his dimensions from his own experience and observations, than from Gautier; and in the doing this, he has found the means of saving to the city, at least one third of the tunnage of Portland stone, that would be necessary upon Gautier's rules..."

Gautier in 1714 had advised, on purely empirical grounds, that the curve of arches should be a semicircle or, if not, a circular arc as near to a semicircle as possible;[5] and in a subsequent paper (1717) that the

157

ratio arch span/arch thickness should not exceed 15 to 1 and the ratio arch span/pier thickness should be 5 to 1.[6]

Smeaton had rejected these rules in favour of dimensions based on his own observations and measurements of existing bridges, and a scientific analysis of his intended middle arch and piers. A list of his measurements[7]—most of them made on actual bridges, but one or two on published drawings—which has been given elsewhere,[8] shows a preponderance of arches which were circular arcs of 120° or less and ratios arch span/arch thickness up to 36 to 1. It had been shown by scientists, such as Emerson in 1758, that such arches were more stable than semicircles when the spandrels were of common shapes[9] but they made no distinction between stability (the absence of a tendency to bend) and adequate strength (the absence of a tendency to crush). The distinction was seldom made clearly by engineers even in the nineteenth century, but Smeaton made it almost perfectly in the first quotation given above, affirming that while the stability of an arch depends on its shape ("figure") the strength depends on its thickness. A modern correction would only substitute the words "more stable" for "stronger" in the second sentence. His derivation of the structural dimensions by theoretical analysis combined with knowledge of precedents at full scale conforms to the best principles of design practice today.

The proportion arch span/arch thickness in the Blackfriars design was 31 to 1, and he continued to design arches much thinner than Gautier recommended (and other designers built) throughout his career (see Table 3). The proportion arch span/pier thickness was 7.3

Table 3.   Structural proportions

Date	Design	Dimensions of largest arch			Proportions	
		Degrees of arc	Span (ft)	Thickness (ft)	Arch span/ Arch thickness	Arch span/ Pier thickness
1759	Blackfriars★	120	110	3.5	31 to 1	7.3 to 1
1760	Glasgow★	90	76	2.5	30 to 1	5.8 to 1
1763	Coldstream	134	60.7	2.5	24 to 1	4.3 to 1
1764	Perth	134	75	3.0	25 to 1	4.4 to 1
1772	Banff	134	50	2.0	25 to 1	4.2 to 1
1777	Hexham	134	51	2.25	23 to 1	4.1 to 1

★ Unexecuted designs.

to 1 (measuring thickness at the thinnest part of the pier between low- and high-water) but in later designs he used thicker piers with proportions (Table 3) conforming more to Gautier's rule.

He adopted the low arch profile which theoretical writings suggested in a design for a bridge at Glasgow made in 1760 (segments of 90° arc) and for another bridge intended to be built in the estate of Wentworth Woodhouse and probably designed in the same year (segments of 65°). In 1762 he commented on a proposed arch of 150 ft span at Bristol that "no limit to the span of arches, in proportion to their rise, has as yet been found"; but he never actually built arches of less than 120° or more than 75 ft span (see Table 3). Neither did he ever again claim to have analysed arches or piers by theoretical methods. It is likely that he chose the dimensions of all his designs after 1760 by precedents and rules of thumb, including some rules established by his own analysis of the Blackfriars design. More than once he expressed the opinion that increasing the spans would cause an increase in the overall cost of a bridge and this would be a sufficient reason for his use of only moderate spans. Nevertheless, the proportions listed in Table 3 would suggest that in this respect he grew more cautious as the years passed.

Foundations

"It cannot now be said that in the course of thirty years practice... not one of Mr. Smeaton's works have failed." These words, which he repeated in at least two letters to different people, show how deeply he felt the failure of Hexham Bridge. It was the only serious failure in all his engineering works, a catastrophic failure of foundations. Yet he had begun his pamphlet in 1760 with the words. "The principal strength of a bridge consists in its foundation... this being well secured, the superstructure... seldom fails." It is inevitable that an assessment of Smeaton's bridge-building should dwell at length on his design of foundations.

He described his intended method of laying the foundations at Blackfriars as follows:

"Mr. Smeaton proposed and recommended the laying the foundations of his piers upon the *dry*, as the best and only sure method where it can be practised; and this he proposed to do by a method... invented... by himself.... This he is sure of from experience, that it is the best method of founding abutments [where the depth of water would be less than at the piers], may be practised in some of the piers, and that there is great reason

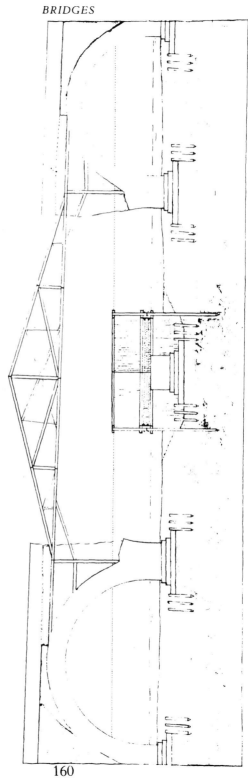

160

*Fig. 32. Cofferdam proposed for repairs to Westminster Bridge, 1748 (Designs, **4**, f. 172)*

to think, will equally succeed in all . . . gradual tryal thereof, will demonstrate how far it can be practised with security, and will by no means obstruct the putting other methods in practise . . . and in this light only Mr. Smeaton proposed it, not precluding himself from the building in Caissons, the practice of which he has been frequently eye witness to at Westminster. . . . "

His intended method of laying foundations in the dry was undoubtedly a single-walled cofferdam of timber piles. He therefore differed from Charles Labelye, the engineer of Westminster Bridge (built 1738–50), who had believed it impossible to pump out the quantity of water which would seep into cofferdams through the gravel bed of the Thames at high tide, when the depth would be up to 24 ft; Labelye had invented and used the floating caisson as an alternative.[10] He also differed from George Semple, the architect of Essex Bridge in Dublin (built 1753–55), who in a river of similar depth and similar bed had made step-sided cofferdams with six walls of planks and a large body of clay packed into the spaces between them.[11] Smeaton certainly knew that double-walled, clay-filled cofferdams had been specified for the largest recent bridges in France such as the Pont Royal at Paris (1685), the bridge of Blois (1724) and the bridge of Compiègne (1735), these three bridges being fully described in print by Gautier[12] and Belidor.[13] Moreover, no other engineer in the next 70 years even attempted to use single-walled dams for a bridge in the tidal reaches of the Thames and the details of Smeaton's proposed method would therefore be of great interest. Unfortunately he gave no details in 1760; but his other designs of single-walled dams give some indication of what he was intending.

His earliest known scheme for a single-walled cofferdam was addressed to the Commissioners of Westminster Bridge in 1748. One pier of Labelye's bridge, just after its completion, had settled more than 2 ft into the river bed, distorting the adjacent arches. Smeaton believed that the only sure mode of repair was to take down the arches and the pier right to its foundation, and he proposed to do this by enclosing it in a single-walled cofferdam.[14] The sketch he submitted (Fig. 32) shows a continuous wall of piles about 12 in. square with their heads just above low water, and a further wall of vertical timbers placed on top of the piles and extending to just above high water. The joint above low water is made with double walings both inside and out, and presumably a caulking compound. The piles were to be driven to a stratum which could both hold their ends firmly and limit the water percolating under the dam to an amount which could be removed by pumps. Smeaton asserted that both these requirements could be satisfied in either clay or gravel "of any tolerable consistance"; he was undoubtedly right about the firmness of hold on the piles, but it is very doubtful if the water flowing in through a bed of gravel at high tide could have been pumped out by contemporary machines. Yet his claim was more than a pious hope, for he wrote in his report to the Commissioners that he had already tested his method by "a working model" in both soft clay and loose gravel.

The report claimed that he had invented a "new kind of cofferdam" in which "the juncture of the several parts . . . are rendered much more perfect than by any other method". This would seem to be a reference either to a special method of driving the piles or to a special form of joint between contiguous piles. He used two special details in his subsequent designs of sheet-pile cofferdams. One was intended for economy, not extra watertightness: the interlock was obtained by grooving both sides of each pile, thus retaining their full widths, and inserting a separate hardwood tongue (Fig. 33c). The other was for improved watertightness: the pointed end of each pile was cut to a slant (Fig. 33d) so that the force of driving would press it into closer contact with the contiguous pile already driven.[15]

Attention had been directed in 1721 to the details of sheet piles by

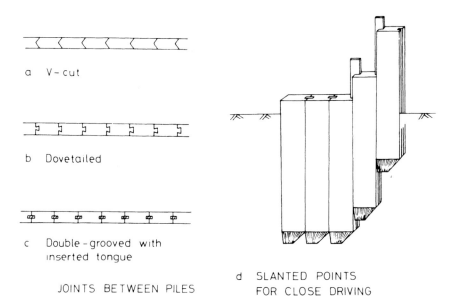

a   V – cut

b   Dovetailed

c   Double – grooved with
        inserted tongue

JOINTS BETWEEN PILES

d   SLANTED POINTS
        FOR CLOSE DRIVING

Fig. 33.   Sheet piling

162

John Perry in his description of the closing of a breach in the tidal defences of the Thames estuary at Dagenham.[16] Perry attributed his success in that work largely to the driving of a wall of sheet piles to cut off percolation under his new embankment. He criticised the use of piles with V-cut edges which had been used in some important French works (Fig. 33a), insisting on dovetailed tongue-and-groove connections between contiguous piles (Fig. 33b). He claimed to have made single-walled dams of dovetailed piles in Russia and to have successfully excluded water 20–26 ft deep. It was for similar depths that Smeaton proposed single-walled dams in the Thames in 1748 and 1759–60 and we may speculate that like Perry he was putting his faith in a special type of interlocking piles of his own "invention".

In his actual construction of bridges between 1763 and 1780 he used single-walled dams with reasonable success, but only in rivers of moderate depth. In the gravel bed of the Tweed at Coldstream in 1764–65 he attempted to excavate down to rock at 8–10 ft below the bed but the gravel proved porous and water entered much more quickly than he expected; only with difficulty could it be lowered enough to place the lowest course of masonry 3 ft below the bed.[17] The river was non-tidal. At Perth (Fig. 34) in 1766–67 the problem was almost the opposite: the gravel was so dense that the piles could not be driven more than about 2 ft and so, to lengthen the percolation paths under the dams, Smeaton ordered a mound of mixed gravel and earth to be placed against the outside of the wall. Similar earth was scattered on the river bed outside the dams at Coldstream at one time. The dams at both these sites were placed at some distance from the faces of the piers, but for his third large bridge at Banff he designed dams with a joint at low water, like his proposal for Westminster Bridge, but with the piling right against the face of the lowest course of stone in the piers and thus forming a wall in the ground under the edge of the foundation. The timbers above low water were to be removed after the pier had been built. He designed the dams at Perth and Banff to stand no more than 6 ft high from the river bed although the tide would rise higher than that for several days around the springs and so flood the excavations. He thought it uneconomic to provide dams and pumps to keep the excavations dry at the highest tides, and he may have already revised his estimate of the depth of water which could be excluded. When underpinning the piers of Hexham Bridge in 1778 he found that the water could not be lowered 6–8 ft inside a single wall of tongued-and-grooved piling driven 5–10 ft into the gravel river bed and so introduced a diving bell.

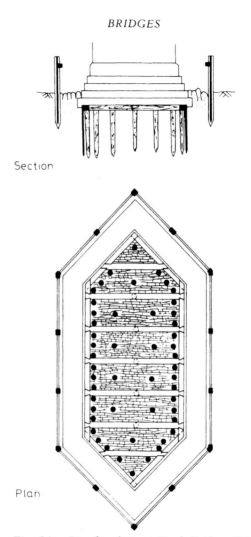

Section

Plan

Fig. 34.   Pier foundations, Perth Bridge, 1766

Once the cofferdams were pumped dry it was Smeaton's practice to excavate to 3 ft below the surface of the river bed. If there was a chance of reaching rock he dug deeper, but most of the piers of his bridges had to be founded on gravel. In the bottom of the excavation, bearing piles were driven and capped with a "grating", or pile-capping frame, of timbers approximately 12 × 6 in.; a further wall of sheet piles 5 or 6 in. thick was then driven tight against the outside members of the grating and spiked to them (Fig. 34). These piles were usually about 5–6 ft long (at Banff these piles were driven first and formed the cofferdam, as noted above). He differed from common practice in not nailing a floor of thick planks on top of the grating to form a base for

164

the masonry. Instead, he packed the spaces within the grating with rubble stones, either filling the voids with gravel (as at Coldstream) or grouting them with lime mortar (as at Perth), and then laid the first course of freestone directly on this bed, so creating a continuous body of masonry right through the pier to the gravel of the river bed. He expressed concern more than once about the risk of decay of timber used in foundations, and another good reason for omitting the floor was its compressibility under load. Some lateral tying of the pier was lost by omitting the planks but he dovetailed the ends of cross-members of the grating and made generous use of iron cramps at one or two levels at and below low water. For additional tying in the bottom course of the piers at Coldstream and Perth all the outside stones of the bottom course were cut as headers with a 9 × 3 in. nib overhanging the edge of the grating and sheet piling (see Fig. 34), thus restraining the piling from outward movement. At Banff the same restraint was obtained by iron ties passing through the sheet piles and built into the masonry.

Placing the gratings 3 ft below the surface of the river bed did not remove all risk of undermining by scour because the building of a bridge always caused changes in the rate or the "set" of the current. Usually there was new scour of the bed between the piers due to an increase in the velocity or the turbulence of flow. Smeaton's answer to this was to dump coarse stones of irregular shape in scoured hollows and allow the flow of the current over and through them to shake them into a dense packing. He sometimes threw in gravel and sand to fill the voids between the stones but he also expected the voids to be filled by the ordinary sediment of the river. He usually also ordered a mound or slope of coarse stones to be placed all round the foot of each pier. At Coldstream the river in flood proved too strong for these defences several times, and by 1785 he was recommending that the first stones thrown in be ½–1 ton in weight, with smaller stones to fill the voids. When he wrote his last report on Coldstream Bridge, only 2 years before his death, scour was still a threat to the foundations, as it has continued to be ever since. The same protection against scour was perfectly successful at Perth, however, and presumably at Banff, although it appears that Smeaton had little or nothing to do with the construction of Banff Bridge. When he came to build Hexham Bridge he found a local quarry rubble which he considered to be the best he had ever used, but his attempts to protect the foundations with it were a total failure.

Relying on coarse stone protection was not, however, his first

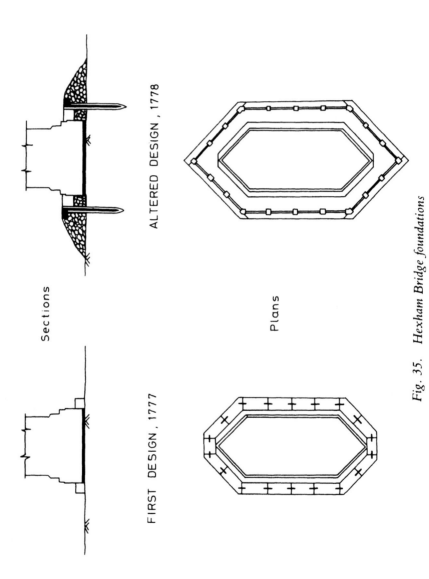

Sections

ALTERED DESIGN , 1778

FIRST DESIGN , 1777

Plans

Fig. 35. Hexham Bridge foundations

mistake at Hexham. On the basis of others' borings and excavations at several sites, and his own probing of the chosen site, he judged that there was a dense crust of gravel some feet deep, under which lay loose silt or sand. Having decided that the crust would resist erosion, he designed the foundations for five of the eight piers with no piles at all and laid the first course of masonry on a thin wooden platform placed on the undisturbed river bed (Fig. 35). They were to be protected from scour by very large stones cramped to form a girdle round the foot of each pier, but serious scour occurred in a flood before the girdles had been placed. The altered design, using both sheet piling and rubble mounds, went more than half-way back towards Smeaton's previous methods but it failed to prevent further scour. The protective mounds were therefore carefully watched and maintained. However, 2 years after the bridge's completion, a violent flood in March 1782 caused erosion of the bed, particularly at the upstream end of the piers, and undermined four of the five piers founded by the method described, as well as two of the three which were founded on piles and gratings as at Coldstream and Perth.[18]

From the difference of water level upstream and downstream (the "fall"), observed to be about 4½ ft just before the collapse, Smeaton calculated[19] that the average velocity of flow between the piers reached the frightening figure of 17 ft/s. Even this is an underestimate as the simple formula he used, $v = \sqrt{2gh}$, where h is the fall, makes insufficient allowance for the velocity of approach in the river; the correct value[20] is probably about 20 ft/s. However, a more important point is that the only way of safeguarding the bridge against the effects of such velocities, with techniques available in the eighteenth century, would have been to cover the entire river bed between the piers, and for some distance upstream and downstream, with a timber or heavy masonry platform or raft; as was done in the reconstruction (1790–95) by the Northumberland Bridge surveyors, William Johnson and Robert Thompson.[21]

Thus the tragic irony of the Hexham affair is that having misjudged the possible magnitude of a flood, all the care and attention to economy devoted by Smeaton to the foundations proved quite useless while a simple if expensive solution, which he was loath to use, lay readily at hand.

Spandrels

Smeaton acknowledged the interdependence of arches and spandrels when he referred in his 1760 pamphlet to "a great load of rubble work necessary in the haunces, in order to preserve the form of the arch when unnatural". He was using the concepts of the contemporary theory of "equilibrium" (in modern terms, stability) of arches. Although, due to the assumption that voussoirs were frictionless, the theory led to absurd conclusions when applied to some shapes of arch, including the semicircle, its first finding was correct and useful: that the distribution of weight in the spandrels could either improve or detract from the stability of the arch. For "equilibrium" the vertical load, i.e. the height of spandrel, must increase from the crown of the arch to the springing but at a non-uniform rate depending on the shape of the arch.

As well as permanent stability with the full weight of spandrels acting, the arch required stability at the moment of removing the centring when only part or none of the spandrels might be built. It was doubtless partly to provide this initial stability that designers often tapered their arches to a greater thickness at the haunches, but some may also have felt that the spandrel filling was too vaguely specified to place any reliance on it, even as mere weight. Both Labelye, in Westminster Bridge, and Robert Mylne, in Blackfriars Bridge, increased the arch thicknesses in this way, but Smeaton never did so. A more common way of avoiding instability near the spring-ings was to fill the spandrels between the backs of adjacent arches up to some height with rubble masonry; for considerations of stability the springings were effectively raised to the top of the filling. Smeaton always specified rubble filling to a height of 6 ft, which was common practice in Britain. In France the spandrels were generally filled with masonry to the full height of the arches.

From 6 ft above the springings to the top of the spandrels was filled with loose material, both in British practice generally and in Smeaton's first large bridge at Coldstream. The material might be good gravel or quarry rubble but was also often the rubble of demo-lished buildings and correctly called "rubbish". It had to be retained by the outer spandrel walls and as arches and spandrels grew in size the thickness of walls required became a matter of concern and of uncer-tainty.

A third consideration in the design of spandrels was the weight which they applied on the piers. Lightness of spandrels was clearly beneficial to the foundations and this might conflict with the need for weight to give stability to the arch.

In the years before 1760 cylindrical voids had been both proposed and used to answer one or other of these three problems of spandrel

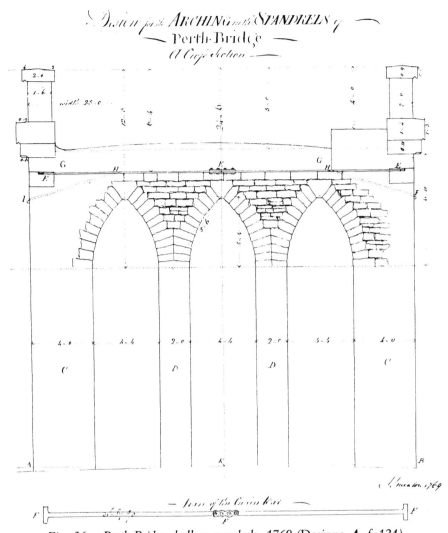

Fig. 36. Perth Bridge, hollow spandrels, 1769 (Designs, **4,** f. 124)

design.[22] Gautier in his book of 1714, and Batty Langley in a design for Westminster Bridge in 1736, had proposed voids to reduce the load on foundations. Langley had also proposed voids of unequal size to equalise the loads on the haunches of an arch which carried spandrels of unequal height, and so improve the arches' stability. A series of voids was made in each spandrel of the single-arch bridge at Pontypridd in 1756 to obtain a distribution of load corresponding closely with that required by the "equilibrium" theory, and there is a suggestion that Smeaton may have given some advice on the design.[23] In

1768 and 1769, however, he produced a different method of hollowing spandrels which solved all three problems at once. It was to build the spandrels over each pier as a set of parallel longitudinal walls abutting on the backs of the arches, leaving longitudinal voids between the walls and bridging over the voids with slabs or vaults to carry the road.

The use of the new method seems to have been prompted by failures. He first proposed it for the bridge at Dumbarton in 1768 after one foundation of a pier had settled catastrophically due to overload.[24] When after a collapse of rubble arches and a retaining wall in one of the approaches of the new North Bridge in Edinburgh in 1769 Smeaton found cracks in the pier foundations,[25] he recommended "any method of arching in the spandrils between the great arches, that will effectively save weight", in order "as well to relieve the piers, with their foundations, as to prevent the lateral pressure of the earth against the spandril-walls, from producing any ill effect".[26] The method, chosen by others, was cylindrical voids, but it was probably in reaction to the Edinburgh failure that Smeaton in 1769 designed hollow spandrels of the parallel-wall type for his own bridge at Perth. In each spandrel at Perth there are four parallel walls enclosing three voids, the voids covered by pointed arches of rubble and any lateral thrust which these arches might exert resisted by iron "chain-bars" or ties running from face to face of the bridge over the tops of the arches. "Chain courses" of cramped masonry were also laid parallel to the chain-bars (Fig. 36).

Perth Bridge is the first which is known to have been built with spandrels of this type.[27] Smeaton used them again in Hexham Bridge, and they were adopted by most leading engineers and used in virtually all the great stone bridges and aqueducts of the years 1780–1830. If not the most daring of his innovations in bridge construction, they were certainly the most successful.

Centring

A sketch survives of the centring Smeaton proposed for erection of his Blackfriars Bridge design. Each rib was a truss with a horizontal tie at high-water level, a king-post at midspan and crossing diagonal struts. Spanning from pier to pier, in order to allow the passage of boats at least at low tide, it was supported on the offsets at the foot of each pier by three long raking struts. For the centring of his bridges at Coldstream and Perth he designed similar trusses but because there was little or no navigation at either site he was able to support them by

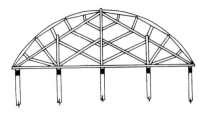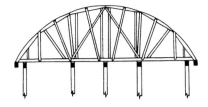

Coldstream & Perth   Banff & Hexham

Fig. 37.   Designs of centring

lines of piles at three points in the span, as well as by single lines of
posts on the offsets (Fig. 37). He retained the truss form only, he
wrote, so that "if any one pile, or row of piles, should settle, the
incumbent weight would be supported by the rest". If the piles did
not settle, or all settled equally, the weight of the arch would be
carried directly to their heads by the vertical and diagonal struts.

There was probably no serious settlement, for he abandoned the
truss form in the centres for Banff and Hexham Bridges. The arches
there were supported simply by fans of struts which converged from
the rim of the centre on to the heads of each row of piles, and as there
were no truss connections to be made Smeaton was able to suggest
that local round fir timber (that is, unsawn trees) should be used for
the struts in the Banff centre. This was but one of the expedients he
proposed to save money on centring; nothing shows more clearly
than his reports on centring how much importance he attached to
economy. He designed the Coldstream centre to be made with whole
or half timbers although smaller scantlings would have done, because
the larger pieces could be sold for re-use more easily at the end of construction. A most important principle he adopted at Coldstream, and
adhered to for his other large bridges, was that all the arches were
drawn of the same radius so that the centre made for the smallest arch
could be used for all the others by adding only a few extra timbers at
each end to support one or two courses of stone above the springings.
To achieve the saving all the arches had to be built successively on a
single centre and at Coldstream the resident overseer, Robert Reid,
objected to the resulting slowness of construction. Smeaton,
however, insisted that the saving was worth while. At Perth, two
centres were used, but there were more arches to be built and money
was much less scarce.

An unusual and probably unprecedented device was used for

171

economy in the centring of the Forth & Clyde aqueduct over the Luggie at Kirkintilloch. The span is 45 ft but the width of the arch is no less than 90 ft because the canal is carried over the bridge with its full width of water and earthen banks—most unlike the walled trough only slightly wider than a single boat which was common on English canals. A centre was used which was 30 ft wide and the arch was built in three parts, shifting the centre sideways on small rollers after each of the first two parts was finished.[28] Unfortunately no details are recorded, and there is no direct evidence that Smeaton designed the centre; but his constant search for economy and his technical ingenuity make it seem likely that he did so.

Architecture

Of his Blackfriars design Smeaton wrote:

> "Mr. Smeaton studied to avoid every ornament that did not naturally arise out of the subject, looking upon simplicity to be the greatest beauty.... Even the Gothick builders... when they set about to build bridges, strictly adhered to the simple and chaste... from whence arises... a kind of elegance, that stands in no need of ornament drawn from foreign subjects."

About elliptical arches, he was quite particular:

> "An humble imitation of an ellipsis is commonly practised by joiners and plaisterers made up of segments of circles, from different centers, which they call an oval; but this is so very imperfect, that not appearing as a fair curve, even to a moderate eye, the better artists in those branches use what is called by them a *trammel*, by which they describe their ellipses, as they ought to be, from two centers at a time...."

This prejudice against the approximate ellipse can hardly have been formed by viewing real arches, because elliptical arches were not common in buildings and probably non-existent in British bridges, and if they had been common it is very doubtful if contemporary architects could have detected the difference. Robert Mylne was proposing to build the arches of Blackfriars Bridge with the three-centred approximate ellipse, and actually did so (1760–69). Smeaton was therefore expressing the sensitivity, not of an aesthete, but of a scientist and instrument-maker. He retained the prejudice throughout his practice, sending detailed instructions on the setting-out of true ellipses to the workmen at all the bridges in which he designed elliptical arches (Perth, 1766–71; Amesbury, 1777; and Hexham, 1777–80).

It was almost true of the Blackfriars design that the ornament "arose naturally out of the subject"; of Smeaton's later designs it was less true. The general form of the elevation was always determined by the practical needs of flow through the bridge and traffic over it, and structural strength and stability as discussed above; but to this form he almost always added some projecting ornament. For a bridge which he himself called "the ornamental bridge", in the estate of Amesbury Abbey, he made his only classical design, drawing large-scale details of the ballusters, scrolls and mouldings. In other designs he made no attempt to conform to an established style; he seems rather to have allowed the overall form of the elevations to suggest geometrical ornaments, and as a result the architecture of his bridges was always original. In his designs for Glasgow and Wentworth Woodhouse in 1760 he devised unique types of ornament but neither bridge was built. In his four large bridges he created a "Smeaton style" with a large projecting circle on each spandrel over the middle of the pier (Fig. 38). The centre of the circle being the middle point of the spandrel, the circles gave the elevation a clear geometrical logic which obviously appealed to Smeaton. It is virtually certain that he first copied the circles from a design by Robert Reid for Coldstream Bridge, but he must have known that their ultimate source was in prints of ancient Roman bridges where the circles of masonry were the ends of flood-relief passages through the spandrels. To emphasise the circles Smeaton gave them a moulded section and four keystones on the ends of the vertical and horizontal diameters, and also filled the area within them with black rubble masonry. The contrasting black rubble was lost when the spandrels were rebuilt at Hexham (1796) and Banff (1881), but it is still to be seen at Coldstream and Perth.

Perversely, the architectural intention of this "Smeaton style" has not been recognised, for from his day to ours almost every writer on bridges has asserted that the four bridges were built with open cylindrical voids like the Roman bridges. In fact, as has been shown already, Smeaton used voids of a different form invented by himself but hid them behind the circles which were closed by masonry from the start, and whose purpose was only adornment.

Despite the fact that his designs now appear both able and original in their architecture, he was quite reserved, for much of his career, about advising on matters of appearance. On being asked his opinion about the finishes of the masonry at Coldstream, for instance, he replied that "this being a matter of taste it must be determined by the trustees only"; but he nonetheless gave a firm opinion and the trustees duly acted on it.[29] He probably became used to this experience, and

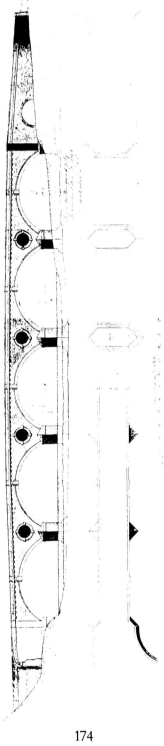

PLAN & ELEVATION for a Bridge over the TWEED at Coldstream.

Fig. 38. Plan and elevation of Coldstream Bridge, 1763 (Designs, 4, f. 154)

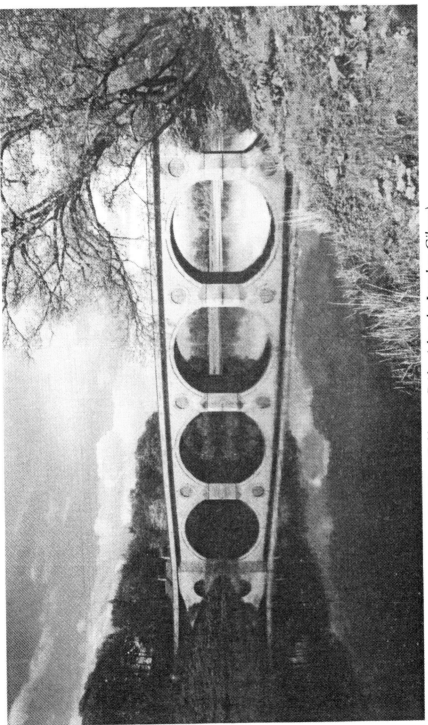

Fig. 39. Coldstream Bridge (photo by Jonathan Gibson)

towards the end of his life he did not trouble to hide a concern for the beauty of his bridges. For instance, in 1790 he reported on proposed alterations to the small dam which had been built downstream of the bridge at Coldstream to help protect it from scour, but in a second letter to Lord Swinton he said:

"I find myself somewhat jealous of the beauty of the bridge. The dam being of equal height in every part, the bridge in the lowest water times will appear to stand in a level pool... terminated by an extensive cascade, a noble sight. . . ."[30]

It is indeed as fine a sight as any surviving bridge of the eighteenth century (Fig. 39).

Materials
The finish of masonry had an important effect both on appearance and costs. The arches of large bridges were generally built of smooth-hewn ashlar and the piers of hewn, but often rough-faced, stone. The question of taste which Smeaton referred to the trustees at Cold-stream was whether the piers could be built with smooth-hewn stone which had already been prepared while some of the upper parts were of rough or "scrabled" masonry. At the same time he gave his own opinion that:

"he would not only make the piers rough but the whole bridge, the projections only excepted which he would make very smooth work and this contrast will look prettier than if the whole bridge was smooth and at the same time save a deal of money".

This choice of finishes remained his common practice throughout his career. He visited quarries and approved the stone in use—wisely, it would seem, from the small amount of decay to be seen on the bridges today, but how he recognised durable stone is not at all clear. It is certain from a list of the materials he specified for the Stonehouse Creek Bridge at Plymouth that he thought very carefully about the properties of stone required in different parts of a bridge. It was a single arch of 40 ft span, but he recommended the use of four different types of stone: Portland stone for the arch, facings, cornice and copings; "moor stone", or Dartmoor granite, for the rustic part of the pillars; Plymouth marble with cut ashlar finish for the parapets (except copings); moor stone or Plymouth marble, whichever was cheaper, for the body of the abutments (but with a preference for moor stone as "taking more kindly to the mortar, especially when constantly wet"); and rubble from the nearby rocks for the inside core of the abutments. For mortar, hydraulic lime from Watchet or Aber-thaw was to be used for the joints of all the exterior, but a mixture of one of these with Plymouth lime could be used for the interior.

The wide knowledge of local stones at Plymouth shown by this list was gained during Smeaton's work on the Eddystone Lighthouse in 1756–59. At other bridge sites he was seldom able to specify types of stone in advance. His knowledge of limes for mortar, which began with experiments at Plymouth in 1756, grew with his practice until he knew the properties of most of the limes in Britain. When adequate hydraulic lime was not available, he ordered the imported materials pozzolana or tarras to be used and often gave detailed mix proportions for the mortar.

His confidence in the durability of hydraulic mortar is a possible ex-planation for the omission from his bridges of a sealing layer of clay on the extrados of the arches or under the road-metal. Without such a layer rain water was able to seep through to the arches where, by satu-rating the stone and mortar, it both leached out lime and other salts to form efflorescence on the soffits and rendered the arches subject to frost damage. Hydraulic mortar might be stronger to resist such damage but it was certainly not immune to it. Among other designers it was already a common practice to prevent the entry of rain water by a layer of clay. For instance, the four large bridges over the Thames designed by James Paine in the years 1774–89 at Richmond, Chertsey, Walton and Kew all had clay seals laid on the extrados of every arch; and a clay seal just under the road-metal was placed on Coldstream Bridge by Sir John Rennie about 1830. When the longitudinal vaults had been built in the spandrels of Perth Bridge in 1770, however, one of the tradesmen asked what thickness of clay was to be placed over them before the road-metal, and Smeaton replied that he proposed none at all.[31] It was safer there than in a bridge with gravel-filled span-drels, but later engineers regularly used clay, and later concrete, over the cover-stones of hollow spandrels.

A related observation can be made about his two surviving designs of aqueducts. It was common to place a bed of clay up to 3 ft thick over the top of an aqueduct under the bed of the canal, but in Smeaton's design for the Luggie aqueduct the clay is drawn only 6 in. thick over the crown of the arch, and no clay at all is shown over the arch of the Camelon aqueduct. In view of his evident distaste for large aqueducts at an earlier date, this skimping of clay is extremely puz-zling.

A final puzzling omission, not so much from Smeaton's bridges as from his correspondence, is any mention of iron as a material for bridge-building. There is not even among his drawings a copy of any of the prints of the iron bridge at Coalbrookdale which were published in the 1780s. It would be fascinating to know what the old master thought of this revolutionary development, but his letters are absolutely silent—and one cannot help guessing that in Smeaton's correspondence silence meant dissent.

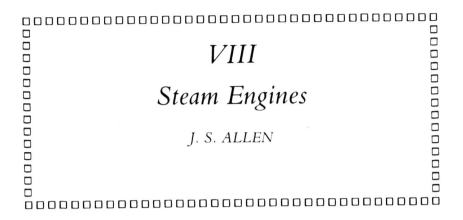

VIII

Steam Engines

J. S. ALLEN

Thomas Newcomen constructed his first successful steam pumping engine at a colliery in the parish of Tipton, Staffordshire, near Dudley Castle, in 1712. It made use of low-pressure steam beneath a piston in an open-topped cylinder; the steam from a boiler below the cylinder was condensed by the injection of water, which thus created a partial vacuum, and atmospheric pressure then drove down the piston. Above the cylinder was a large balance or working beam fitted at each end with arch heads. The piston was attached to one end by a chain, and to the other end were attached the pump rods, which passed down the mine shaft to the bottom of the pit. Each working stroke activated the pumps via the pumping rods and thus raised water out of the mine.[1]

Newcomen's invention was so sound in principle that it formed an indestructible foundation upon which posterity could confidently build. Already by 1740 more than 150 of these engines had been erected. They were known as atmospheric engines or, more usually in the eighteenth century, simply as "fire engines".

The early Newcomen engines were quite small, developing less than 10 hp but gradually as knowledge and confidence increased larger engines were built; so that from cylinders not exceeding 30 in. in diameter the maximum size rose to 42 in. by 1734, to 48 in. in 1754 and 74 in. by 1763. This 74 in. engine, built by William Brown at Walker colliery, near Newcastle-upon-Tyne, developed 43 hp and ranked as just about the most efficient and the most powerful engine before Smeaton came on the scene. Its *duty* was 7·2 million ft.lb/ bushel of coal (84 lb). More typically the best engines of the period achieved a duty around 6½ million, as we shall see, but even so this

179

figure represents an increase of something like 30–50 per cent over the performance of engines before 1730.

Smeaton, then, was not the first to tackle the problem of improving the steam engine; but he did so in a manner combining scientific enquiry with practical insight, and achieved notable results.

One of his earliest drawings, made when a boy of 17, is of a Newcomen-type engine, probably at a colliery near Leeds.[2] His first design dates from 1765; it was for a 4 hp engine which could, without great difficulty, be transferred from one site to another.[3] In this so-called "portable engine" he substituted for the beam a pulley wheel 6½ ft in diameter over which passed a chain connected at one end to the piston shank and at the other to the pump rod. The engine appears not to have been built, though he used the same principle very successfully for the winding engine at Prosperous Pit, Long Benton colliery, in 1777 (see later).

The portable engine already shows a good grasp of technical details, but Smeaton's deep involvement with steam engines began 2 years later in 1767.

New River Head engine

His second commission was for a more conventional pumping engine; the object being to satisfy an increasing public demand for water from the high-level pond at the premises of the New River Company in Islington, of which Robert Mylne was engineer.

Smeaton started his investigations in 1766 by testing the existing horse-mill pumps, worked by four horses, and after dismissing the possibility of using a waterwheel effectively at this location, recommended a steam engine which, he calculated, would raise twice as much water in 12 h as the horse machine did in 16 h, at an expenditure of 3 bushels of Newcastle coal.

His advice having been taken, Smeaton set about the design. He recognised that the stoppage of the column of water in the pumps, and putting the heavy machinery into motion from rest twice at every cycle, caused a great loss of energy, and therefore decided to work the engine at a slower rate than usual with larger pumps and a longer stroke. His designs, made in 1767, include details of the engine and engine house.[4]

The engine was erected in 1768 and set to work at the beginning of 1769, but on testing it Smeaton found the results to be very disappointing.

"By good luck [he says] the Engine performed the Work it was expected to do, as to the raising of Water, but the Coals by no means answered calculation."[5]

After trial-and-error modifications he improved the duty to 7 million, a respectable figure for the period, but neither he nor Mylne were at all pleased and, admitting a lack of proper understanding, Smeaton resolved if possible to make himself master of the subject. To do this he decided to build a small engine at home on which experiments could be carried out, and also to conduct a systematic study of existing engines.

Engine tests

In 1769, therefore, Smeaton obtained from William Brown a list of engines in the Newcastle district. Of these 57 were in action and Smeaton made, or caused to be made, exact observations on fifteen of them.[6] He expressed the results in terms of the engine's power, defined as the *great product*, and its efficiency or *effect*, and in this way introduced (apparently for the first time) correct quantitative measures of engine performance.

Without changing the concepts these quantities were redefined by Watt in 1782–83 and became known as *horse power* (hp) and *duty* respectively;[7] and it is more convenient to use these familiar units.

It is worth considering the results of this first comprehensive set of engine tests. On the basis of efficiency there is a clear separation into two groups. In the better group, which includes nine engines with cylinders from 42 to 74 in. in diameter, the duties range from 5·9 to 7·4 with an average around 6½ million, and the mean piston loading is about 7½ lb/sq. in. But the loading tends to decrease with increasing engine size (as does the number of strokes per minute) and the power therefore does not increase so much as might otherwise be expected in the larger engines.

As for the engines with a relatively poor performance, these generally had inadequate and poorly designed boilers, imperfectly bored cylinders or faulty pump-work. Nevertheless the average duty of about 5½ million for the thirteen engines with cylinders more than 40 in. in diameter seems, from the scanty data otherwise available, to be fairly representative of general practice at this time. Smaller engines achieved a distinctly lower duty.

Another locality where good engine performance could be expected was Cornwall, with its deep metalliferous mines and costly coal. It is therefore interesting to note, if somewhat out of chronological order, the results which Smeaton obtained in 1779 from a similar survey to that made 10 years earlier around Newcastle. Twelve Cornish engines were fully examined but this time only those with cylinders 60–70 in. in diameter.[8] The duties ranged from 5 to 7 and averaged 6½ million; a figure by coincidence exactly the same as that for the nine best Newcastle engines.

Two of the engines, at Poldice Mine, are of special significance as they had been selected in the previous year (1778) as providing an agreed basis for comparison with the first Boulton & Watt engine to be erected in Cornwall. They, too, had a duty of about 6½ million so this figure can confidently be adopted as typical of the best performance before Smeaton introduced his improvements first embodied in the Long Benton engine, designed in 1772.

Experimental engine
Smeaton's experimental engine, which he built in the grounds of his house at Austhorpe, is shown in Fig. 40. It had a 10 in. cylinder and developed just over 1 hp expressed as the rate of work achieved by the pump.[9] All relevant measurements were made, including pressure in the cylinder, barometric pressure, temperature in the hot-well, quantity of water evaporated per bushel of coal, and so on.

Starting in 1770 he made some 130 tests, the procedure being to adjust the engine to good working order and, after observing its performance, to alter one particular factor and again observe performance, all other circumstances being kept as nearly as possible unchanged.[10] In this way he learnt to optimise the piston loading, the timing of the valves, and the form of the injection nozzle; he realised the benefit of insulating the piston and using the hot-well tank as a feed-water heater or heat exchanger, and studied the relative evaporating power of different coals.

No one of these and other points discovered in the tests was of outstanding importance, comparable to Watt's invention of the separate condenser, but together they formed a basis for major improvements.

With the knowledge thus gained, after research continued over a period of 2 years, Smeaton felt justified in drawing up a table for the proportions and characteristics of engines for all sizes from 10 to 72 in. dia. cylinders, with corresponding figures for length of stroke, rate of working, quantity of injection water, coal consumption, and the resulting power and duty to be expected.[11] He was now, in 1772, ready to embark on his great period of engine building.

Long Benton engine
The request to design a pumping engine for Long Benton colliery,

Fig. 40. Smeaton's experimental steam engine, 1770 (engraving by Wilson Lowry—Rees' Cyclopaedia)

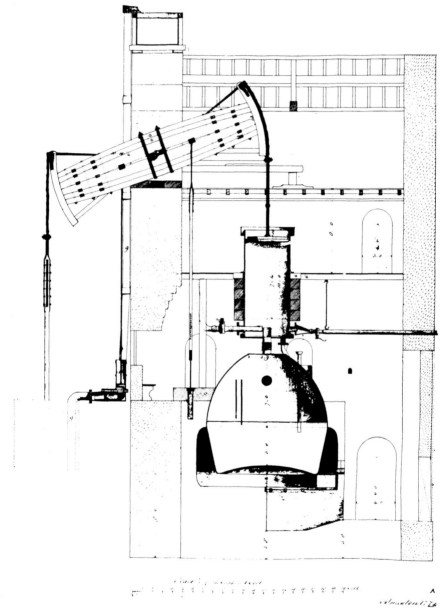

Upright Section of a FIRE ENGINE *at Long Benton.*

*Fig. 41. Long Benton pumping engine, 1772 (Designs, **3,** f. 73v)*

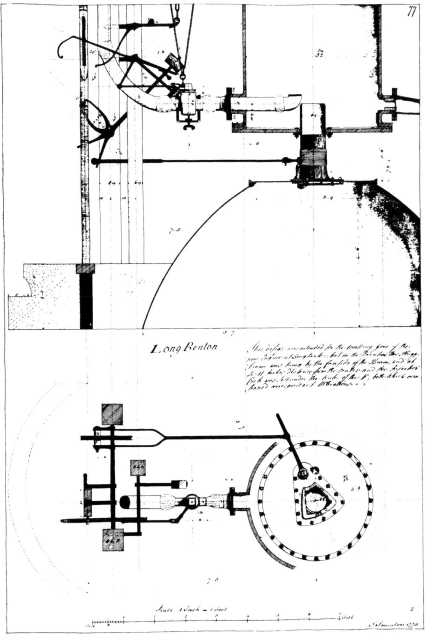

Fig. 42. *Long Benton engine working gear, 1772 (Designs, 3, f. 77)*

185

Northumberland, came in the summer of 1772, obviously at an opportune moment. Tests made in July on the old 52 in. engine there showed that it developed 30 hp at a duty of only 4.6 million.[12] Smeaton produced his drawings (Figs 41 and 42 are two of the fifteen which survive), erection was completed by the end of 1773, and the engine started in February 1774.

It had a 52 in. cylinder, a 7 ft stroke, and worked 12 strokes/min with a piston loading of 7·5 lb/sq. in. when operating the two columns of pumps of 12¼ in. bore each 148 ft in depth, making a total lift of 296 ft. There were two boilers, one 12 ft in diameter beneath the cylinder and another, slightly larger, alongside. Together the boilers evaporated 1·5 cu. ft of water/min. The beam was 22 ft long, 24 in. wide and 50 in. deep at its centre, having a cast iron axis with gudgeons 7 in. in diameter running in brass bearings which supported a load of 27 tons during the working stroke.[13]

Tests were made in May 1774 with the principal results that the engine developed 40 hp at a duty of 9·1 million;[14] a figure very little short of Smeaton's expectation. This duty represented an increase of 25 per cent on the most efficient engine previously built and an improvement of 40 per cent on the typical good performance of the period. The Long Benton engine is therefore a landmark in the history of steam power.

No details of the cost of this engine have been found but Farey gives figures for the construction cost of a colliery engine of similar date, size (48 in. cylinder), and depth of working (276 ft):

engine house	£580
engine and 2 boilers	745
pit-head gear and pump work	652
total	£1977

The cylinder with its bottom plate and piston weighed 4 tons. For the giant 74 in. Walker engine of 1763 the cylinder alone came to 6½ tons.[15]

Chacewater engine

Smeaton's next engine was erected in 1775 at Chacewater mine in Cornwall. This, too, established a new record as it exceeded the power of the Walker engine by about 65 per cent.

It replaced two engines, with 64 and 66 in. cylinders, which together developed 60 hp and achieved a duty of 6·9 million. One of the existing granite-walled engine houses was adapted for Smeaton's engine, accommodating a 15 ft dia. boiler beneath the cylinder and one of the same size on each side of the house. All the cast iron parts, including the cylinder, boilers, piston, steam valves and beam axis, were executed at the Carron Ironworks in Scotland and shipped to Cornwall.[16]

Again a practically complete set of Smeaton's drawings (sixteen in number) have survived[17] but in this case we also have his report and explanation of the drawings, both written in February 1775.[18] The report summarises the performance of the existing engines, as noted above, and gives details of the new engine which he designed to develop 72 hp with a duty of 10 million.

The main characteristics of the Chacewater engine were: 72 in. cylinder, 9 ft stroke, 9 strokes/min, piston loading 7.7 lb/sq. in. (a notable increase on previous practice for engines of this size) and three columns of pumps each of 16¾ in. bore lifting 102 ft or 306 ft in all.[19]

Test results for the duty are unfortunately not available, but there is every reason to suppose the engine came close to expectation as four others of almost identical dimensions were subsequently designed: one for returning water in dry seasons to the reservoir at Carron iron-works (1780), and the others for collieries at Dunmore Park in Stir-lingshire (1779), Middleton in Yorkshire (1780) and Bourn Moor in County Durham (1783); see Appendix III.

Kronstadt engine

In 1773 data concerning the docks at Kronstadt, near St Petersburg, were sent to Smeaton with a request for designs for an engine capable of pumping out the docks far more expeditiously than could be done by the two windmill pumps then in use. In his reply Smeaton said that a 66 in. engine, developing 60 hp, would do the required work at an expenditure of about 12 bushels of coal/h; but as the supply of this quantity of coal at Kronstadt will be a considerable expense, the better of the two windmills should be preserved to supplement the steam engine pumps.[20]

This advice having been accepted Smeaton drew up the plans in 1774 and the parts were again made at Carron. In March 1775 we find him writing "Directions to be observed in adjusting the Engine at Cronstadt to its work"[21] but there seem to have been some delays and it did not come into operation until 1777.

The main features of the engine were: 66 in. cylinder, with a stroke of 8½ ft working 10–13 strokes/min depending on the level of water

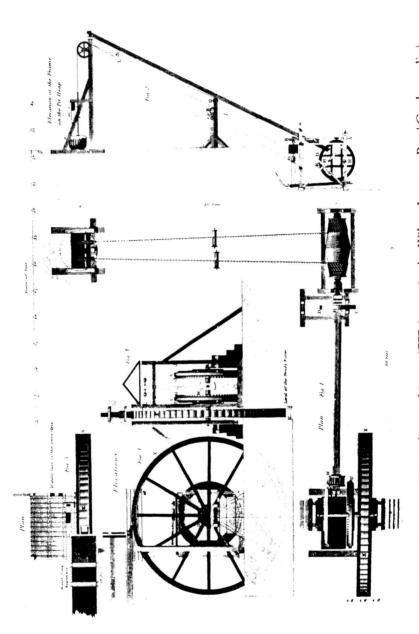

Fig. 43. Prosperous Pit winding machinery, 1777 (engraving by Wilson Lowry—Rees' Cyclopaedia)

in the docks; a lift of 33 ft when pumping began and 53 ft when the water was completely drained. As at Chacewater there were three boilers, but of modified design, taller and narrower with a spiral flue encompassing the lower part.

John Farey, who saw the engine during a visit to Russia in 1819, says the boilers answered the purpose very well and the engine performed its work satisfactorily without having to be modified in any way. He also remarks that a similar design was adopted in 1780 for the three boilers of the 72 in. returning engine at Carron ironworks.

Prosperous Pit engine

Smeaton produced one of his most masterly designs in 1777 for a returning engine, waterwheel and winding machinery to raise coals from a depth of nearly 500 ft at Prosperous Pit, Long Benton colliery; having shown by calculations in August 1776 that such an arrangement would be more economical than the existing horse-gin. Referring to Fig. 43 the winding drum was operated through gearing by a 30 ft dia. waterwheel, and the water returned to the wheel by the 9 hp engine shown in Fig. 44. As many as twenty of his drawings have survived, together with a long letter on the subject, and he even designed a machine for cutting the screw-thread on the conical winding drum.[22]

The engine, again with all the ironwork supplied by the Carron Company, started work at the end of 1777. It proved so satisfactory that a second, identical one, was built the next year and a third, of somewhat larger dimensions, in 1785.[23]

The 1777 engine had a 26 in. cylinder, a stroke of 5 ft 8 in. and worked at 14 strokes/min with a piston loading of 7½ lb/sq. in. Steam was supplied from a single 10 ft dia. boiler, and the engine delivered 140 cu. ft of water/min to the wheel. The corves, each holding 700 lb of coal, were raised at a rate of 30/h.

As a loaded corf ascended the shaft so an empty one descended, but at the start of an ascent the whole weight of the rope (nearly 500 lb) had to be lifted with practically no rope on the empty side. For this reason the winding drum was made conical to ensure that the empty corf exerted a maximum counterbalancing torque at the start of its downward journey. Waste coal was used to fuel the boiler—that is coal which otherwise would be left in the mine—and a sufficient quantity for 12 h working could be raised in 12 min.

It may be noted that the winding machinery at Long Benton was developed and improved from an earlier design by Smeaton in 1774

189

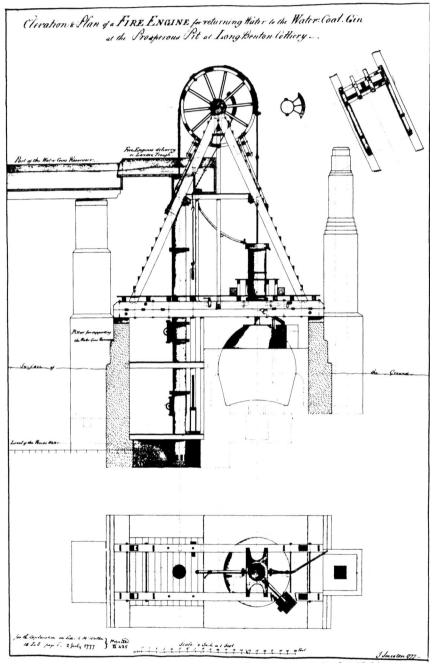

*Fig. 44. Prosperous Pit engine, 1777 (Designs, **3**, f. 163A)*

for Griff colliery, Staffordshire. Here he arranged a 37 ft waterwheel operating a winding drum which raised the coals alternately from two separate but adjacent shafts. Normally there was an adequate water supply from a reservoir, but in dry seasons an existing steam engine returned water from a neighbouring canal up to the reservoir.[24]

Walker winding engine

The success of the Long Benton winding engines led to the spread of such machines in the North East coalfield, and Smeaton himself designed one in 1783 for Walker colliery.[25] It turned out to be his last steam engine design.

At Walker there was every intention of leaving the winding engine at the same pit for many years, so it had the usual engine house and beam; in other respects it followed the 1777 prototype, though built on a rather larger scale: 36 in. cylinder, 6½ ft stroke, working 13 strokes/min, and with a 12 ft dia. boiler. The waterwheel again had a diameter of 30 ft, but the pit was 570 ft deep and the corves were raised at the rate of 43/h, each carrying 680 lb of coal.

The steam engine developed 17 hp and delivered 260 cu. ft of water/min to the wheel. Tests showed the duty to be about 8½ million, an excellent figure for an engine of moderate size, especially since second-grade coal was probably used for firing the boiler, as at Long Benton Prosperous Pit.

From Smeaton's journals we can follow rather closely his progress on this job.[26] Preliminary site visits occupied the 18th and 19th December, 1782. After settling down in his new quarters at Gray's Inn he began designing on 28th February, 1783. Various letters to Henry Eastburn followed, doubtless enclosing sketches, and after a total of about 38 h work he dispatched the "general Design" to Eastburn by the Leeds coach on 6th April with a letter 2 days later asking him to send off immediately to Walker colliery, by the Newcastle "fly", any drawings that had already been completed; particularly those for the waterwheel, working beam, boiler and cylinder beams. A letter "on the Walker Machine" also went to the Carron Company. Another drawing, of which Smeaton himself made a copy, was sent to Carron with an accompanying letter on 22nd April.

On 12th May he wrote to Thomas Barnes, the viewer (i.e. mining engineer) at Walker, who would have been responsible for directing construction. Smeaton visited the site again on the 23rd June. Design of the brakes and reversing gear took 6 h in August, and the "pencil sketch" was sent off on the 29th of that month with written instructions. A further 8 h on more details of the winding machinery followed early in September. Eastburn dispatched what must have been the last drawing in October, whilst acknowledging the receipt of several letters from Barnes, and on 11th December Smeaton visited Walker to arrange the engine trials. These took place, in his presence, on 18th–20th December; a practice run was made on the 22nd, the engine began normal working next day, and on 24th December he set off home from Newcastle.

In all, Smeaton had spent 9 days on site and about 62 h in design; to which must be added Eastburn's time in copying drawings. Of these, fifteen are in *Designs*, the last one being a modification of the safety device on the winding machine made in 1784.

Blowing engines
Mention has already been made of the 72 in. engine installed at Carron ironworks for returning water to the reservoir in dry weather, the water being required to keep four furnace-blowing machines in operation. Smeaton also designed two returning engines, linked directly to waterwheels, for furnaces at Seacroft in Yorkshire (1779–80) and at Beaufort ironworks in South Wales (1782).[27] The blowing machinery is described in Chapter III.

Finally, we note that Smeaton was consulted on improvements of steam pumping engines at London Bridge (1771) and York Buildings waterworks in London (1777), and he remodelled the engine at York waterworks.[28] Tests on the latter in 1785, as compared with the performance of the original engine, showed that the duty had been rather more than doubled.[29]

Boulton and Watt
Smeaton's important work on the steam engine was soon overshadowed by the brilliant contributions of Watt and the developments made by the partnership of Boulton and Watt in the period 1775–1800.

After long delays and much difficulty Watt successfully ran his experimental engine at the Soho manufactory in 1775, and the first full-scale engines on the new principle were erected in 1776.[30] Smeaton, of course, understood the advantage of condensing the steam outside the cylinder, the main point covered by Watt's patents, but thought (correctly) that the higher capital cost of Boulton & Watt engines, coupled with the heavy premiums charged, would inhibit, or at least delay, their acceptance in the coalfields. However, in other localities the case was different and in January 1778 he asked the partners whether they would grant a licence for the application of a condenser to a 26 in. engine he was designing at Hull.[31] The engine would be used mainly for water supply to the town and also as a returning engine for an oil-mill.

Though greatly respecting Smeaton and his works, and wishing to help him in any way they could, Boulton and Watt were not happy with the idea of adding a separate condenser to a Newcomen-type engine even in its improved form; their design incorporated several features, other than the condenser, on which the overall success depended. An interesting correspondence followed in which, among other things, Smeaton expressed a strong desire to know exactly the performance of the Watt engine, as some of the figures which had been quoted he knew to be theoretically impossible.[32]

The opportunity for making a test came in April 1778 when he was asked by the Birmingham Canal Company to carry out trials on a newly erected engine at Smethwick lock. The results, communicated to the Canal Committee by their engineer Samuel Bull, showed a duty of nearly 18 million;[33] about the upper limit of what Smeaton had anticipated.

In an earlier letter to Watt,[32] Smeaton had written that "your Idea, of condensing in a separate vessel from the cylinder . . . I look upon as a greater Stroke of invention, than has appeared since Newcomen", and he followed this tribute by saying:

> "I most heartily wish you all the Success that your ingenious discoverys, and indefatigable labours have deserved, and shall endeavour to promote your Interest, not only in speaking more particularly to the quantum of Product of your Machines . . . but in recommending to your Execution all such Subjects as occur to me, where the price of Coals is a consideration so material as to make it worth the while of the Proprietor."[34]

He also hoped that Watt would communicate his research and promised "if you chuse to give a paper to the Philosophical Transactions, I will do myself the pleasure of presenting it". Moreover, when Watt came up for election to the Royal Society it was Smeaton's name (followed by those of Priestley and Cavendish) that headed the proposal form submitted in April 1785.

Smeaton kept his word, advising his client at Hull to order a Boulton & Watt engine. This was duly built, for the waterworks and to operate the millwork already constructed to Smeaton's design, and he himself carried out the tests in 1779; the duty again being nearly 18 million, with a piston loading of about 10 lb/sq. in.[35]

He also recommended that Boulton & Watt should supply the engine for a double corn-mill which he was designing for Deptford dockyard, but as a returning engine rather than operating directly through a crank. Part of his report, which is dated 23rd November, 1781,[36] is quoted in Chapter III. The very fine millwork is fully described and illustrated by Farey in Rees' *Cyclopaedia* but he says a Newcomen-type engine was used to return the water.[37]

IX

Harbours

A. W. SKEMPTON

Smeaton's reports and drawings on harbours are more numerous than those on any other civil engineering topic, and refer to no less than 30 different sites in England and Scotland.[1] In some cases he is dealing with relatively minor improvements, but quite often he is tackling the complex problems of deciding how best, with limited funds, to create a harbour where hitherto only inadequate shelter had been provided. A complete story of his contributions in this field cannot be attempted in a single chapter. Instead, we shall outline some of the smaller schemes constructed in accordance with his designs and deal more fully with the works at Aberdeen and Ramsgate, adopting a chronological treatment.

St Ives
In his report and drawings of 1766 Smeaton planned a new pier much larger and in much deeper water than the structure already existing.[2] He proposed that the pier should be founded by the method of *pierres perdues* some 9 ft below low water springs on sand proved by probing to be quite dense at this depth—about 6 ft below the sea bed. The pier was to be 360 ft in length with a top width of 24 ft and a height of 36 ft above the foundations, surmounted by a 9 ft parapet wall rising 15 ft above high water of spring tides. On the large, random stones of the foundation the core of the pier would be built of rubble masonry encased between external walls of coursed masonry battered at ½ to 1 on each side.

Constructed in this way, and containing about 35,000 tons of stone, the pier was built during the years 1767–70 at a cost of £9,480

Fig. 45.   Eyemouth harbour (engraving by James Cooper after a sketch by R. P. Leitch—Smiles' Lives of the Engineers, Vol. 2)

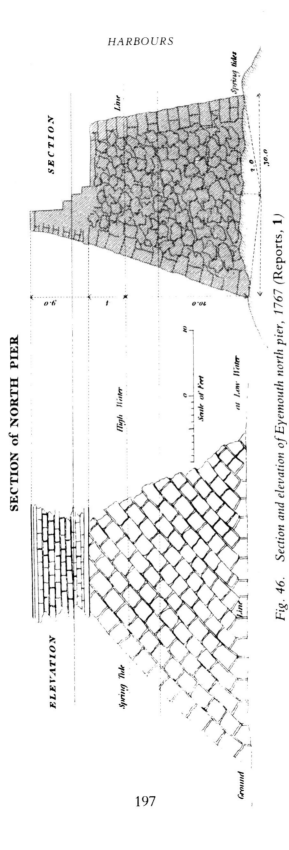

Fig. 46. Section and elevation of Eyemouth north pier, 1767 (Reports, 1)

197

by Thomas Richardson,[3] undoubtedly the "very careful and diligent" Thomas Richardson of Plymouth who had served Smeaton so well as foreman mason on the Eddystone Lighthouse.[4]

The original light at the end of "Smeaton's Pier" (it is the only work which still actually commemorates his name) was replaced by a stone-built lighthouse in 1831, and the pier was extended to its present length in the 1890s.

Eyemouth

The pier which can be seen on the left of the view shown in Fig. 45 had been constructed in 1747, but the harbour remained exposed to northerly gales. In 1767 Smeaton designed a pier 340 ft in length to give the required protection and also to act as an additional landing place. It was to be founded on rock at low water level, with the external masonry built in steeply sloping courses (Fig. 46) so that the foundation stones of each course need not be set at exactly the same elevation.[5]

Probably this method of construction was introduced here for the first time. It must have proved successful as Smeaton adopted the technique in many of his later designs, and several examples occur in harbours built in the nineteenth century.

At Eyemouth the contractor, Cramond of Dunbar, following Smeaton's plans, completed the work in 1770. The pier, the end of which appears on the right in Fig. 45, remained practically unchanged until recently. The massive stones, weighing up to 3 tons each, in the external courses can still be seen and the core masonry when examined in 1965 was found to be in good condition.[6]

Portpatrick

Portpatrick provided a terminus for the shortest sea passage to Ireland, but originally it was equipped simply with a landing stage in a sandy bay partly surrounded by rocks and offering little protection against the violent storms on the west coast of Scotland. The creation of a harbour, properly so called, at this place followed Smeaton's report and plans of 1770.[7]

It was perhaps the Duke of Queensberry who called on Smeaton for advice, and he certainly paid Smeaton's fees, but the scheme was part of the Government's plans for improving communications in Scotland. The War Office contributed £2,000 annually to the harbour and a road leading to it, under the general direction of Colonel Skene, though some funds may have come locally; as for Banff Bridge which, coincidentally, also came under Colonel Skene as Inspector of Roads in North Britain.[8]

Whatever may have been the nature of the administration, it is clear that Smeaton's plans were quickly approved and in the autumn of 1770 he arranged for John Gwyn to leave Perth Bridge, then nearing completion, in order to become resident engineer at Portpatrick. By the end of the 1773 working season the main pier had been built out from the shore in a westerly direction across a gully about 100 ft wide on to a reef of rocks exposed at low tide. The pier as then built had a length of 270 ft and formed the south side of the harbour. As at Eyemouth, the external walls had sloping courses of masonry.

From the start, Smeaton envisaged a flank pier branching off almost at right angles to the main pier, from a point just short of its 1773 termination, to provide a protected inner harbour. He had also planned the main pier to run out a good deal further. Assessing the situation, he now decided to concentrate on the flank pier and in January 1774 presented a report, with drawings and instructions to Gwyn, for a somewhat modified design of this structure.[9] It was to be 175 ft long, founded for the most part on sand by the *pierres perdues* method, and particular attention was paid to details of the rounded pier head where the external masonry was to be formed "Edystone fashion" with interlocking dovetail construction.

The flank pier was well advanced by the end of 1774 (the site being sheltered) when some of the construction equipment was sold to Aberdeen, and Gwyn left in January 1775. However, work continued on the pier and on deepening the harbour near the junction of the two piers, by excavating rock as ordered by Smeaton in 1774, and the harbour was judged to be completed in 1778.

After finishing at Banff Bridge, James Kyle took charge at Portpatrick. Repairs had to be made occasionally to damage caused by winter storms attacking the main pier, and in 1782 Smeaton reported again, by letters and a drawing, on defending this pier by a sloping "bulwark" of huge blocks of stone to break the force of the waves.[10] By 1797 the harbour had cost government about £15,000[11] and although it is difficult to say how much was spent on the original work up to 1778 the sum can hardly have been less than £10,000.

Starting in 1821, from designs by John Rennie, the harbour was further deepened and the main pier extended; much along the line shown in Smeaton's drawings but with even more massive protection.[12]

199

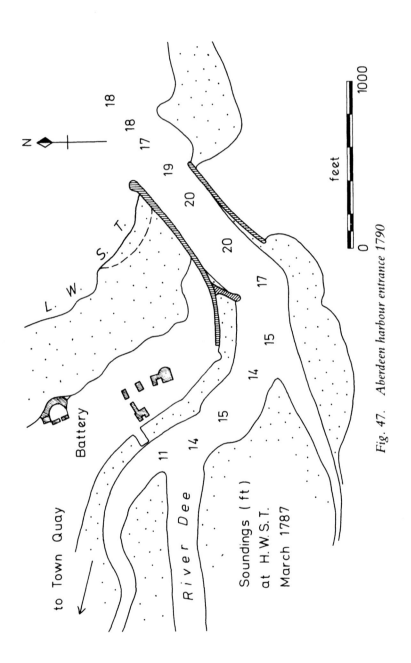

N

L. W. S. T.

18
18
17
19
20
20
17
15
14
15
14
11

Battery

to Town Quay

River Dee

Soundings (ft)
at H.W.S.T.
March 1787

feet

0   1000

Fig. 47.   Aberdeen harbour entrance 1790

Aberdeen

So late as the 1760s little had been done to improve this harbour from its natural state. Ships entered the mouth of the River Dee and navigated up a branch channel leading to the town quay about a mile upstream; but in May 1768 the Lord Provost wrote to Smeaton saying:

> "The Magistrates of Aberdeen have for some years had in view the reparation and improvement of their Harbour but have been at a loss for want of a well qualified Person to give them a proper plan for that purpose. As they are now informed of your being in Scotland . . . they are sollicitous (if your business permits) you should come to this place . . . and after viewing and considering the present State of our Harbour give us your Advice and opinion how far the same can be improved and the most effectual method of executing such Improvements, which we will esteem a favour conferred upon our Community and at the same time be ready chearfully to gratify you for your trouble.[13]

With the best will to comply with such a polite and important request, Smeaton could not manage a visit that summer, but did so in August 1769 and submitted his report with estimates and drawings in February 1770.[14] His fees and expenses came to £40–16s–0d. The Lord Provost, acknowledging, said the proposals "seem very clear and satisfactory and I hope it will all be carried into Execution so soon as the state of our Finances will permit". He thought the fees "extremely moderate", enclosed a draft for their payment, and begged leave to present his best respects to Mrs Smeaton.[15] Meanwhile, surveys had been and were being made by John Home, though Smeaton himself had taken the soundings.

As he correctly realised, the main problem was the existence of a bar just outside the river mouth, and in a single page of his report Smeaton gives a dissertation on the formation of such bars in general and at Aberdeen in particular. Clearly, all other measures would be pointless until the bar was reduced, and in his opinion the only means by which this could be effected was to build a pier along the north side of the mouth of the Dee (Fig. 47) which he planned to be 1,400 ft in length, projecting 370 ft beyond the present low water mark of spring tides; and to dredge outside the pier-head from time to time.

> "The pier (he says) will not indeed stop the continual driving of the matter [sand and gravel] coastwise from the north, but after the back of the pier is filled up with sand to a certain degree, it will then go round the pier head, and by the action of middling freshes and spring ebbs will be kept in deeper

201

water . . . without getting into the harbour's mouth, or at least not in such a degree as to obstruct the navigation. By this means, as the bar will not only be kept clean down to the stone bed, but by lifting the larger sort of stones by art, the remaining gravel will wash out into deeper water, so as to make, as may reasonably be expected, full two feet more water than there now is in its best state."

As usual he pays much attention to economy but estimates that construction costs of the pier would amount to £10,000. He then goes on to make proposals for improving the inner part of the harbour, by training walls etc., which add another £1,000 to the estimates.

The necessary Act was eventually obtained in 1773 (13 Geo. 3, c. 29). Smeaton gave further advice, perhaps verbally in Edinburgh as no letter is recorded, and in February 1774, evidently on his recommendation, John Gwyn visited Aberdeen to make preliminary arrangements for quarrying stone (granite, obtained locally), building a lighter and the purchase of "machinery" from Portpatrick; though in a letter written before his visit Gwyn emphasised that "it will be the Latter End of this year before I can possibly be finally aquitted from my present Engagement at Portpatrick".[16]

Quarrying began in September 1774 and orders were given for a lighter.[17] With permission from Colonel Skene, Gwyn got the machinery shipped on 30th December for Glasgow en route for Aberdeen via the Forth & Clyde Canal. He took up his post as Superintendent and Director of Works towards the end of January 1795, with an annual salary of £120 for 5 years back-dated to 1st January, and he received £15 "as the expense of removing his family from Portpatrick".[18] Materials, including 58 tons of pozzolana, were now being delivered, the machinery arrived in April, and the laying of the foundation stone took place in June.

Work proceeded steadily, using direct labour under Gwyn's direction, with the assistance of a clerk of accounts and the Town Clerk acting as secretary to the management committee; contracts were made only for the supply of stone, timber, etc. Perhaps as the cost began to exceed the estimate it was decided to limit the length of the pier to a projection of about 180 ft beyond low water mark, for in December 1779 Gwyn wrote to the Lord Provost saying "the North Pier to the Length of 1200 feet is nearly compleated agreeable to Mr Smeaton's general design, and all parts thereof are in a safe sufficient Situation, answering the Intentions expected", and adding that as the operations will henceforth be on a smaller scale he wished to leave in 6 months' time.[19]

In March 1780 the Magistrates issued a circular stating that "the town of Aberdeen has now an exceeding good Harbour of easy entrance much frequented by ships of considerable burden". The last payments to workmen were made on 19th October, 1780, which can be taken as the date of completion. Gwyn himself stayed on until 1st October, when he received a gratuity of £75 in recognition of his highly satisfactory conduct of the works.[20] The final cost, from 1768 to the end of 1780, including legal charges, salaries and all incidentals, came to £16,060.[21]

The pier, containing some 45,000 tons of stone, was built to a height of 6 ft above high water springs and its cross-section increased in three stages; the outermost portion having a top width of 24 ft, a base of 36 ft and a height of 24 ft surmounted by an 8 ft parapet. The length of the pier, according to a survey of 1787, was 1,208 ft.[22] The same survey shows, as expected, that the beach had built up behind the pier, but the depth of water over the bar at high tide now measured 17 ft (Fig. 47) as compared with 13½ ft in 1769. A hand-operated dredging machine, probably of the "bag and spoon" type used on the Thames, was fitted on a barge at about this time to remove the larger gravel "by art", as Smeaton said.

However, the lowering of the bar led to increased wave action further upstream in strong easterly winds. To examine this effect Smeaton visited Aberdeen in October 1787 and reported in March of the following year.[23] He designed a "catch pier" projecting at an angle from the main pier (Fig. 47) and rising only just above high tide level. He also recommended that the old South Pier, which was really no more than a training wall, should be rebuilt and reduced in length at its westward end, to allow the waves to dissipate their energy by running up the sloping beach opposite and upstream of the catch pier.

These works started in July 1788 and were finished by December 1790, at an expenditure of about £1,500, by the mason Alexander Gildavie operating a "cost plus" contract. They served their purpose well.

When paying Smeaton's fees in 1788 the Magistrates took a belated opportunity of adding a gratuity "for the Success that has attended the Execution of the North Pier". In all, on this occasion he received £267, no other payment having been made to him since 1773.

Use of the harbour increased so substantially that by 1810 further important works could be put in hand, but the history of this second phase of development, for which Telford and John Gibb were largely responsible, is another story involving an extension of Smeaton's pier, the acquisition of an early steam dredger and major improvements of the inner harbour. However, at the great port which Aberdeen has now become Smeaton is remembered as the engineer who made the first, vital steps towards its prosperity.

Peterhead

The old south pier of this harbour being in a bad state, Smeaton was consulted in 1772. In a brief report accompanied by a sketch plan he advised complete rebuilding on a new alignment, with the pier slightly concave to the sea (instead of convex) in order to throw the seas away from the entrance.[24] He also replanned the short west pier or jetty, to make an entrance 80 ft wide between the pier heads. Gwyn then made drawings and estimates, and added as an idea of his own a wet dock. For the south pier (350 ft in length, containing 150,000 cu. ft of masonry) he estimated £2,023 without contingencies; a very low figure as stone from the old pier could be re-used for 70 per cent of the core of the new structure. Excavating rock to deepen the harbour came to £2,500 and there were further items for a quay wall and the west jetty.[25]

After a struggle to raise the necessary funds, work began in 1775. Gwyn visited Peterhead from time to time as supervisor of construction, obviously with approval of the Aberdeen authorities. Much damage to the partly completed pier was caused by an unexpectedly severe summer storm in August 1776, and Gwyn made urgent repairs to safeguard the structure for the winter.[26] Deepening of the harbour went on concurrently with work on the pier, the whole job being finished in 1781. By then upwards of £6,000 had been spent, of which the pier cost £2,900. The entrance provided a depth of 14 ft of water at spring tides and the innermost part of the harbour (the total area of which amounted to 5 acres) was only 3 ft shallower.[27]

The next developments took place under Rennie's direction. They included completion of the west pier in 1807, to a slightly greater length than Smeaton had proposed, and a further general deepening of the harbour (by about 4 ft) carried out 1808–10.[28]

Cromarty

Smeaton's drawings for the north pier of this small harbour are undated,[29] but work probably began in 1781 and the pier had been built to a length of 230 ft by 1783, with John Gwyn as resident engineer. Rather than making the pier longer, Smeaton then decided to terminate it and construct a detached pier or breakwater 130 ft long, almost parallel to the shore and about 70 ft from the north pier head.[30] By this arrangement he considered that adequate protection would be provided for shipping without too much deposition of sand within the harbour;[31] for here, in contrast to the sites previously mentioned, he was dealing with a relatively sheltered situation and the problem, as he wrote to Gwyn, was that "of harbour making upon a sandy shore where there is no backwater".

Smeaton's client was the landowner and industrialist George Ross who created the "new town" of Cromarty in the 1770s and had already built a stone jetty out to low water mark which was incorporated as the south pier of the harbour.[32]

A point of special interest is that we can gauge the extent to which Smeaton and his resident engineer kept in touch, as we find that during the period January 1782 to June 1783 Gwyn wrote nine letters to Smeaton and received four letters in reply, all on this job.[33] Of course there would have been others before and after but no records of them are available. Smeaton writes in the most friendly way, with quite lengthy discussions on the work and adding pieces of family and general news; but it is clear how much detail he had to leave to Gwyn's initiative and experience.

With work at Cromarty drawing to a close in the summer of 1784 poor Gwyn was worried about his future prospects. Fortunately, as Trevor Turner has related in delightful detail,[34] Smeaton managed to arrange for him to take a job at Hull as engineer for a new bridge there. Gwyn left Cromarty in December 1784 but got stormbound, ironically at Peterhead, and then, having decided to travel by road, got stormbound in Aberdeen where (he wrote): "the roads are Impassible from this to Edinbro by either fly chaize or horse, the Mail being for numbers of miles carried on mens backs". This reminds us to mention that, as Smeaton meticulously notes both the dates of writing and receipt of letters sent to him, we know Gwyn's letters from Cromarty usually took between 8 and 12 days to arrive in London or Austhorpe.

If Gwyn felt concern about the effect his lateness of arrival could be having on his future employers at Hull, Smeaton was worried about the impression Gwyn's grammar might be making on them. So he wrote to the Town Clerk saying:

"I never recommended him as a writer or as a Speaker: and indeed if the Gentlemen judge of him from the style of his letters, or indeed of his discourse, they will not conceive any high opinion of his abilities. I dont mean that he is not sufficiently intelligible, but having served his apprenticeship in London he both Speaks and Writes the London Vulgar; and withal has such a knack of misapplying an heap of fine Words and Phrases as by no means to do justice to his Mechanical abilities: and this I think it is but justice to him to say; as we are very apt to judge from first impressions."[35]

It is scarcely necessary to add that Gwyn had done fine work at Cromarty, as elsewhere; after nearly 200 years much of the original piers remain as part of the present harbour.[36]

Ramsgate

In the following account specific references are made to Smeaton's reports, letters and drawings, but otherwise it can be taken for granted that the facts are given in his *Historical Report on Ramsgate Harbour*, published in 1791,[37] and in a recent paper which presents a reassessment of the subject and brings the story up to 1850.[38]

Under authority of an Act obtained in 1749 the harbour at Ramsgate had been very greatly enlarged by the construction of two piers, as shown in Fig. 48(1), during the period 1750–73. The works were carried out under a Board of Trustees with Thomas Preston, master mason, acting in effect as resident engineer. They created what was potentially one of the largest harbours in England, with an enclosed area of 46 acres (including the old harbour which can be seen in the north-east corner of the plans in Fig. 48).

However, as the piers advanced seawards so an ever-increasing quantity of sand was deposited inside the harbour, with the result that by the time the piers reached completion the harbour had become choked up to levels in most places well above low tide; this state of affairs existed despite the removal by spade and dredger of more than 50,000 tons of sand during the past 2 years.

In the summer of 1773 the Trustees sought Smeaton's advice. He could not come to Ramsgate immediately, as he was about to visit Ireland, but would be very ready to attend at any further convenient season. Another call for help came early next year; he made his site investigations in April and reported on 24th October, 1774.[39]

The report is a pleasure to read. It starts with a clear discussion of the general principles, proceeds to analyse the remedial measures available, then makes detailed recommendations for the works required and finally gives estimates of the cost. With the type of material being deposited, a fine sand interbedded with thin seams of mud, and in the absence of any river to provide a backwater, he concludes that only two methods are technically feasible to clean the harbour: (1) by a combination of spadework at low tide and dredging when the sand is under water, using the type of large hand-operated machine employed for raising ballast in the Thames; or (2) by sluicing. Observations and calculations on the amount of sand already in the harbour (upwards of 300,000 tons) and the rate at which it is being deposited (about 400 tons/week), coupled with calculations on the rate and cost of removal by method (1), show this to be hardly a practical proposition. Smeaton, of course, was writing long before steam dredgers had been thought of, but he seems to have dismissed rather too lightly the capacity of horse-operated dredgers (the "mudmills" which he has seen in Holland), thinking they were not well suited to working in sand. However, the quantities involved were certainly formidable and he was probably correct in deciding that method (2) had to be used.

This he proposed to achieve by constructing a basin in the inner part of the harbour, see Fig. 48(1), from which, having been filled at high tide, water could be discharged at low tide through sluices; the power of the issuing streams being sufficient to erode the sand and carry the particles out to sea. He realises that the eroding streams will only form channels, down to the chalk bottom of the harbour, but the intermediate ridges will subsequently in large part be washed into the channels, to be removed by later sluicing operations, and where this does not take place the sluice streams can be re-directed by sinking a temporary caisson, shaped like a bridge pier, at an appropriate place and shifting it around from time to time when needed.

As a refinement he proposes the basin could be divided into two parts, so that either one can be used in turn to scour out the other; a neat arrangement, though it has to be admitted that there would be no great difficulty in cleaning out the basin by spadework and dredging, it being reasonable to suppose that the rate of deposition therein must be far less than in the harbour.

The sluices, Smeaton says, would normally be operated in spring tides, the range of which is up to 18 ft. He estimates the cost of building the basin wall and six sluices, together with the capitalised equivalent of men's wages in operating the system, will be around £10,000.

Soon after Smeaton's report Preston proposed a modification, with a wall going right across the harbour and a pair of gates in the wall to permit access for ships into the basin (and the old harbour). Faced with such radical and expensive schemes, the Trustees took some

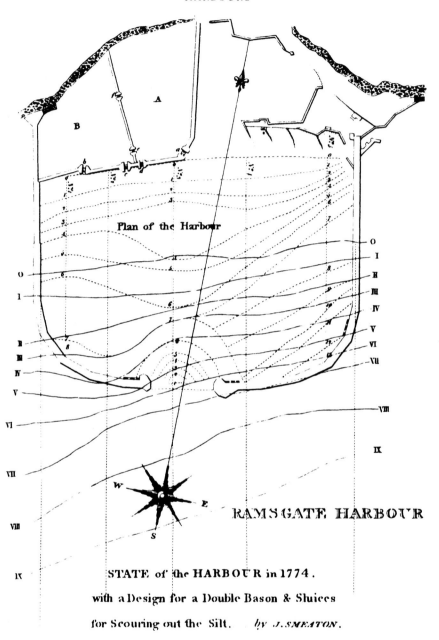

Plan of the Harbour

RAMSGATE HARBOUR

STATE of the HARBOUR in 1774.

with a Design for a Double Bason & Sluices

for Scouring out the Silt.   *by J. SMEATON*.

Scale of Feet

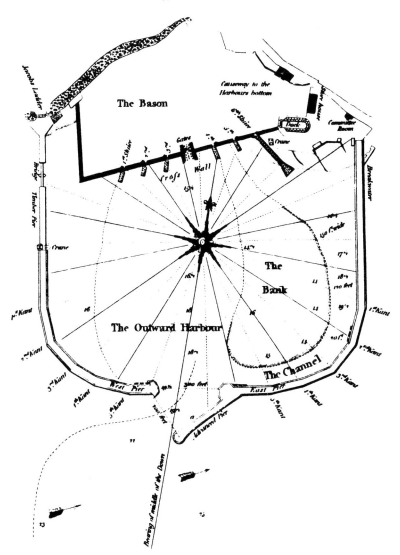

STATE of the HARBOUR in 1790.

with the Principal Works then Executed.

Fig. 48 (above and left). Plans of Ramsgate harbour in 1774 and 1790 (Reports, 3). The Advanced Pier had been built to point a in 1790.

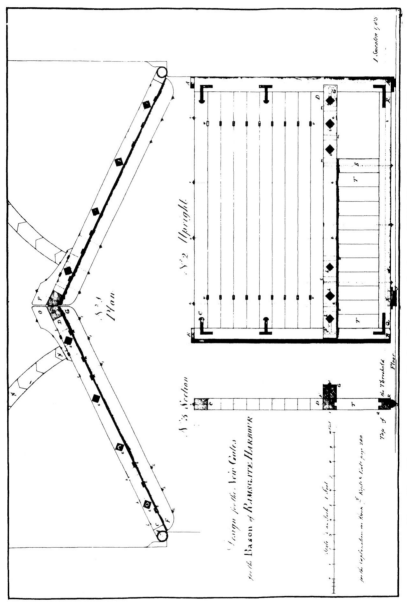

Fig. 49.   Entrance gates to Basin, Ramsgate harbour, 1783 (Designs, 5, f. 127)

time to reach a decision, but finally did so, favouring Preston's revised plan, and work began in 1776.

By the end of the year the cross-wall had been built from the west pier almost to the position of the first sluice. Smeaton then submitted a further report with working drawings for the sluices: masonry, door and lifting mechanism.[40] Each sluice had a waterway 4 ft wide and 6 ft high, with a long downstream apron to prevent undermining of the wall and the sluice itself, and the sill was 12 ft below high water level.

At about this time Preston died and was succeeded by Edmund Hurst, previously foreman mason. By 1779, when the works were nearing completion, a trial run of sluices No. 1 and No. 2 produced quite remarkably encouraging results. However, the cross-wall caused increased agitation of water in the harbour at high tide, by wave reflection, so part of it was then removed and a return wall made to the shore, as shown in Fig. 48(2); an opening was also made in the west pier, spanned by a timber bridge.

All these works, including the six sluices and the basin entrance gates, were finished in 1781 and, as Smeaton says in his *Historical Report*: "from this era Ramsgate Harbour began to put off that forlorn appearance of a Repository of Mud, and to assume a more respectable aspect than it had for 15 years past". Indeed the Chairman of the Trustees on a visit 2 years later reported that the sand was now almost entirely cleared away, and ships of 200–400 tons burden could be accommodated with ease and safety.

Smeaton was consulted again, in August 1782, when he surveyed the site for a dry dock, suggested some modifications to the fifth and sixth sluices, and promised to provide designs for improved entrance gates as well as for the dock. In connection with the latter he went to Liverpool in October to study the dry docks there, and in the early part of 1783 produced the required drawings with fair copies made by his assistant (Henry Eastburn at Austhorpe) for the Trustees.[41] In all Smeaton spent 22 days on this work.[42]

The gates, 14 ft high and spanning a clear width of 30 ft (Fig. 49), were also to be provided with new entrance wing walls. Work on the walls began towards the end of 1783. The following year Henry Cull followed Hurst as master mason (annual salary £70) and construction started on the dock to his designs. It had a very flat inverted arch in masonry instead of the timber floor proposed by Smeaton. The entrance gates, finished in 1785, were satisfactory but the dock proved otherwise; for, when emptying the dock, the unbalanced hydrostatic uplift acting on the underside of the floor, through fissures in the chalk, caused the inverted arch to thrust sideways to such an extent as to cause serious cracking of the north wall.

Smeaton, reporting on this event, which he witnessed in August 1787, shows by calculation that the thrust (17 tons/ft run) is amply large to explain the failure.[43] He goes on to consider the possibility of reducing the horizontal pressure by building an inverted arch of greater curvature, and produced a sketch design, but suggests it would be best to start again with a timber floor. The uplift pressure is the same, obviously, but the timbers simply act as beams supported at their ends by the vertical weight of the walls, on which there is in this case no lateral thrust.

Meanwhile the Chairman of the Trustees died in the autumn of

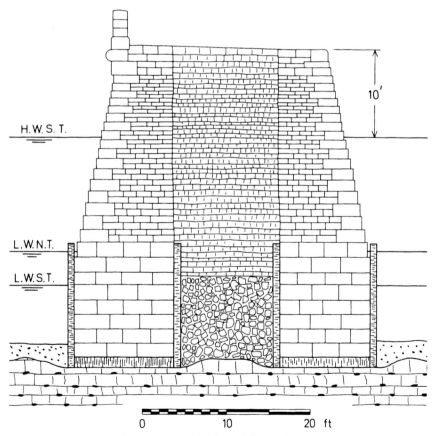

Fig. 50. Ramsgate harbour Advanced Pier, 1788

212

1787 and was succeeded by Alexander Aubert. One of Mr Aubert's first decisions was to appoint Smeaton as engineer to the harbour, instead of using him as a consultant occasionally and then not always taking his advice. Moreover he recommended to the Board, no doubt after discussion with Smeaton, that John Gwyn (who had just finished the bridge at Hull) should become resident engineer, with Cull remaining as master mason. At last a proper organisation on the engineering side had been achieved. Smeaton was to receive £250 a year and Gwyn the not excessively generous annual salary of £100.

After these affairs had been settled Smeaton visited Ramsgate again in December, in company with Mr Aubert, and presented a lengthy report on 9th January, 1788.[44] This reviews the progress made since his first visit in 1774, highly gratifying as far as the sluicing operations are concerned but not so in regard to wave action within the harbour. The construction of an "Advanced Pier", to give additional protection, had been under discussion and Smeaton now submits drawings for this structure.[45] It is to be 360 ft long, pointing so as to make the harbour mouth face SSW with a distance of 200 ft between the pier heads—see Fig. 48(2). The foundations are 36 ft wide formed by two parallel rows of timber caissons, spaced 12 ft apart, sunk onto the levelled chalk sea bed at depths of 7–10 ft below low-water springs; the caissons are 20 ft long and each is to contain about 250 tons of cut stone brought up to a level just above low-water neaps. On this masonry the walls are built to a height of 10 ft above high-water springs, the external faces being battered to a top width of 26 ft, and the internal space between the caissons and walls is to be filled with rubble masonry (Fig. 50).

Also with this report Smeaton sent new drawings of the dock.[46] It has a top width of 50 ft and a depth of 19 ft. The floor consists of built-up beams placed 12 in. apart, spanning 31 ft between the foot of the walls, and covered with 6 in. thick longitudinal planks; the beams being made of two superimposed 13 in. square timbers, with shear connectors, extending 6 ft under each wall (Fig. 51).

Gwyn arrived in January. Smeaton wrote to him shortly afterwards, and also to the secretary remarking that Gwyn "having got an house to his mind, seems to think himself very happily scituated; and I doubt not but that as soon as the Season comes favourable every thing will go on Chearfully at Ramsgate".[47]

And so it did. Machinery of various kinds was designed, ordered and delivered. Smeaton went to the site in April. Next month he visited Dorset with Gwyn and Cull to examine stone quarries at

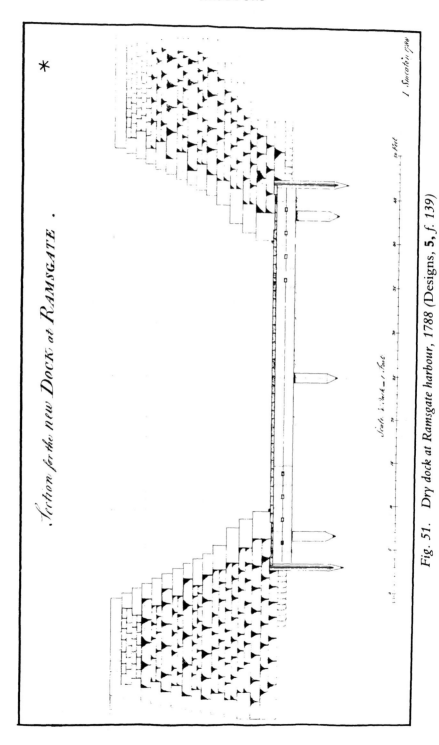

Fig. 51. Dry dock at Ramsgate harbour, 1788 (Designs, 5, f. 139)

Purbeck and Portland, and quarries at Lyme for Blue Lias hydraulic limestone.[48] Random stones which had been deposited for protection around the east pier head were removed, partly by lifting tackle but mostly with the aid of a diving bell. Designed by Smeaton,[49] as an improvement on the bell used at Hexham this comprised a cast iron chest, weighing 2½ tons, large enough for two men to work within, and supplied with a steady flow of air pumped in at sufficient pressure to keep out all but a few inches of water.

It came into operation in July 1788, with Smeaton personally demonstrating its use, and by mid-August enough stones had been cleared away (140 tons of them) for work to start on levelling the chalk bottom ready for the first two caissons. The diving bell was again used for fixing the caissons to the existing pier head; a matter on which Smeaton wrote detailed instructions to Gwyn.[50] The two caissons were safely and properly established and filled with masonry in September, Smeaton being present on site, and the next pair followed in November.[51] Work then ceased for the winter, but meanwhile good progress had been made on the dock; the walls were taken down, sheet piling driven around the floor, and about one-half of all the 52 great "double beams", as Smeaton called them, were in place.

He wrote further instructions about the dock in January,[52] and after a site visit in March.[53] By his next visit in May the dock floor had been completed and a few courses of masonry. Work also had been resumed on the Advanced Pier. Tragically, Gwyn died after a short illness in mid-June; "a real loss to the public", Smeaton said, "as well as lamented by his family and friends". Henry Cull then took full charge of the work, and it was he who showed the diving bell and levelling operations to Rennie, from whom we have an interesting description recorded in his notebook of 3rd August, 1789.[54]

Three weeks later Smeaton "had the honour to attend the Chairman down to the Bottom of the Sea", in the diving bell, to inspect the caisson foundations. They stayed down for three-quarters of an hour and on ascending "were received with great joy by our Friends, whom we found surrounding us in boats, and who by this time were beginning to be apprehensive that some thing might have happened to us".

By the end of 1789 another eight caissons had been sunk, and after his visit in November Smeaton made designs for a breakwater wall in the external corner of the east pier at its landward end.[55] He also surveyed sections across the harbour and examined the west pier head with a view to designing a small lighthouse to be built there.

215

In 1790 the masons concentrated their efforts on the Advanced Pier and breakwater, leaving the dock alone for the time being. The breakwater was completed in May, and by October a total length of 180 ft of the pier had been built up to high-water mark. Smeaton made four site visits that year and wrote most of his *Historical Report*.

Work on the dock was resumed, and completed, in 1791. Henry Cull continued building the Advanced Pier, still under Smeaton's supervision, and the *Report* was published. In the summer he drew up estimates for work still to be done.[56] This shows that £28,000 had been spent on the Advanced Pier up to the spring of 1791 and £9,500 more would be spent by the end of the year. To complete a total length of 360 ft Smeaton estimates a final expenditure of £57,000 but in 1792 the pier was terminated at 320 ft, presumably as it then proved to be adequate for its purpose. The other items in his list, not all of which were destined to be carried out, indicate how busy he had been in the early part of the year planning further improvements.

If Smeaton made a site visit in the spring of 1792 it was his last. With deteriorating health, he must have asked the Board to end his appointment, for on 18th July they resolved:

> "That a letter be written by the Chairman ... to Mr Smeaton, their Engineer, expressive of the concern the Trustees feel at his intention to withdraw those activities from their service, which have hitherto been employed so much to his own honour and to their satisfaction, and particularly that they lament the cause of it."[57]

They were in fact quite unwilling to accept his resignation, but he died in October, still in service to the Board.

Further engineering works were undertaken, notably by Rennie (1807–21) and his son Sir John Rennie (1821–50); but the success of the harbour had been established under Smeaton and with justifiable pride he ends his *Historical Report* by remarking that:

> "Within the last seventeen months upwards of Six Hundred sail of ships and vessels have taken shelter in the Harbour, of which above Three Hundred were bound to and from the port of London. Evidence can be produced, that the Harbour has been this Winter [1790–91] the means of saving ... property to the amount of between two and three hundred thousand pounds, with a great number of valuable lives, which otherwise would have been driven upon the flats and rocks, and in all probability lost."

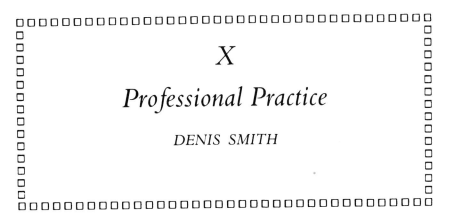

X

Professional Practice

DENIS SMITH

To some it may seem surprising that the word *professional* can properly be used in connection with an engineer's career in the mid-eighteenth century, but Smeaton regularly used the term himself during his 40 years as a consulting engineer. In this respect Smeaton is of particular interest and differs significantly from most of his predecessors in civil engineering. His letters and reports testify not only to his technical competence but, more importantly for our present purpose, reveal his design principles, professional ethics, and the manner of organising his practice. Smeaton obviously thought of himself as an independent professional designer and would begin a report by saying: "I take the opportunity of reporting my opinion, as a professional man, upon the subject before me";[1] and on another occasion: "I think it necessary to give my opinion with that freedom that becomes me in a matter wherein I am consulted, and . . . where my opinion is desired in the way of my profession."[2] He also strongly maintained the independence of the engineer and on one occasion sharply commented: "the commissioners of the harbour, I presume, did not pretend to professional skill in *civil engineering*".[3] An aspect of Smeaton's ethics is revealed when, asked to comment on a bridge design in which he was not personally involved, his unequivocal reply was:

"it is contrary to the usual practice of professional men to give their opinions upon each others work unless regularly called upon in the way of their profession; and upon reflection you will readily see the want of confidence in the persons employed, and confusion, that in many cases a proceeding of this kind would naturally create."[4]

From 1760 Smeaton ran his consulting practice from his family home, Austhorpe Lodge near Leeds, where he had an office and workshop built in the grounds. He also made regular trips to London on Parliamentary and other business. On these occasions, during the last 10 years of his life, he lodged at Gray's Inn and in 1783 advised a client:

> "My direction is to Mr. Smeaton, Engineer, No 2 Grays Inn London. My present stay I expect to be till towards the end of this month and as I have got fixed chambers here; when in Town you may also at a future time, direct to me as above."[5]

He frequently enlisted the services of his friend John Holmes in financial transactions, and Holmes' watchmaker's shop "4 doors from Somerset House",[6] in the Strand, was also effectively Smeaton's London office before moving to Gray's Inn.

The Austhorpe office and workshop
Smiles described Smeaton's purpose-built structure adjacent to the house:

> "The building was in the form of a square tower, four stories high. . . . The basement contained his forge; the first floor his lathe; the second his models; the third was his drawing room and study; and the fourth was a sort of lumber room and attic."[7]

While in this tower he gave strict orders not to be disturbed, and his daughter Mary described his working routine:

> "The arrangement of his time was governed by a method, as invariable as inviolable; for professional studies were never broken in upon, by any one; and these ... wholly ingrossed the forenoon. ... His afternoons were regularly occupied by practical experiments, or some other branch of mechanics. And not more was his mind devoted to his profession in one division of his time, than abstracted from it in another."[8]

He used the top of the tower for early-morning astronomy, and his journal provides a detailed glimpse of an August day in 1781:

till $9\frac{1}{2}$	Observations, breakfast, and Minutes
till 11	Mill and Mill minutes
till 2	Report on Scarborough Pier
till $2\frac{1}{2}$	Computing time
till $3\frac{1}{2}$	Dinner
till $8\frac{1}{2}$	Mill, Mr. Brooke and Mr. Colley till night.[9]

It is clear that Smeaton regarded himself as the designer of schemes for which others would contract to supply materials and carry out the construction. He described his own role thus:

> "They who send for me to take my advice upon any scheme I consider as my paymasters; from them I receive my propositions of what they are desirous of effecting; work with rule and compass, pen, ink, and paper, and figures, and give them my best advice thereupon."[10]

Smeaton regarded drawing as an important part of his work saying: "the rudest draft will explain Visible things better than many words";[11] and again: "I do not think it within the compass of human knowledge, to form the best possible Design *at once*. Things are far better finished by touching and retouching as is usual, and necessary to the greatest Painter."[12] John Farey, a friend of Jessop, described the activity of the third-floor drawing office:

> "Mr. Smeaton was a man of laborious habits and made all his drawings with his own hands. . . . His earliest designs, which were executed under his own inspection, show signs of having been used as working drawings . . . [but] After he became more established and employed a draughtsman he still continued to draw the lines of all his drawings to the proper scale in pencil on cartridge paper. . . . These sketches were fair copied on drawing paper by the draughtsman Mr. Wm. Jessop at first and afterwards Mr. Henry Eastburn, and Mr. Smeaton's daughters frequently assisted in the shadows and finishing, in indian ink which was very well executed."[13]

The collection of Smeaton's excellent drawings in the library of the Royal Society are amongst the earliest examples of their kind. That Smeaton intended them to be used on site as scale drawings is clear from a typical remark in a report:

> "The position and shapes of the other parts will be readily determined from the eye, or by measurement from the design; but it must be carefully observed, that wherever the measures marked upon the plan differ from those resulting from the scale, the figured measures are to be adhered to."[14]

The assistants mentioned above are the only ones Smeaton had in his office throughout his career. Indeed, up to the mid-1760s he effectively had none, for when William Jessop arrived in 1759 it was as a pupil aged 14 and he ranked as a qualified assistant only from 1767 until he set up on his own in 1772.[15] Henry Eastburn followed Jessop as a pupil in 1768 and, after 7 years' training, stayed on at Austhorpe until about 1788.[16] Thus, as Smeaton explains in reply to a letter asking if he had a vacancy for a pupil:

> "I have never trusted my reputation in business out of my own hand, so

my profession is as perfectly personal as that of a Phisician or councillor at Law. . . . One person therefore brought up in my office as my assistant, is capable of making every thing fair, that I am capable of producing and setting in the rough; the labouring oar, is in reality with myself. . . . Thus you see my dear friend I have at present no opening for any fresh Pupil."[17]

Smeaton's correspondence reveals that he was often asked to recommend suitable engineers. For example a letter from Dublin in 1771 asked if he "could recommend an Engineer that would come over, of high character, for Integrity, Knowledge, and Experience, and that had actually executed some Navigations to satisfaction".[18] Smeaton replied:

"I beg leave to recommend to you John Grundy, Esq; Engineer, at Spalding, Lincolnshire; a Gentleman of great Experience in the branches of Inland Navigation and Drainage, and who is in first rate Reputation, by the Works of that kind whereof he has acquitted himself. As his Terms may be different from mine, I apprehend it may be proper to apply to him upon that head."[19]

In the beginning Jessop's very distinguished career owed almost everything to the help and encouragement of his master.

Fees
When Smeaton started business in London in 1748, as an instrument-maker, he had an allowance from his father, and later he inherited the Austhorpe estate. He also had a small income from rents in property he owned in York, and for 12 years, from 1765, he was employed as an agent for the Derwentwater Estates of Greenwich Hospital, "an employment worth near £500 a year".[20]

For his first big job after completing the Eddystone, that is, as engineer to the Calder & Hebble Navigation, he received an annual salary of £250 for which he had frequently to be on site, though not of course full-time. At this period, in the early 1760s, his consulting fees were 1 guinea a day, plus travelling expenses;[21] the usual rate charged by consulting engineers and land surveyors at that time. Then, in May 1767, came a fairly drastic increase when Smeaton announced that:

"his lowest fee for a consultation at home, is one guinea; but if sent for, two guineas: and if employed the whole morning or day in London, five guineas."[22]

This was again altered slightly in the next year, as we learn from a letter written in 1782 which explains that:

"For 14 years past Mr. Smeaton's Terms of Business abroad have been and are 2½ guineas p. day during the whole time of being away from home, with the addition of 2½ guineas upon each day actually employed upon the Business in hand; the above includes his personal Expenses but to be allowed what he pays out of pocket in Coach and Chaise Hire."[23]

Smeaton provided such precise statements because "most Gentlemen desire to know the Expenses beforehand",[23] but sending in accounts was one thing—getting paid was another. In 1764 he said:

"The case is I find it more difficult to persuade my Customer that Engineers are like other Men in needing money to maintain themselves and Familys than I find in procuring their employment."[24]

On another occasion his polite request was:

"As this is the time of the year when tradesmen call for their bills on engineers and Philosophers, as well as other men; will it be agreeable to you to settle my account."[25]

As well as these fees and expenses for site visits Smeaton had a fixed scale of charges for more routine work at home. Writing in August 1782 (again in the third person) he says:

"As making the Designs for the direction of Workmen is a work of Time he always does it at home. His constant Price for water Mills for Corn, Oil, &c for 30 years past has been, and is 25 guineas each Sett, that is a Sett of Designs for Corn will be 25—and for Oil the same price—Wind mill 30 guineas."[26]

Thus the charge for this class of work remained constant from the very beginning of his engineering career, even though, as we learn from a letter written to Holmes, the time involved in designing a mill might amount to as much as 48–50 h.[27]

Despite this precision in the submission of accounts Smeaton would often, somewhat surprisingly, introduce such escape clauses as:

"but as I always make it a point to make my charge agreeable to my employers; if you think the charge more than you would have wished, or expected, please to settle it to your own liking, and at such time as will be agreeable."[28]

Smeaton's modest financial independence, based on what he described as "my *original* fortune", may account for his lenient attitude. His daughter Mary spoke of "The disinterested moderation of his pecuniary ambition"[29] and Smeaton himself found that:

"notwithstanding the successful exertions of so many years in favour of others, I had not done more for myself and family, than saved the accumulated income of my paternal Estate during the course of 35 of those years, that I had possessed it. It appears therefore clearly, that all this while I had been labouring for a meer maintenance."[30]

Nevertheless in raising his basic fee to 5 guineas a day Smeaton made a bold step which reflected his conviction that he was as fully a professional person as any doctor or lawyer.[31] His lead was followed exactly by engineers such as Mylne, Jessop, Rennie and Telford as they in turn reached a position of eminence in the profession. To arrive at present-day values the various figures mentioned above should be multiplied by at least 40; a necessarily approximate factor but of the correct order.[32]

Estimates

Smeaton's reports and estimates are documents combining a wealth of detail with a clear overview of feasible alternatives. All this was done with commendable clarity as, for example, in his introduction to a report in 1780 where he said:

"I have endeavoured to assemble the following properties,—that is, strength and durability of all the matter, materials, and fundamental parts; ease of repair of such as are most liable to decay by weather or wear; to have all possible simplicity, so as to be as little subject to be out of order as may be when suddenly wanted upon an exigency; and the whole of such form and construction as to be capable of being adequately repaired and kept in order by the proper artificers in the country."[33]

Such clear statements of philosophy are characteristic of Smeaton. As an appendix to a report he would, where necessary, attach an estimate of costs. Some 68 are known and these were obviously important to clients, particularly where alternative schemes were costed. Apart from new works he would also estimate for repairs to existing structures. Points-of-no-return in repairs were carefully computed as, for example, on a dam repair where he said: "If the rubble cannot be put in place for 2s. 6d. per yard, or under, I believe it will be advisable to begin a new dam in a new place."[34] Smeaton usually did not separate material and labour costs. Portland stone blocks were priced per cubic foot "laid in place" and timber piling as "every thing fixed in place, iron work included". Having evaluated the cost he said "for contingent expenses I generally allow 10 per cent upon the whole",[35] and that this surcharge was "exclusive of all expenses preceding the application, and procuring an act of parliament, and also interest of money, and law charges, &c. during the procedure of the work".[36] One item Smeaton never priced was land, and he would say: "I have done nothing more than give the quantity of acres, cut and covered, as I apprehend that no engineer should venture to name a price for it".[37] He would also occasionally produce estimates of return on capital received from tolls and other sources, and would estimate the cost of maintenance of works over a given period. Smeaton's largest estimate for a job was £293,440 in connection with the Forth & Clyde Canal in 1767.

Careful though he always tried to be in making realistic estimates, Smeaton had no illusions as to the difficulties involved:

"The longer I live [he wrote] I every year see more into the reasons why estimates are generally exceeded in the execution, and how impossible it is, without repeated proofs from experience, to conceive how this can happen in so great a degree."[37]

On another occasion he explained that: "such is the difference between the Computations, and the Out-goings, that no estimate can be made to keep pace therewith".[38] Things have not changed very much in this respect in the last 200 years!

Site management and other professional matters
Smeaton's reports and letters provide clear details of his ideas on construction supervision in general, and of canals in particular. In March

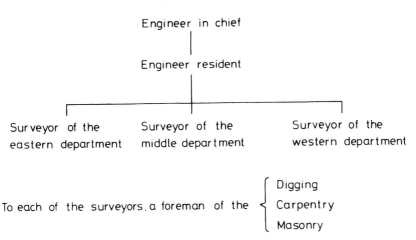

Fig. 52. Management structure for work on the Forth & Clyde Canal

223

1768 he produced "A Plan or Model for carrying on the mechanical Part of the Works of the Canal from Forth to Clyde",[39] in which he proposed the management structure shown in Fig. 52.

Smeaton's descriptions of the duties of the engineers are so succinct yet explicit that they are worth quoting in full:

Engineer in chief

1st. To make plans for execution of such works as shall be directed by the committee.

2dly. To pitch upon the ground whereon the said works are to be constructed.

3dly. To correspond with the committee upon such points as they shall think necessary.

4thly. To correspond with the engineer resident, and send such directions from time to time as himself or the resident shall find necessary.

Engineer resident

1st. To attend such meetings of the committee as he shall be ordered to attend, or such meeting as he shall think necessary to procure directions.

2dly. To see the plans and directions of the engineer in chief put into execution.

3dly. To mark out the grounds to be purchased, and to enter into such treaty with the proprietors as he shall be directed by the committee.

4thly. To supply such plans and directions for the lesser part of the works as he shall be desired by the engineer in chief, or which his absence, or the necessity of the case shall make expedient.

5thly. To correspond regularly with the engineer in chief.

6thly. To give a monthly account of the state of the works to the committee, or oftener, if required, and to send a duplicate to the engineer in chief.

7thly. To attend each part of the work upon any emergency or difficulty, and also to see all new matters or methods put rightly in hand.

8thly. To survey the materials, and make such purchases thereof as directed by the committee.

9thly. To visit all the works from end to end as often as possible.

N.B. It is supposed that the resident engineer ought to have power of employing a land surveyor, on occasion, to measure and survey the lands, and to have power of discharging any officer under him on neglect of duty.

Surveyors of particular districts

1st. To attend to the orders of the engineer resident.

2dly. To see the proper quantities, qualities, and conversion of the materials committed to his care.

3dly. To order the foremen concerning the works whereon they are to employ themselves.

4thly. To transmit an account weekly of the progress of the works to the engineer resident, and of what materials &c. are wanted.

5thly. To receive the necessary wages from the pay-clerk, and account with him for the money.

6thly. To reside as near as may be to the place where the principal works are under his care, to visit them daily, and the most distant once a week, or as often as possible.

This is a good example of the clarity of Smeaton's directions and it would be hard to improve upon them. He appreciated the problems of the site engineer, saying:

> "The greatest difficulty of all therefore, is to get a proper person for the Resident Engineer; Practical Knowledge in Mechanics is not the only thing wanted to equip a man fully, for this employment requires so great a number of qualifications that I look upon it as impracticable to find them united in one person. I therefore take it for granted, that he will of course be capitally defective in something."[40]

Having advised on management Smeaton was not averse to telling his employers, the Committee of Proprietors, how they should act. He stated the importance of communication in management and, in particular, the need to "preserve a good understanding between the Resident Engineer, and the Committee that directs him", and went on:

> "I would wish the Committee to exert themselves, not in drawing the burthen or directing how it is to be drawn, but in seeing that every Horse in the Team draws steadily, and takes his own share of it. Stone, Wood and Iron, are wrought and put together by mechanical methods, but the greatest work is to keep right the *Animal* part of the Machinery."[40]

He obviously drew on experience when he added: "but the great difficulty is to keep Committees from doing either too little, or too much; too little when any case of difficulty starts, and too much where there is none". Of the day-to-day matters he considered that the Committee should "make all capital Bargains for Land, Stores, Work, &c. and as much as possible enter into these matters". Smeaton was consulted on the merits of doing the work by contract or otherwise, to which he replied: "I look upon it as eligible to do all the Work you properly can by contract", and added:

> "Advertising for Contractors or Materials, if any scarcity of either, I do not disapprove, provided it is not made a *condition* to *prefer* the lowest bidder; the merit of the Tradesman, and the goodness of the Materials, are in those things of superior consideration to the lowness of the Price."[40]

As a consulting engineer Smeaton was also involved with the legal aspects of his clients' business, particularly in the arbitration of disputes. That Smeaton's father was an attorney with a successful law practice in Leeds was obviously an important influence on his son's career. Apart from being sent to London to study law, where he must have absorbed the lawyer's respect for precise language, Smeaton's concept of what is meant to be a professional man, both in terms of ethics and the scale of fees, must surely have been influenced by the legal atmosphere in which he grew up. Even as a civil engineer, however, John Smeaton has claim to a place in legal history.

This relates to a case brought to the Norfolk Assizes in 1782 between Sir Martin Folkes and the Trustees of Wells harbour. The Trustees threatened to cut down an embankment, built in 1758 on land belonging to Folkes, which they claimed had caused the harbour to silt up. At the Lent Assizes Folkes was granted an injunction against the Trustees at which trial Robert Mylne gave his opinion that the embankment was not to blame. In the Easter term a new trial was granted after the defendants appealed saying that they "were surprised by the doctrine and reasoning of Mr. Mylne".[41] The parties were directed to print and exchange the engineering opinions they intended to produce at the next trial. This occurred in the summer term when "They also called Mr Smeaton, an eminent engineer, to show that, in his opinion, the bank was not the cause of the mischief, and that the cutting the bank would not remove it". The judge rejected his evidence as being matter of opinion. The plaintiff's lawyers obtained yet another trial on the basis that the judge had improperly rejected Smeaton's evidence. This last trial came to Court on Thursday 21st November, 1782, and Lord Mansfield delivering the opinion of the Court said:

> "It is objected that Mr Smeaton is going to speak, not as to facts, but as to opinion. That opinion, however, is deduced from facts that are not disputed—the situation of banks, the course of tides and of winds, and the shifting of sands. His opinion, deduced from all these facts, is, that, mathematically speaking, the bank may contribute to the mischief, but not sensi-

bly. Mr Smeaton understands the construction of harbours, the causes of their destruction, and how remedied. In matters of science no other witness can be called.... I have myself received the opinion of Mr Smeaton respecting mills, as a matter of science. The cause of the decay of the harbour is also a matter of science, and still more so, whether the removal of the bank can be beneficial. Of this, such men as Mr Smeaton alone can judge. Therefore we are of opinion that his judgement, formed on facts, was very proper evidence."

The Law Report comments: "This may be regarded as the principal case on the admissibility of matter of opinion. It has been followed and confirmed by a variety of similar decisions."[42]

A study of Smeaton's career shows him to have been a man with a professional view of his life's work. His articulate letters and admirably clear reports speak of his philosophy of approach to design problems and management issues, together with a sense of public service. He was greatly respected both by his contemporaries and subsequent engineers and it was said that he "examined every circumstance connected with his profession with great accuracy".[43] In 1858 Robert Stephenson said: "Smeaton is the greatest philosopher in our profession this country has yet produced",[44] but perhaps James Watt came closest to an accurate assessment of Smeaton's contribution to the development of the profession when he wrote: "his example and precepts have made us all engineers".[45]

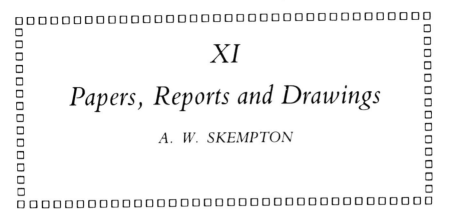

XI

Papers, Reports and Drawings

A. W. SKEMPTON

After Smeaton died Sir Joseph Banks purchased an almost complete set of his drawings and a substantial number of his report books, letter books and so on. These manuscripts were catalogued in some detail. Other papers and notebooks remained at Austhorpe, but they also were listed. We know, therefore, rather exactly the nature and extent of Smeaton's professional papers.

Many of these, not surprisingly, have disappeared during the past nearly two centuries. Some may have been destroyed after his death and a fire in 1850, in London, was probably responsible for the loss of an important part of the missing documents, including the report books. But the whole of Banks' collection of the drawings has survived, as well as several letter books and diaries. Moreover, before it was too late, practically all of Smeaton's reports were published in 1812 in three quarto volumes well illustrated with engraved plates.

Meanwhile in 1791 Smeaton himself published his *magnum opus* on the Eddystone Lighthouse and a long historical report on Ramsgate harbour. All his scientific publications are of course still available in the original journals, but the eighteen papers which he contributed to *Phil. Trans.* were conveniently reprinted in a collected edition in 1814 and, of these, the three on mechanics were reprinted on several other occasions in London and Paris. The *Reports* also appeared in a second edition and the Eddystone book had three editions.

The bibliographic history of this material is outlined in this chapter with brief accounts of the reports printed in Smeaton's lifetime, the two lists of his professional papers, his drawings, and the use made by John Farey in the early nineteenth century of the Banks collection. Some references are also given to surviving letters, reports and plans sent by Smeaton to various clients and friends. Notes on his library and mathematical instruments will be found in Appendix I.

Printed reports and plans

Smeaton followed the normal practice of sending a handwritten report to the client and entering a copy, usually written by a clerk or assistant, in "report books" kept as a permanent record for future reference. In many cases that was the end of the matter, though sometimes the client might have a few further copies made, again by hand. Plans and drawings were dealt with in a similar manner, a copy being kept in the engineer's office.

For some public works, however, especially in the early stages of planning and submission of schemes to Parliament, it would be necessary to distribute a report, and often a map, to the proprietors or commissioners and to people interested in the proposals. Also, a report on work in progress or the results of an enquiry might require quite wide circulation. For these reasons the manuscript would have to be printed and a plan engraved, and this was commonly done within a few weeks after the report and drawings had been received.

At least 26 of Smeaton's reports were printed in this way. Ten of them are accompanied by a map or plan and in addition five maps were issued separately. The canal engineer Robert Whitworth had more maps published but, so far as reports are concerned, Smeaton's outnumber those of any other engineer in the eighteenth century.

It seems to have been usual to issue more copies than were immediately needed (for instance, 1,000 copies of Smeaton's report on the River Lee Navigation were ordered to be printed)[1] and spare copies circulated among the profession, much as offprints do today. To quote a single example, Rennie had nearly a dozen of Smeaton's printed reports in his possession around 1796 even though few, if any, of them related directly to works on which he was or had been engaged.[2] Nevertheless, demand sometimes outstripped supply and second editions had to be produced. This applies to both of Smeaton's reports on the Forth & Clyde Canal. A report, when relevant to later investigations, might also be reprinted many years after its first issue; as happened with his report on King's Lynn harbour.

The following list is believed to be complete, though one or two particularly elusive reports may have been missed.[3] The separate printing in 1760 of the "Experimental Enquiry" *Phil. Trans.* paper is included, and also the printed correspondence on the Grand Canal of Ireland.

Calder & Hebble Navigation, map	1757
Calder & Hebble Navigation, report	1757
River Clyde improvement, map	1758
River Wear Navigation, map	1759
Experimental Enquiry, paper + 3 plates	1760
Blackfriars Bridge, tract	1760
Trent & Mersey Canal, map	1760
Louth Navigation, report	1761
Witham Drainage, report	1761
(jointly with John Grundy and	
Langley Edwards)	
Rye harbour, report + map	1763
Holderness Drainage, map	1764
(jointly with John Grundy)	
Forth & Clyde Canal, report + 2 maps	1764
Bristol harbour, report + plan	1765
River Lee Navigation, report + map	1766
London Bridge waterworks	1767
Forth & Clyde Canal, 2nd report + map	1767
Forth & Clyde Canal, review	1768
King's Lynn harbour, report	1767
Lewes Laughton Drainage, report + map	1768
North Level Drainage, report	1768
(+ section by William Elstobb)	
Dover harbour, report + plan	1769
Edinburgh North Bridge, report	1769
(jointly with John Adam and	
John Baxter)	
Aberdeen harbour, report	1770
Tyne Bridge, report	1772
(jointly with John Wooler)	
Haddlesey Canal, report	1772
Grand Canal, Ireland, letters	1773
Grand Canal, Ireland, report	1773
Hatfield Chase Drainage, report + map	1776
Bridlington piers, report	1778
Sunderland harbour, report	1780
Wells harbour, report	1782
Hexham Bridge, memorial	1783
Ramsgate harbour, report + 2 plans	1791

A

R E V I E W

O F

SEVERAL MATTERS

RELATIVE TO

The FORTH and CLYDE Navigation,
as now settled by Act of Parliament :

W I T H

Some OBSERVATIONS on the Reports

O F

Mess. Brindley, Yeoman, and Golburne.

By JOHN SMEATON, Civil Engineer, and F. R. S.

[*Published by order of a General Meeting of the Company of Proprietors
of the* Forth *and* Clyde *Navigation* (1st November 1768.)
for the use of the Proprietors.]

Printed by R. Fleming and A. Neill.
M,DCC,LXVIII.

Fig. 53. Title page of Review of Forth & Clyde Canal, 1768

Smeaton's *Historical Report on Ramsgate Harbour* occupies a special place among the printed reports, on account of its length (94 pages in large octavo) and its comparatively frequent presence in libraries. It was written by order of the Harbour Trustees, and presumably printed at their expense, but clearly the circulation must have been widespread. There are two editions: one issued in the spring of 1791 and the second, with an extra page of text, in the autumn of that year.

Typically the reports run to about 20 pages of quarto or about 8 pages of foolscap; in grey or marbled wrappers or "stitched as issued", with or without a folding engraved plan and a title page. The shortest reports are printed simply on two or three sides of a double foolscap sheet with a docket title on the back page.

It is interesting to note that the words "civil engineer" appear for the first time on the title page of any eighteenth-century publication in Smeaton's *Review of Several Matters relative to the Forth and Clyde Navigation*, written and printed in 1768 (Fig. 53). Indeed there is only one earlier known example of the term, in a London directory of 1763 where Smeaton and Thomas Yeoman are both described as "surveyor and civil engineer".[4]

Just as the reports are often fine examples of printing, so the maps display the art of engraving. Moreover the maps exemplify the change from an early, more decorative style (as in the Calder & Hebble map of 1757) to a plainer but more precise form of topographic representation (as in the River Lee map of 1766).

Smeaton's printed reports are tangible and evocative mementoes of his work as a civil engineer. They have become scarce and desirable collector's items; but examples can be seen in major libraries such as the British Museum, the National Library of Scotland, the Universities of London and Cambridge, and the Institution of Civil Engineers.

The Eddystone book
In his introduction to this book Smeaton remarks:

"I have myself always found that exact accounts of buildings which were in any degree remarkable, and actually executed, were much more instructive to my mind, than *systematical* writings; and when a new method of operation, or a new Idea is once set forth, it is impossible to say, to how many good purposes it may by ingenious men be applied."

With these sentiments one can heartily agree, and be thankful that

Smeaton took the trouble to write this classic of engineering literature.

> "Some progress [he says] was made in the present work, between the time of compleating the building and the year 1763; and his Majesty having signified his pleasure to honour the design with his patronage, several drawings were prepared, and engraven, some of which were executed by the late celebrated Mr Edward Rooker: but by the time matters were brought into this train, I found myself so exceedingly pressed with business in my profession of a civil Engineer . . . and the consequent succession of engagements . . . that a total stop [was put] to any further proceeding upon a description of the Edystone Lighthouse till the year 1783."

He then resumed work on the book but "found much more difficulty in writing, than in building; as well as a greater length of time, and application of mind, to be required", and not until 1790 was the task completed. The volume, of 142 pages in large folio, with 23 plates (mostly engraved by Rooker and James Record), is printed on the highest quality paper supplied at no extra charge by "my friend Mr Whatman". Smeaton gratefully acknowledges the help of three other friends: John Michell and Nicholas Walton, in revising the text to improve its style, and Charles Blagden,

> "who has been so obliging as to overlook the greatest part of the printed proofs, with much advantage to the work. I say the greatest part, as in justice to him, I must observe, that I was obliged to send several of the sheets to the press, without his seeing them. Whenever therefore a more than ordinary deficiency occurs, my reader may conclude *that* sheet never went to Dr Blagden."

The book appeared early in 1791 in a limited edition produced at Smeaton's own expense. He modestly anticipated a restricted sale, but a second edition had to be issued in 1793; this time with the bookseller George Nicol acting as publisher, and with a few textual corrections by Alexander Aubert. The second edition sold at £3–3s–0d in boards. By about 1810 the stock must have been practically exhausted and, with help from the Society of Civil Engineers in the form of a loan of the original copper plates, which had come into their possession from Smeaton's daughter Mary Dixon, Messrs Longman published a third edition in 1813. This was issued in a printing of 300 copies selling at £6–6s–0d in half leather.[5]

There is ample evidence that Smeaton took enormous care in writing the Eddystone book and considered it to be one of his greatest achievements. He presented a copy, perhaps one of the earliest to come from the press, to the Royal Society on 21st January, 1791.

Scientific publications

A youthful account of some electrical experiments appeared in the *Gentleman's Magazine* in January 1747 and one of his last contributions, on Westgarth's water pressure engine, was printed in *Trans. Soc. Arts*, vol. 5 (1787); but all the rest of Smeaton's scientific papers were published in *Phil. Trans. Roy. Soc.*

The first six of these, dating from 1750 to 1754, include four papers on scientific instruments, one on a new pulley tackle and another on a steam engine; then came two in 1757–58 describing field observations on the effects of lightning and on air temperatures. His first contribution to engineering science was the famous "Experimental Enquiry concerning the Natural Powers of Water and Wind...", presented in 1759. Nine busy years of practice followed without any further published papers, but three on astronomical topics were read in 1768–69 and, after a short note on a new hygrometer, Smeaton wrote up his experimental investigations on mechanic power in 1776. The companion paper on impact came out in 1782, a masterly account of methods of dividing (i.e. graduation of instruments) appeared in 1785, and finally two astronomical papers in 1787–88.

All eighteen of the *Phil. Trans.* papers were reprinted in 1814, employing the original copper plates loaned by the Royal Society. John Rennie acted as editor and in a few cases used copies which had belonged to Smeaton with corrections in his own hand; these were lent by Mary Dixon. Longman published the volume, under the title *Miscellaneous Papers of John Smeaton, Civil Engineer*, in an edition of 500, price £1–11s–6d in boards.[5]

The "Experimental Enquiry" was issued as a separate monograph in 1760. With the original plates, but a new setting of the type, this is now one of the rarest of Smeaton's publications. The three papers on mechanics (i.e. the Experimental Enquiry and the papers on mechanic power and impact) were reprinted in 1794 in the form of a book of 114 pages with 5 plates published by I. & J. Taylor. A second edition had to be printed in 1796. Then in 1810 these three papers appeared in a French translation by P. S. Girard, published in Paris, and this also required a second edition in 1827. Finally, they were included (together with papers by Venturi and Thomas Young) in Tredgold's *Tracts on Hydraulics*. First published by Josiah Taylor in 1826, this too had a second edition in 1836 and even a third so late as 1862. Thus, following its first appearance in *Phil. Trans.*, the "Experimental Enquiry" was reprinted no less than nine times during a period of just over 100 years.

Professional papers

Smeaton died in October 1792 and his will was proved 3 months later. Soon afterwards Sir Joseph Banks, President of the Royal Society, arranged with Smeaton's daughters to purchase a mass of their father's engineering papers. This he did partly as a keen collector of scientific manuscripts but also as an admirer, and friend, of Smeaton himself. The material arrived at Banks' house in Soho Square in September 1793 and was then listed, on 14 foolscap pages, under the title "A Catalogue of the Papers of the late Mr Smeaton, purchased from the Executors by Sir Jos. Banks".[6] The contents may be summarised as follows (with editorial comments in square brackets).

    (i) Reports and Estimates.
        Vol. 1 from Aug 1760 to Sep 1763
        Vol. 2 from Sep 1763 to Dec 1764
        Vol. 3 from Dec 1764 to Sep 1767
        Vol. 4 from Sep 1767 to Jun 1769
        Vol. 5 from Jul 1769 to Dec 1773
        Vol. 6 from Jan 1774 to Apr 1778
        Vol. 7 from Apr 1778 to Aug 1787
        [With some other pieces, these were published in the
        three volumes of *Reports* (1812); see below.]

   (ii) General Letter Books, being Letters sent & received.
        [Vols 1–8, May 1759–July 1767.]

  (iii) Letter Books of Letters sent.
        [Vols 9–17, July 1767–June 1792.]

  (iv) Letter Books of Letters received.
        [Vols 9–14, Jan. 1767–Apr. 1779.]

   (v) Bundles of Letters received.
        [Jan. 1780–July 1792.]

  (vi) Philosophical Letters sent & received.
        [Vol. 1, 1770–78; Vol. 2, 1778– .]

 (vii) Calder Navigation Journals.
        [2 Vols, May 1760–Dec. 1765.]

(viii) Calder Navigation Letter Books.
        [3 Vols, Jan. 1760–Feb. 1766.]

  (ix) Wear Navigation Letter Book.
        [Oct. 1760–Aug. 1761.]

   (x) Forth & Clyde Canal Letter Books.
        [4 Vols, Mar. 1768–Apr. 1779.]

  (xi) Loose papers chiefly originals that have been copied into the Books
        of Reports and Estimates, also printed Reports of Mr Smeaton and
        other Engineers.
        [Listed as site locations under the following headings: Harbours

Docks & Lights, 34 items; Fen Drainage, Supply of Water, Coal Pits, Fire Engines, 17 items; Canal Navigations, 18 items; River Navigations, 15 items; Bridges, 18 items. About three-quarters of these can be identified in *Reports* (1812); the remaining 25 items are probably printed reports by other engineers.]

(xii) Bundles of Papers.

[Classified under headings such as: Astronomical Instruments, Astronomical Observations and Computations, Philosophical Instruments, Papers published in Transactions, Fire Engines, Geering Wheels, Experiments relating to Engineery, Mechanic Powers, Mills Mines & Coal Pits.]

(xiii) Things unarranged.

[Includes three short papers on Coal Measure, Mills (executed) and Mortar, all printed in *Reports*, and various other items together with Tables and Inventions.]

(xiv) Calculation Books.

Nos. 2–6,   1755–65
Nos. 8–15, 1767–

[No. 1 is noted as missing and No. 7 as lost in the box of papers stolen coming from London, 4th March, 1767.]

(xv) Miscellaneous Observations. No. 1; No. 2, begun in 1765.

(xvi) Plans and Drawings.

[The list of these runs to 6 pages, under headings such as Bridges, Navigations, Mills, Fire Engines, Drainage, Harbours, Piers and Lighthouses. This is the collection of drawings later arranged and annotated by John Farey, and now in the Royal Society: see below.]

To this catalogue can be added

(xvii) Machine Letter Books.

[Vols 1–4, 1781–92. So called as they contain copies of outgoing letters, made on Watt's copying machine: presumably duplicates of those in the Letter Books of letters sent. Banks received them in May 1794. They were sold at Sotheby's in 1886,[7] and purchased by the Institution of Civil Engineers through a book dealer. Several letters are missing from these volumes.]

It has long been known that some other Smeaton manuscripts are in Trinity House, London:

MS.114   Journal of a Five Weeks Tour in Flanders & Holland in the Year 1755.
[This was published in 1938 by the Newcomen Society.[8] Fig. 54 is a facsimile of the first page, in Smeaton's handwriting.]

MS.113   Copy of a Journal to Flanders & Holland.
[A fair copy of the above, in a different hand.]

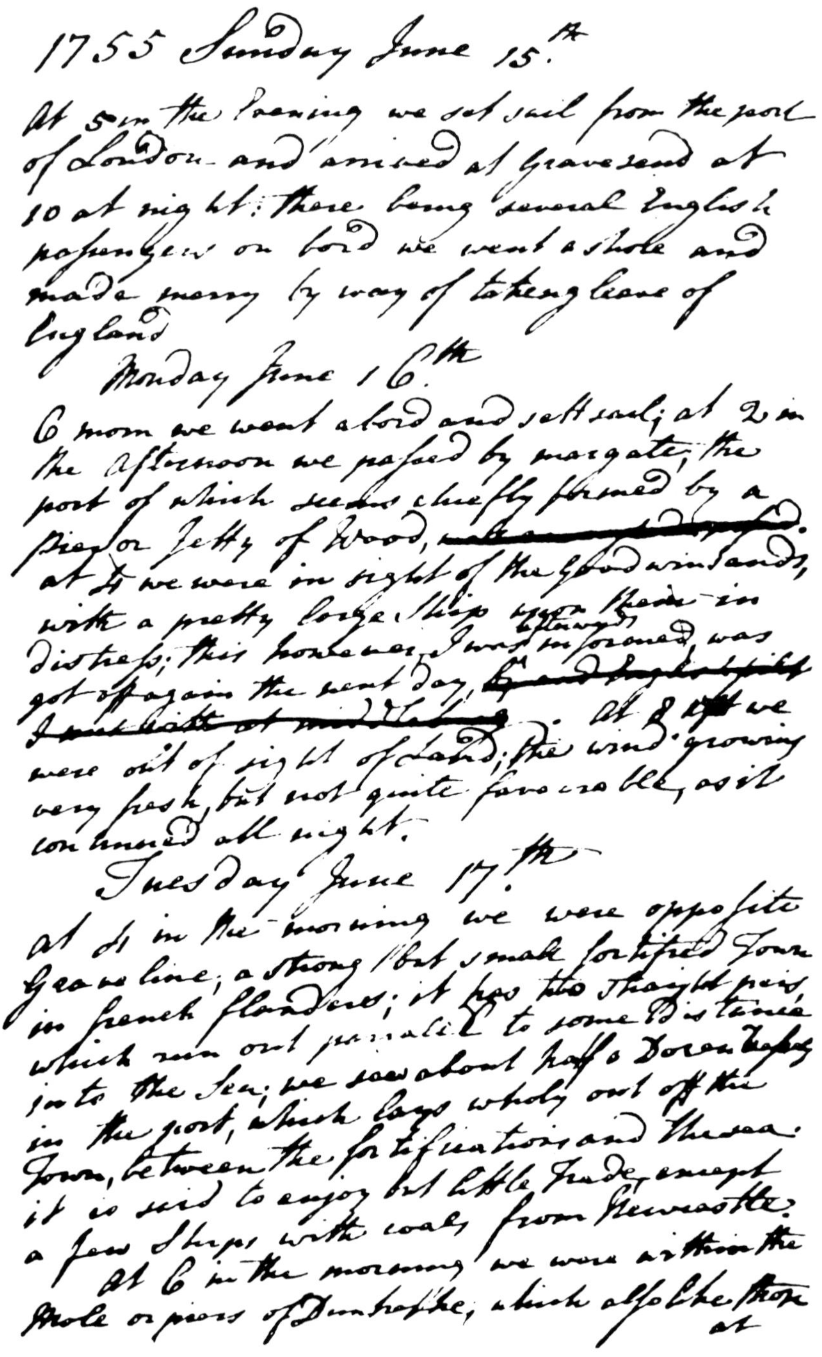

1755 Sunday June 15th.

At 5 in the Evening we set sail from the port of London and arrived at Gravesend at 10 at night: there being several English passengers on board we went ashore and made merry by way of taking leave of England

Monday June 16th

6 morn we went aboard and set sail; at 2 in the afternoon we passed by margate; the port of which seems chiefly formed by a Pier or Jetty of Wood, ~~————~~. at 4 we were in sight of the Goodwin sands, with a pretty large Ship upon them in distress; this however, I was afterwards informed was got off again the next day, ~~————————~~. At 8 we were out of sight of Land; the wind growing very fresh, but not quite favourable, as it continued all night.

Tuesday June 17th.

at 4 in the morning we were opposite Gravesline, a strong but small fortified Town in french flanders; it has tho' the straight pier which run out parallel to some distance into the Sea; we saw about half a Dozen ships in the port, which lays wholly out of the Town, between the fortifications and the sea. it is said to enjoy but little Trade, except a few Ships with coals from Newcastle; At 6 in the morning we were within the Mole or piers of Dunkirk; which also like those at

Fig. 54. Facsimile of the first page of Smeaton's diary of his journey to the Low Countries, 1755

MS.115   [A 45-page portion, untitled, of what appear to be early notes for the Eddystone book.]
MS.116   Austhorpe Journal 1781.
         [Smeaton's day-to-day Austhorpe diary.]
MS.117   Minute Book 1782 & 1783.
         [A similar journal for London and out-of-town visits with some interpolated notes.]
MS.118   Watch Book.
         [Records of the "going" of a very accurate watch kept at Austhorpe, from April 1785 to October 1791.]

These documents, or some of them, were purchased in 1899 from Miss A. E. Croft Brooke,[9] Smeaton's great-granddaughter. The notebooks were rebound in 1909 by Douglas Cockerell. There are also two copies of the 1760 reprint of the "Experimental Enquiry".

Robert Mylne, in the Preface (1797) to *Reports*, stated that Banks had purchased all of Smeaton's papers, and this has been the general view ever since. However, following the comparatively recent discovery of the Banks catalogue some doubts have arisen because it was found not to include the Trinity House material or a letter book acquired by the Institution of Civil Engineers in 1972. There has always been a difficulty also in explaining the conspicuous absence in the Royal Society collection, which came from Banks (via John Farey), of any of Smeaton's drawings for the Eddystone.

However, these problems were resolved in 1980 when I found on five back pages of MS. 118 another list of Smeaton's papers. As this notebook was certainly kept at Austhorpe the papers listed in it surely must have been there; and only one conclusion seems to be possible, namely that this batch of material remained at Smeaton's home and was preserved, at least in part, by the Brooke family.

The list, not in Smeaton's hand, was written after 1790. Its contents are summarised below.

(1)   Private Letter Books.
      [One of these, for 1764, eventually came into the possession of Sir Alexander Gibb. It is now, along with the Machine Letters, in the Institution of Civil Engineers.[10] By an extraordinary chance the back pages contain the daily accounts of Smeaton's instrument-making workshop from September 1751 to February 1752.]
(2)   Derwentwater Letter Books.
      [These would be official letters relating to the Greenwich Hospital estates for which Smeaton, jointly with Nicholas Walton, was agent from 1765 to 1777.]
(3)   Ravensbourn Letter Books.

(4)   Clyde Navigation Book.
(5)   Perth Bridge Accts.
(6)   Calder Bridges.
(7)   Printed Papers relating to the Calder.
(8)   Mr Eyes's Plan of the Calder extension to Sowerby Bridge.
(9)   Papers relating to Leeds & Selby Canals.
(10) Aire & Calder Navigation, Papers.
(11) Ditto, Plans as delivered to the Committee 1774.
(12) Mr Smeaton's MSS Papers on Aire & Calder.
(13) Prints of Aire Navigation.
(14) Temple Newsam Engine Papers.
(15) Ramsgate Harbour Book.
(16) Original Draughts of Edystone Book.
(17) Edystone Plans.
(18) Edystone Papers.
(19) Printers Proofs of Edystone.
(20) MSS Books relating to Edystone L.H.
      [Trinity House MS. 115 may be from this lot.]
(21) Spurn Papers.
(22) Calculation Book.
      [Presumably the missing Vol. 1, see item (xiv) in the Banks catalogue.]
(23) Original Journal to Flanders & Holland 1755.
      [i.e. Trinity House MS. 114.]
(24) Minutes and Investigations on Building Materials.
(25) Mill Book, 1st.
(26) [The "Watch Book" (Trinity House MS. 118) can be added as it contains the list itself.]

There are several other entries and a few "Printed Books", or tracts, including spare copies of the five reprinted *Phil. Trans.* papers by Smeaton, his Dover harbour report, and a reprint of the celebrated paper "Experiments on Air" by his friend Henry Cavendish.

In 1858 Thomas Sutcliffe, researching for Samuel Smiles,[11] heard a story that long after Smeaton died "a fire was made in the yard [at Austhorpe] and lots of papers and books burnt", being then reckoned as so much "rubbish". Though probably an exaggeration this may explain the loss of some of the above items; and it is easy to suggest that the collection bought by Banks came from Gray's Inn. However that may be, the two lists together appear to constitute a full record of Smeaton's professional papers as they existed in 1792.

In addition he had an extensive library of printed books. This was purchased by the London bookseller John Egerton and offered for sale in 1794; unfortunately along with books from other owners.

Nevertheless it is possible to identify with reasonable certainty about 50 of the technical books which belonged to Smeaton. These are listed in Appendix I together with notes on a sale catalogue of his mathematical instruments and workshop equipment.

Other original documents
Apart from the papers and books in Smeaton's own possession there were of course many letters, plans and manuscript reports sent to his friends and clients. Some of these have been preserved in various archives. Further research is required before a complete list can be compiled but the following may be mentioned by way of illustration.

British Museum
  Letters to Benjamin Wilson, 1744–64.
Birmingham Reference Library
  Reports on River Clyde, 1755 and 1758.
  Letters to Boulton & Watt, 1778–79.
Newcastle University Library
  Plan for a bridge at Hexham, 1756.
Royal Scottish Museum
  Drawings and models of Eddystone Lighthouse; most if not all made by Josias Jessop in 1757 and sent by Smeaton to Robert Weston.[12]
Leeds City Archives
  Plan of Adlingfleet Drainage, 1764.
  Letters on Aire & Calder Navigation, 1771–73.
Metropolitan Water Division
  Report on New River Head engine, 1766.
  Report on New River gauge, 1781.
Ramsgate Public Library
  Reports and letters on the harbour, 1774–91.
National Library of Scotland
  Report on Dysart harbour, 1758.
  Further reports and letters on Ramsgate harbour, 1777–88.
Sheffield Public Library
  Report on Greasborough Canal, 1775.
York Waterworks
  Drawings of the steam engine, 1781–84.
Bristol Record Office
  Report on proposals for the floating harbour, 1789.
Gloucestershire Record Office
  Reports on Thames & Severn Canal, 1789.

Reports, 1812

The 26 reports printed in Smeaton's lifetime represent a small (if important) part of his total output, and in any case few of them would have been readily available by the end of the century. So in 1795 the Society of Civil Engineers resolved to appoint a committee to carry out the task of publishing a complete set of his reports, which would be a service to the profession and an appropriate memorial to their great founder-member.[5] Banks generously waived any financial claim to copyright, and the seven Report Books (item (i) in Banks' catalogue) were delivered in May of that year to Robert Mylne, Treasurer of the Society and chairman of the committee. The other committee members were William Jessop, Captain Huddart, John Rennie and Sir Joseph Banks. A few months later Dr Charles Hutton agreed to act as editor and copying of the reports began.

Samuel Brooke, a leading London printer and Jessop's brother-in-law, took on the job of printing the first volume and William Faden, the cartographer, accepted responsibility for selling it. Each committee member paid £40 towards the cost of publication. Page proofs were ready by 1797. Mylne then wrote an interesting Preface, Mary Dixon contributed a lively sketch of her father's character and Hutton composed a brief biography. It was decided to include a portrait frontispiece, the preparation of which caused a short delay, and Vol. 1 finally appeared on sale in March 1798 at 18s in boards.

Without plates, except for the portrait, and covering only a third of Smeaton's career, the volume had limited appeal and sold slowly. Nevertheless the committee kept to their original plan. In February 1806 a call was made on all members of the Society for a 5 guinea subscription towards the cost of printing the remaining reports, in two further volumes, and of engraving a considerable number of plates. The response was quite good but even so it fell short of the estimates, and 3 years passed before a publisher, Messrs Longman, could be found to undertake the business.

The rest of Banks' collection of Smeaton papers was then handed over to John Farey, a young man already highly skilled as an engineering draughtsman, whose father, John Farey senior, was well known to Banks and other members of the committee as a practical geologist and writer of technical articles. Farey began the delicate process of reducing the drawings selected for reproduction, to quarto size, ready for the engraver Wilson Lowry; and the production of 72 plates, the number finally decided upon, took a further 3 years. Several of the plates are reproduced in the present book.

Meanwhile Mylne delivered to Longman the remaining stock of the printed sheets of Vol. 1; the printing of Vols 2 and 3 and the plates reached completion in 1812 and all three volumes, in an edition of 500 copies, came on sale in August of that year at a price of £7–7s–0d in boards. As then issued the *Reports* comprised:

Vol. 1 with portrait frontispiece and the original (1797) letterpress, except for a new title page, and 33 plates: 446 pp.
Vol. 2 with 23 plates: 452 pp.
Vol. 3 with 16 plates: 428 pp.

A second edition in two volumes, but with an unabridged text and all the plates, was published by M. Taylor in 1837.

No other printed collection of an engineer's reports is in existence. It is, however, not quite complete and the missing items as known at present are:

Westminster Bridge cofferdam	1748
Lochar Moss Drainage	1754
River Clyde improvement	1755
Adlingfleet Drainage	1755
Calder & Hebble Navigation	1757
Dysart harbour	1758
River Clyde (two reports)	1758
New River Head engine	1766
London Bridge Waterworks	1767
Peterhead harbour	1772
Ramsgate harbour	1774
Greasbrough Canal	1775
Ramsgate harbour	1777
New River gauge	1781
Ramsgate harbour	1787
Ramsgate harbour (two reports)	1788
Bristol floating harbour	1789
Thames & Severn Canal	1789

Presumably the Ramsgate reports were omitted in favour of the long historical account of this harbour which is reprinted in Vol. 3. The five other reports of the period 1760–87 appear not to have been copied into the report books. All pre-1760 reports were either overlooked or rejected, but of those later than 1787 the committee missed only the reports on Bristol and the Thames & Severn Canal; and to put the matter in perspective, the *Reports* contain about 250 items as compared with the twenty listed above.

It is to be noted, however, that a number of progress and interim reports, which can be found in minute books such as those of the Forth & Clyde Canal, may have been entered by Smeaton in his letter books and are not included in the three volumes published in 1812.

John Farey and the Smeaton papers
Farey, while working on the *Reports*, had permission from Sir Joseph Banks to select and use other drawings from his Smeaton collection as illustrations to articles appearing in Rees' *Cyclopaedia*.[13] From about 1812 Farey himself began contributing articles to this publication and in doing so drew quite substantially on the Banks papers. Thus he provides descriptions and drawings of Smeaton's experimental steam engine of 1769, the Long Benton winding engine of 1777, and a flour-mill at Deptford dockyard designed in 1781, to mention only three examples. Moreover he made use of a manuscript on hydraulic machines[14] and gives the only published account of Smeaton's work on the flow of water in pipes (Chapter II).

Then, in 1827, Farey issued his monumental *Treatise on the Steam Engine*, long sections of which are based, often with quotations, on Smeaton's notes, calculations and letters. Indeed the *Treatise* depends to an important degree on this material, just as Chapter VIII of the present book depends largely on the *Treatise*. Farey also contributed several notes to the Institution of Civil Engineers (of which he was a member from 1826) summarising or reproducing material from the Smeaton manuscripts: the measurement of horse power, for instance, and a letter on flow in open channels (Chapter VI).

Smeaton's drawings
After Banks' death in 1820 it seems that the Smeaton papers, which had been on loan to Farey, now came into his possession. In 1821 he arranged the drawings in six very large volumes under the headings:

I   Windmills and Watermills for Grinding Corn
II Mills for various Purposes
III Fire Engines for Raising Water
IV Bridges and Buildings
V   Canal Works, Sluices and Harbours
VI Canals, River Navigations [and Fen Drainage].

Many of the drawings are annotated by Farey, using the letter books and other papers as source material. The 72 plates in *Reports* were selected for this collection and Farey similarly reproduced another seven, also engraved by Lowry, in his *Treatise*, while a further ten appear as illustrations to his own and other articles in Rees.

It is clear that Farey still had the papers and drawings in the 1830s and 1840s. Then in 1850 considerable portions of his library were damaged or destroyed by fire in his London house and poor Farey, who soon afterwards suffered the loss of his wife, never fully recovered from the shock.[15] He died in 1851.

The probability is that most of the Smeaton papers disappeared in the fire. However, the drawings did survive and passed to Farey's son who bequeathed them to the Royal Society in 1913.[16] They have been catalogued and rebound, keeping to Farey's own folio numbering system.[17]

This wonderful collection includes rather more than 1,000 drawings from Smeaton's office, about 50 drawings by other engineers, and 100 engravings. As previously explained, the drawings left at Austhorpe, such as the Eddystone plans (which he obviously had to hand when writing the book), and some others, were never incorporated. In general, however, the collection is remarkably complete, in excellent condition, and of unique interest.

APPENDIX I

Smeaton's Library and Instruments

In 1794 the London bookseller John Egerton issued a printed *Catalogue of Books, including the Library of John Smeaton, Esq. FRS . . . and many other collections lately purchased*. The books belonging to Smeaton are not identified specifically, with the exception of ten volumes of tracts, but it cannot be mere coincidence that most of the works (Belidor, Desaguliers, Maclaurin, Wren, and a dozen others) to which he refers in his own publications happen to appear in the catalogue. The catalogue also includes Clare's *Motion of Fluids*, a copy of which with Smeaton's signature is in Leeds Reference Library, and Pryce's *Mineralogia* to which he was a subscriber; he often refers to "Dutch mill books" and, significantly, two of these (by Boeckler and Leupold) are listed; and though it may seem odd to find Carburi's account of the statue to Peter the Great, this is mentioned in the *Eddystone* and the reason becomes clear when we find the sub-title to be "relation des travaux et des moyens méchaniques pour transporter à Petersbourg un rocher des trois millions pesant, destiné à servir de base à la statue équestre de cet empereur".

By this kind of detective work it is possible to establish about 30 books as having been in Smeaton's possession. Moreover, as the catalogue does not list many books on mechanics, while giving prominence to his name on the title page, it seems a fairly safe assumption that the majority of works on this and related topics were his. Some cautious guesswork therefore is admittedly involved in adding a further 20 books on this basis, but the results are thought to be worth recording as a more or less reliable record of the technical section of Smeaton's library. Doubtless his collection contained numerous books of a more general nature, though there is no way of separating these from the hundreds of such items in Egerton's catalogue.

With Smeaton's youth can be associated several of the books on mathematics and physics published around 1740; certainly Clare's *Fluids* and Smith's *Optics*, while in 1744 he was writing from Austhorpe to Benjamin Wilson on the translation (from the Latin) of various passages in Flamsteed. Stone's *Mathematical Instruments* was probably another early acquisition, so were the works of Gravesande and Desaguliers, and he was well acquainted with Belidor and the Dutch mill books before setting off on his journey to the Low Countries in 1755. For civil engineering, in the strict sense, Belidor stands out as the main source, though as we have seen in Chapter XI about 25 printed reports by other engineers were among Smeaton's professional papers (item (xi) in the Banks collection). Further, there were in his library the ten volumes of tracts "collected by Mr Smeaton", and a few words of explanation concerning these may be given.

They would have contained reprints of papers by Smeaton's scientific acquaintances, various pamphlets and short works (of which Labelye's *Foundations of Westminster Bridge* is a likely example). It was common practice to bind such items together, either on a subject basis or simply in groups as they came to hand. Such collections, some still in their original bindings, can be seen in the British Museum, the Institution of Civil Engineers, and other libraries; but regrettably not one of Smeaton's volumes has so far been traced.

Finally, a note on prices. The tracts were offered at 4½ guineas; folios ranged from about 15s to 3½ guineas for the *Eddystone*; quartos from 7s–6d (for a probably well used Maclaurin) to a guinea for Emerson's *Mechanics*, listed as "scarce", and 2½ guineas for the two volumes of Desaguliers; octavos were typically around 4s to 7s.

Titles in the following list have been expanded from those given by Egerton, the dates checked and details of editions added, using the *British Museum Catalogue of Printed Books* (1965) supplemented by the *National Union Catalog* (1968–80).

Acts of Parliament on canals.

Alberti, L. B. *The Architecture of Alberti* (trans. by Leoni). London, 1755. fol.

Badeslade, T. *Ancient and Present State of the Navigation of King's Lyn.* 2nd edn. London, 1766. fol.

Bailey, W. *Mechanical machines . . . adopted by the Society of Arts* (revised edn). 2 vols. London, 1782. fol.

Barrow, I. *Geometrical Lectures* (trans. by Stone). London, 1735. 8vo.

Belidor, B. F. de. *Architecture hydraulique.* 4 vols. Paris, 1737–53. 4to.

Birch, T. *History of the Royal Society.* 4 vols. London, 1756–57. 4to.

Boeckler, G. A. *Theatrum machinarum novum.* Cologne, 1662. fol.

Boyle, R. *Philosophical Works of the Hon. Robert Boyle* (ed. by Shaw). 3 vols. London, 1725. 4to.

Carburi, M. *Monument élevé à la gloire de Peirre-le-Grand.* Paris, 1777. fol.

Chambers, W. *Treatise on Civil Architecture.* London, 1759. fol.

Clare, M. *The Motion of Fluids.* London, 1735. 8vo.

Cotes, R. *Hydrostatical and Pneumatical Lectures.* London, 1738. 8vo.

Cumming, A. *Elements of clock and watch-work.* London, 1766. 4to.

Desaguliers, J. T. *A Course of Experimental Philosophy.* 2nd edn. 2 vols. London, 1744–45. 4to.

Du Buat, P. L. G. *Principes d'hydraulique.* 2nd edn. 2 vols. Paris, 1786. 8vo.

Dugdale, W. *History of Imbanking and Draining* (ed. Cole). 2nd edn. London, 1772. fol.

Emerson, W. *Principles of Mechanicks.* 2nd edn. London, 1758. 4to.

Ferguson, J. *Lectures on select subjects in Mechanics, Hydrostatics, Pneumatics and Optics.* 2nd edn. London, 1764. 8vo.

Ferguson, J. *Select Mechanical Exercises.* London, 1773. 8vo.

Flamsteed, J. *Historia ceolestis.* 2nd edn. 3 vols. London, 1725. fol. [Smeaton seems also to have had the single-volume 1712 edn.]

Fréart, R. *Parallel of the ancient architecture and the modern* (trans. by Evelyn). 4th edn. London, 1733. fol.

Gravesande, W. J. S. *Mathematical Elements of Natural Philosophy* (trans. by Desaguliers). 6th edn. 2 vols. London, 1747. 4to.

Gregory, D. *Elements of physical and geometrical Astronomy* (trans. by Stone). 2 vols. London, 1726. 8vo.

Hammond, N. *The Elements of Algebra.* London, 1742. 8vo.

Hatton, T. *An introduction to the mechanical part of clock and watch work.* London, 1773. 8vo.

Le Monnier, P. C. *Histoire céleste.* Paris, 1741. 4to.

Leupold, J. *Theatrum machinarum.* Leipzig, 1724. fol.

Maclaurin, C. *An Account of Isaac Newton's philosophical Discoveries.* London, 1748. 4to.

Martin, B. *The young Trigonometer's Compleat Guide.* 2 vols. London, 1736. 8vo.

Martin, B. *Logarithmologia: or the whole doctrine of logarithms.* London, 1740. 8vo.

Maskelyne, N. *The British Mariner's Guide.* London, 1763. 4to.

Maskelyne, N. *Astronomical Observations made at the Royal Observatory 1765 to 1769.* London, 1774. fol.

Newton, I. *Principia Mathematica* (trans. by Motte). 2 vols. London, 1729. 8vo.

Newton, I. *Opticks.* 4th edn. London, 1730. 8vo.

Perrault, C. *Recueil de plusieurs machines.* Paris, 1700. 4to.

Priestley, J. *History and present state of Electricity.* 2nd edn. London, 1769. 4to.

Priestley, J. *History and present state of discoveries relating to Vision, Light and Colours.* 2 vols. London, 1772. 4to.

Pryce, W. *Mineralogia Cornubiensis.* London, 1778. fol.

Semple, G. *Treatise on building in water.* Dublin, 1776. 4to.

Smeaton, J. *Experiments upon a machine for measuring the way of a ship at sea.* [London], 1754, 4to.

Smeaton, J. *Experimental Enquiry on the natural powers of water and wind.* [London], 1760. 4to.

Smeaton, J. *Observations on the Right Ascension and Declination of Mercury.* [London, 1787.] 4to.

Smeaton, J. *Description of an improvement in the application of the quadrant of altitude.* [London, 1789.] 4to.

Smeaton, J. *Narrative of the building ... of the Edystone Lighthouse.* London, 1791. fol.

Smith, R. *Compleat System of Opticks.* 2 vols. Cambridge, 1738. 4to.

Stone, E. *Construction and principal uses of mathematical instruments* (trans. from Bion with additions). London, 1723. fol.

Stone, E. *Ibid.*, 2nd. edn with supplement. London, 1758. fol.

Switzer, S. *An introduction to a general system of hydrostaticks and hydraulicks.* 2 vols. London, 1729. 4to.

Tracts. Philosophical and other Tracts, collected by Mr Smeaton. 10 vols.

Vitruvius. *Les dix livres d'architecture* (trans, and ed. by Perrault). 2nd edn. Paris, 1684. fol.

Watson, R. *Chemical Essays.* 5 vols. London, 1784–87. 8vo.

Wood, R. *The Ruins of Balbec.* London, 1757. fol.

Wren, S. *Parentalia; or Memoirs of the family of Wren.* London, 1750. fol.

A book not traced in the catalogue but which can be added to the list with some confidence is:

Maclaurin, C. *A Treatise on Fluxions.* 2 vols. Edinburgh, 1742. 4to.

Also two tracts known to have been at Austhorpe:

Cavendish, H. *Experiments on Air.* London, 1784. 4to

Smeaton, J. *Description of a new Pyrometer.* [London, 1755.] 4to.

In April 1793 appeared a printed *Catalogue of the Valuable Collection of curious Astronomical, Philosophical, Optical and Mathematical Instruments ... and Implements for working ... the truly genuine property of John Smeaton, Esq. Civil Engineer and FRS deceased. Which, by Order of the Executors will be sold by Auction by Mr Herring at the Globe Tavern, Fleet Street, on Wednesday the 1st of May 1793.* The sale was arranged in 78 lots; a shortened list is given below.

Small theodolite, with telescope and level, and 3-legged stand: by *Nairne & Blunt.*

Pocket levelling instrument: by *Nairne & Blunt.*

Instrument for trying glass bubbles, for levels.

Waywiser: by *Smeaton.*

Two measuring tapes, and a Ludlam's back liner.

Pocket metal compass.

Two speculums, ground by *Mudge.*

5 ft draw-out acromatic telescope. [1756 by Dollond]

Small reflecting telescope and stand.

Acromatic telescope and stand, with equatorial motions and micrometer: by *Smeaton.* [1770]

42 inch Transit instrument: by *Bird.*

Transit instrument: by *Smeaton.* [1768]

Regulator (clock): by *Hindley.*

Celestial globe, with brass horizon, and quadrant of altitude: by *Smeaton.* [1788]

Variation compass: by *Smeaton.*

Brass sextant: by *Morgan*, and artificial horizon. [1756]

Hygrometer. [1771]

Rain gauge.

Microscope.

Smeaton's original air pump (made by himself). [1752]

Pair of 10 inch artificial magnets: by *Gowin Knight.*

Wood T square and straight edge.

Very fine steel straight edge, 40 inches long, and two shorter ones.

6 inch brass divided scale.

Pair of beam compasses.

Pair of proportional compasses.

Parallel ruler.

Brass semi protractor.

6 inch circular protractor, with vernier: by Troughton.

Brass sector.

Improved 30 inch Gunter's scale: by *Nairne & Blunt.*

Three wood sliding rules, with various lines.

Instrument for drawing in perspective.

Good lathe (for hand or foot) with triangular bar, dividing plate, movable
brass chucks etc.

Two good hand lathes.

Well made brass wheel, in excellent preservation, cut into 360 teeth, with
two fine endless screws . . . supposed to be executed by Mr *Hindley.*

Brass endless screw, cut by Mr *Smeaton*, July 21, 1742.

Numerous wood and metal working tools.

Grindstone.

Sundry models.

Dates have been added from information given in Smeaton's *Phil. Trans.*
papers and the *Edystone* book. In a report of 1764 he speaks of having an
improved level. This is not listed; perhaps he had given it to Henry Eastburn.
The Nairne & Blunt instruments must be later than *c.* 1774, when their partnership began.

Smeaton's waywiser and equatorial telescope and one of the air pumps
made to his design are in the Science Museum, as is a 6 in. circular protractor
by Troughton of *c.* 1785. The catalogue does not specify the models, except
for a pulley tackle of 1752.

His original model of the Eddystone Lighthouse remained at Austhorpe
and is now in Trinity House. The lighthouse models made by Josias Jessop
for Robert Weston are in the Royal Scottish Museum (*Trans. Newcomen Soc.*,
5 (1924) 15–21).

APPENDIX II

Portraits of Smeaton

1. By Benjamin Wilson, 1759. Present whereabouts uncertain. The picture was delivered to Austhorpe in July 1764.
2. Attributed to Jonathan Richardson, *c.* 1765. At the Royal Society. Received in 1824 from the estate of Mary Dixon.
3. By George Romney, *c.* 1770. At the Institution of Civil Engineers. Purchased by the Smeatonian Society in 1926, previous history not known.
4. By Rhodes, *c.* 1775. The original of No. 5. May be the portrait at Strathclyde University received in 1951 from the estate of Donald Smeaton Munro.
5. By Romney after Rhodes, 1779. National Portrait Gallery. Commissioned by Sir Richard Sullivan whose wife was a friend of Mary Dixon.
6. By Thomas Gainsborough, May 1783. Southill, Bedfordshire. Commissioned by Samuel Whitbread.
7. By Mather Brown, September 1783. Present whereabouts unknown. Commissioned by Mr Hilbert, owner of Carshalton mill.
8. By Mather Brown, *c.* 1788. Royal Society. Commissioned by Alexander Aubert and presented by him in 1799.
9. Engraving by William Bromley after Brown (No. 8), 1790. Commissioned by Alexander Aubert. This was retouched and issued February 1798 as the frontispiece to Vol. 1 of Smeaton's *Reports*.
10. Engraving by John Corner after Brown (No. 8), 1792.
11. Engraving by Richard Woodman after Brown (No. 8), 1833.
12. Engraving by William Holl after Brown (No. 8), 1861. Issued in Vol. 2 of Smiles' *Lives of the Engineers*. See frontispiece of present book.
13. By John R. Wildman after Gainsborough (No. 6), 1839. Institution of Civil Engineers. Commissioned by Alfred Burges and presented by him in 1840.
14. Marble portrait bust by H. C. Fehr *c.* 1900 after a plaster cast possibly by Sir Francis Chantrey. At the Institution of Civil Engineers.

APPENDIX III
List of Works

It is important to determine which of Smeaton's many designs were actually carried out and, where possible, to provide dates of construction. Much care has therefore been taken in compiling the following tables, but we cannot claim that they are complete and accurate in all respects.

Smeaton himself drew up a list in 1780 of watermills and windmills executed to his plans (*Reports*, Vol. 2, pp. 439–40). These are tabulated here, together with two horse-mills and the winding machinery at Griff and Long Benton collieries. After 1780 our list is based on evidence from Smeaton's letters and diaries and from notes by John Farey on the drawings and in Rees' *Cyclopaedia*.

Apart from his experimental engine Smeaton designed seventeen steam engines, as well as remodelling the engine at York waterworks and improving some others. Of the seventeen, there is clear evidence that nine were built, and their completion dates are given in the table. It is probable that the four other engines listed were constructed. Of the rest, one was not built and we have found no information, positive or negative, on three others. For the record, these were designed for collieries at Dunmore Park in 1778, Kinnaird 1778–79, and Thwaite 1779–80.

Ample evidence exists for the civil engineering works; in the form of minute books, Smeaton's own writings and, in many cases, the works themselves. It is possible, however, that one or two have been missed.

Design dates are taken from reports and/or drawings. Construction dates have been checked from original sources such as Smeaton's letters and minute books. Where we have been unable to establish a date within a year or so it is simply omitted.

Little information appears to be available on the actual cost of mills in the eighteenth century; but Telford in an unpublished manuscript (in the Institution of Civil Engineers library) gives the following figures for mills erected about 1789 in Shropshire: watermill with two pairs of stones £350 including the building and machinery; with two wheels and four pairs of stones £650; windmill with two pairs of stones £500. John Farey in his *Treatise* (London, 1827, pp. 232–3) gives details of the cost, amounting to £2,000, of a medium-sized steam engine (48 in. dia. cylinder) built in the 1770s, this including the engine house and pumping machinery. For canals and drainage schemes the tabulated costs include land purchase, parliamentary and other charges. For most of the other civil works, the cost relates to construction only. Comparisons with modern figures are difficult to make, but it may be mentioned that in Smeaton's day a building craftsman earned about 15s (£0.75) per week, a resident engineer's annual salary typically ranged from £50 to £120 depending on the scale of the works, and the unit cost of excavation rarely exceeded 6d (£0.025) per cubic yard in soft ground.

An idea of the rates of construction achieved can be gained from (i) the piers of the harbours at St Ives (1767–70) and Aberdeen (1775–80) where in both cases about 8,000 tons of masonry were built per year; (ii) the excavation of approximately 380,000 cu. yd/year on the Forth & Clyde Canal (1768–70), equivalent to something like 750 cu. yd/man per year, and (iii) the steam returning engine and winding machinery at Walker colliery (1783) were built and brought into operation 8 months after delivery of the drawings.

Mills and other machinery

Location	Source of power	Purpose	Waterwheels No.	Type	Diam. (ft)	Design	Built
Halton, Lancs	water	flour	no details				1753e
Wakefield	water	flour	1	LB	20		1754e
Wakefield	wind	oil and wood	smock mill			1754	1755e
Colchester	water	fulling	1	LB	14	1760–61	e
Hounslow Heath	water	copper	2	HB	16	c. 1760	e
Kew Gardens	2 horses	water	Archimedes screw			1761	1761
Stratford, E. London	water	water	1	LB	16	1762	1763e
Thornton, Fifeshire	water	paper	1	OS	15	1763	e
Kilnhurst Forge	water	blowing	4	LB	15		⎫
Kilnhurst Forge	water	hammers	2	LB	15		⎬ 1765e
Kilnhurst Forge	water	slitting	1	LB	18		⎭
Carron ironworks	water	blowing	1	HB	27	1764	e
Sowerby Bridge	water	fulling	1	LB	12	c. 1766	e
Knouchbridge, Yorks	water	flour	2	OS	11	1767	e
London Bridge	water	water	1	US	32	1767–68	1768e
Wandsworth	water	flour	3	LB	14	1768	e
Keswick	water	grist	1	LB	16	1769	e
Carron ironworks	water	blowing	1	OS	20	1769	e
Thoresby	water	water	1	OS	7	1769	1770e
Templenewsam	water	water	pressure engine			1769	1770
Carron ironworks	water	boring	2	LB	18	1770	1771e
Dalry, nr Edinburgh	water	flour	1	OS	11	1771	e
Waltham Abbey	water	powder	1	LB	15	1771	e

Location	Source of power	Purpose	Waterwheels				Built
			No.	Type	Diam. (ft)	Design	
Worcester Park	water	powder	1	OS	9	1771	e
Griff colliery	water	winding	1	OS	37	1774	
Leeds	wind	flint	5-sail mill			1774	e
Woodhall, Northumb.	water	grist	1	OS	32	1775	1776e
Coquet ironworks	water	rolling	2	HB	15	1776	
Scremerston	water	grist	1	N	11	1776	e
Hull	water + steam*	oil	1	OS	27	1776	1778e
Carron ironworks	water	clay	2	LB	18	1777	e
Long Benton colliery	water + steam	winding	1	OS	30	1777	1777
Carshalton	water	oil	1	LB	18	1778	e
Deptford	water	water	1	LB	16	1778–79	e
Cardington	water	flour	1	LB	8	1779	1780e
Seacroft ironworks	water + steam	blowing	2	OS	30	1779–80	
Gosport	2 horses	water	horse-gin			1779–80	
Wanlock Head mine	water	lead	1	LB	14	1780	1780e
Austhorpe (Sykefield)	wind	oil	5-sail mill				1781
Carshalton	water	flour	2	OS	8	1780–82	1783
Beaufort ironworks	water + steam	blowing	1	OS	42	1780–82	
Deptford dockyard	water + steam*	flour	1	OS	30	1781	c. 1784
Newcastle-on-Tyne	water	snuff	1	OS	24	1781	1782
Newcastle-on-Tyne	wind	flour	5-sail mill			1781–82	1782
Walker colliery	water + steam	winding	1	OS	30	1783	1783
Waren, Northumb.	water	flour	1	OS	21	1783	1785
Loose, Kent	water	paper	1	OS	19	1787	
Carshalton	water	paper	1	LB	15	1789	1790
Wandsworth	water	oil	1	LB	16	1789–90	
Custom House, London	2 men	crane				1789–90	
Waddon, Surrey	water	flour	1	OS	8	1789–91	

OS = overshot; US = undershot; N = Norse; LB = low breast; HB = high breast;
water + steam = waterwheel with returning engine;
steam* = steam engine not designed by Smeaton;
e = in Smeaton's 1780 list of "mills executed".

The following mills for which no dates have been found are included in Smeaton's list of "mills executed", drawn up in 1780.

Location	Source of power	Purpose	Waterwheels No.	Type	Diam. (ft)
Nine Elms	wind	flint			
Barking	wind	wood	no details		
Heath	water	pumping	no drawings		
Ridge	water	wood	no details		
Honeycomb	water	? flour	no drawings		
Bretton Furnace	water	blowing	1	HB	20
Hounslow Heath	water	powder	1	LB	16
Bussey, Perthshire	water	flour	1	OS	13
Horsley	water	wire	no drawings		
Horsley	water	tilt			
Alston, Cumb.	water	grist	1	OS	30
Whittle	water	grist	no drawings		
Throckley	water	grist	no drawings		
Welbeck	water	pumping	1	OS	4

The total numbers in the above lists are:

windmills	6
watermills	46
watermills with returning engines	6
horse-mills	2
winding engines	3

Steam engines

Location	Purpose	Cylinder diameter (in.)	Design	Set to work
New River Head	water supply	18	1767	1769
Long Benton colliery	pumping	52	1772–73	1774
Chacewater mine	pumping	72	1774–75	1775
Kronstadt docks	pumping	66	1774–75	1777
Long Benton colliery	winding★	26	1777	1777
Lumley colliery	pumping	34	1777	
Gateshead Park colliery	pumping	60	1778	c. 1779
Seacroft foundry	blowing★	30	1779–80	c. 1781
Middleton colliery	pumping	72	1779–80	
Carron ironworks	returning	72	1780	c. 1780
Beaufort ironworks	blowing★	36	1782	
Bourn Moor colliery	pumping	72	1782–83	
Walker colliery	winding★	36	1783	1783

★ Returning engine with waterwheel.

Civil engineering works

	Design	Construction	Cost (£)	Resident engineer
Eddystone Lighthouse	1756	1756–59	16,000	Josias Jessop
Calder & Hebble Navigation	1757, 1759, 1767	1760–70	75,000	Joseph Nickalls, 1760–61 John Gwyn ⎫ Matthias Scott ⎬ 1762–65 James Brindley, engineer in charge, 1765–66 Luke Holt ⎫ Robert Carr ⎬ 1769–70
London Bridge foundations	1763	1763		
Coldstream Bridge	1763–65	1763–67	6,000	Robert Reid
Potteric Carr Drainage	1762, 1765	⎱1765–68 ⎰1772–77		Matthias Scott, 1765–74 Henry Cooper, 1774–77
Perth Bridge	1763–69	1766–71	23,000	John Gwyn
Adlingfleet Drainage	1764	1767–72	7,000	John Grundy, engineer in charge David Buffery, assistant
St Ives harbour	1766	1767–70	9,500	Thomas Richardson engineer–contractor
River Lee Navigation	1766	1767–71		Thomas Yeoman, engineer in charge Edward Rubie, assistant, 1769–71
Ure Navigation & Ripon Canal	1766	1767–72	16,500	John Smith
Forth & Clyde Canal (Grangemouth–Glasgow)	1767–72	1768–77	164,000	Robert Mackell Alex. Stephen, assistant
Eyemouth harbour	1767	1768–70		
Newark flood arches	1768	1768–70	12,000	
Rye harbour, new channel	1763–64	1769–73	19,000	William Green
Spurn Lighthouse	1767, 1770	1771–76	8,000	William Taylor, engineer–contractor
Portpatrick harbour	1770, 1774	1771–78	10,000	John Gwyn, 1771–75
Banff Bridge	1772	1772–79	9,000	James Kyle
Stonehouse Creek Bridge	1767	1773		
Aire & Calder Navigation, new cuts and locks	1771	1775–79	30,000	William Jessop, engineer in charge John Gott, resident engineer
Aberdeen harbour, north pier	1770	1775–80	16,000	John Gwyn
Peterhead harbour	1772	1775–81	6,000	John Gwyn
Dunipace dam	1773	c. 1775		
Amesbury Turnpike Bridge	1775	1775	2,000	
Nent force level	1775	1776–		

257

	Design	*Construction*	*Cost (£)*	*Resident engineer*
Hatfield Chase Drainage	1764, 1776	1776–89	20,000	Matthias Scott, 1776–83. Work continued and extended by Samuel Foster, 1783–89
Ramsgate harbour, basin and sluices	1774, 1777	1776–81		Thomas Preston, 1776–77 Edmund Hurst, 1777–81
Altgran Bridge	1772	1777		
Amesbury ornamental bridge	1776–77	1777		
Coquet dam	1776	c. 1777		
Hexham Bridge	1777–78	1777–80, failed 1782	9,500	Jonathan Pickernell
Cardington Bridge	1778	1778		
Cromarty harbour	1780, 1783	1781–84		John Gwyn
Hull North Bridge	1784	1785–87		John Gwyn
Aberdeen harbour, catch pier	1788	1788–90	1,500	Alexander Gildavie, engineer–contractor
Ramsgate harbour, dry dock	1783, 1788	1788–91		John Gwyn, 1788–89
Ramsgate harbour, Advanced Pier	1788	1788–92	52,000	Henry Cull, 1789–92

Notes and References

Notes to Chapter I

A bibliography of the principal sources used in this Chapter in chronological order.*

PRIMARY SOURCES

1. *Reports of the late John Smeaton, FRS made on various occasions in the course of his employment as a Civil Engineer*, Vol. 1 (London, 1797); Vols. 1–3 with plates (London, 1812). These cover the period 1760–92.
2. *Designs of the late John Smeaton, FRS* (Royal Society). Original drawings from 1741 to 1791. They are listed in *A Catalogue of the Civil and Mechanical Engineering Designs of John Smeaton*, edited by H. W. Dickinson and A. A. Gomme (Newcomen Soc., 1950). Most of the drawings are signed and dated; where this is not the case dates suggested by the editors should be ignored.
3. *The Miscellaneous Papers of John Smeaton, Civil Engineer, FRS* (London, 1814). Reprints of his eighteen papers in *Phil. Trans.*, 1750–88.
4. *John Smeaton's Diary of his Journey to the Low Countries, 1755* (Newcomen Soc., 1938). Edited by A. Titley from the original MS in Trinity House.
5. Letters to Benjamin Wilson, 1744–64 (British Museum).
6. Private Letter Book, 1764 (Inst. Civ. Eng.).
7. Letters to Boulton & Watt, 1778–79 (Birmingham Ref. Library).
8. Machine Letter Books, 1781–92 (Inst. Civ. Eng.).
9. Journals, 1781–83 (Trinity House).
10. Letter to Mary Dixon, 1790. We are indebted to Mr Michael Lee for a transcript of this letter which belongs to Mr F. J. Ridsdale of Johannesburg, a descendant of Ann Brooke.
11. Smeaton, J. *A Narrative of the Building and a Description of the Construction of the Edystone Lighthouse* (London, 1791). 2nd edn corrected (London, 1793).

* Editor's note: Chapter I is a general chapter on Smeaton's life and has therefore not been referenced in the same way as the other chapters.

12. First minute book (1771–92) of the Society of Civil Engineers. A facsimile of the original was published by the Society in 1893 and has been reprinted several times.
13. Parish registers of Leeds, Whitkirk, St Andrew's Holborn, and St George's Hanover Square.

SECONDARY SOURCES

14. Holmes, J. *A Short Narrative of the Genius, Life, and Works, of the late Mr John Smeaton, Civil Engineer, FRS* (London, 1793).
15. [Mylne, R.] Preface in Smeaton's *Reports*, Vol. 1 (London, 1797) pp. iii–xi.
16. Hutton, C. "Some Account of the Life", *ibid.*, pp. xv–xxiv.
17. Dixon, Mary. Letter to the Committee of Civil Engineers, *ibid.*, pp. xxv–xxx.
18. Articles on Smeaton in early encyclopaedias such as Rees (1816), Britannica (1823, 1842) and Edinburgh (1830) are based on refs 14 and 16 above.
19. Farey, J. Articles on "Mills", "Water" and "Winding-Engine", in Rees' *Cyclopaedia*, Vol. 23 (1813) and Vol. 38 (1818).
20. Farey, J. *A Treatise on the Steam Engine* (London, 1827).
21. Smiles, S. "Life of John Smeaton". In *Lives of the Engineers*, Vol. 2 (London, 1861) pp. 3–90.
22. Beare, T. H. Article on Smeaton in *Dictionary of National Biography*, Vol. 52 (London, 1897).
23. Rowatt, T. "Notes on original models of the Eddystone Lighthouse". *Trans. Newcomen. Soc.*, **5** (1924) 15–21.
24. Kirk, G. E. *A History of the Parish Church of St. Mary, Whitkirk* (Leeds, 1935).
25. Wailes, R. "Notes on the windmill drawings in Smeaton's designs". *Trans. Newcomen Soc.*, **28** (1953) 239–243.
26. Wilson, P. N. "The waterwheels of John Smeaton". *Trans. Newcomen Soc.*, **30** (1955) 25–43.
27. Majdalany, F. *The Red Rocks of Eddystone* (London, 1959).
28. Wilson, P. N. "The Nent Force Level". *Trans. Cumb. & Westmorland Antiqn. & Archaeol. Soc.*, **63** (1963) 253–280.
29. Lindsay, J. *The Canals of Scotland* (Newton Abbot, 1968).
30. de Boer, G. *A History of the Spurn Lighthouses* (East Yorks. Local. Hist. Soc., 1968).
31. Turner, T. "John Gwyn and the building of North Bridge, Kingston upon Hull". *Transport Hist.*, **3** (1970) 154–163.
32. Lee, M. "Builder of lighthouses". *Cumbria Lake District Life*, **21** (1971) 31–32.
33. Law, R. J. "Henry Hindley of York". *Antiquarian Horology*, **7** (1971) 205–221.

34. Skempton, A. W. *The Smeatonians: Duo-Centenary Notes on the Society of Civil Engineers* (London, 1971).
35. Skempton, A. W. and Wright, Esther C. "Early members of the Smeatonian Society of Civil Engineers". *Trans. Newcomen Soc.*, **44** (1971) 23–42.
36. Skempton, A. W. "The publication of Smeaton's Reports". *Notes Rec. Roy. Soc.*, **26** (1971) 135–155.
37. Hadfield, C. *The Canals of Yorkshire and North East England*, Vol. 1 (Newton Abbot, 1972).
38. Lee, M. "A philosopher among engineers". *Country Life Annual*, 1972, pp. 124–125.
39. Turner, T. "John Smeaton, FRS". *Endeavour*, **33** (1974) 29–33.
40. Dorn, H. Article on Smeaton in *Dictionary of Scientific Biography*, Vol. 12 (New York, 1975) pp. 461–463.
41. Smith, D. "The professional correspondence of John Smeaton". *Trans. Newcomen Soc.*, **47** (1976) 179–188.
42. Ruddock, E. C. "The foundations of Hexham Bridge". *Geotechnique*, **27** (1977) 385–404.
43. Turner, T. "The works of John Smeaton, a chronological survey". *Trans. Newcomen Soc.*, **50** (1978), 37–54.
44. Hadfield, C. and Skempton, A. W. *William Jessop, Engineer* (Newton Abbot, 1979).
45. Ruddock, T. *Arch Bridges and their Builders 1735–1835* (Cambridge, 1979).

Notes to Chapter II

1. *Miscellaneous Papers of John Smeaton, Civil Engineer, FRS comprising his communications to the Royal Society* (London, 1814).
2. Smeaton later made a present of one of his air pumps to Joseph Priestley who used it in his electrical experiments (letter from Priestley to John Canton written in 1767: see Schofield, R. E. *A Scientific Biography of Joseph Priestley* (MIT, 1966) p. 52). Tests on a Smeaton air pump in the Science Museum showed that it could produce a vacuum of 1–2 mm of mercury as compared to 6 mm by pumps of the ordinary construction in the mid-eighteenth century (Chaldecott, J. A. *Handbook of the King George III Collection of Scientific Instruments* (HMSO 1951) p. 31).
3. Halton Mill, near Lancaster. *Designs*, **1**, f. 54.
4. A contemporary account of Polhem's waterwheel is given by Martin Triewald, *Lectures on the New Natural Sciences* (in Swedish; Stockholm, 1735–36). See also Holgar Rosman, *Christopher Polhem*, trans. by W. A. Johnson (Hartford, 1963) pp. 209–211.
5. Antoine Parent. "Sur la plus grande perfection possible des machines". *Mém. Acad. Roy. Sci.* (for 1704) pp. 323–338.

6. Desaguliers, J. T. *A Course of Experimental Philosophy*, Vol. 2 (London, 1744) p. 532.

7. Smeaton, J. "An experimental Enquiry concerning the Natural Powers of Water and Wind to turn Mills, and other Machines, depending on a circular Motion". *Phil. Trans.*, **51** (for 1759) 100–174, published 1760.

8. Smith, N. A. F. "The origins of the water turbine". *Hist. Technol.* **2** (1977) 215–259. Borda's work dates from 1767; it was a remarkable contribution for the period.

9. Smeaton, J. "An experimental Examination of the Quantity and Proportion of Mechanic Power necessary to be employed in giving different Degrees of Velocity to Heavy Bodies from a State of Rest". *Phil. Trans.*, **66** (1776) 450–475.

10. For an illuminating discussion of this topic see Cardwell, D. S. L. "Some factors in the early development of the concepts of power, work and energy". *Br. J. Hist. Sci.* **3** (1967) 209–224.

11. Smeaton, J. "New Fundamental Experiments upon the Collision of Bodies". *Phil. Trans.*, **72** (1782) 337–354.

12. Farey, J. Article on "Water" in Rees' *Cyclopaedia*, Vol. 38 (1818).

13. Smeaton probably owned a copy of Du Buat (1786), see Appendix I, but his analysis of pipe flow is earlier and of a different form.

14. Young, T. "Of the Friction and Discharge of Fluids running in Pipes, and the Velocity of Rivers". *Phil. Trans.*, **98** (1808) 164–175.

15. Report of John Smeaton, Engineer, upon the State and Improvement of the Water Service of the City of Edinburgh, 12 Feb., 1780. See *Reports*, **3**, pp. 228–234.

16. Dr Peter Mantz of Imperial College has kindly examined Smeaton's test results in the light of modern hydraulic theory.

17. Hadfield, C. and Skempton, A. W. *William Jessop, Engineer* (Newton Abbot, 1979) p. 226.

18. Farey, J. "On Mr Smeaton's estimate of the amount of Power exerted by a man, or a horse". Inst. Civ. Eng. Original Communication No. 299, Jan., 1839.

19. Dickinson, H. W. and Jenkins, R. *James Watt and the Steam Engine* (Oxford, 1927) pp. 353–356.

20. Smeaton, J. *A Narrative of the Building . . . of the Edystone Lighthouse* (London, 1791). See Ch. IV on "Experiments to ascertain a complete composition of Water Cements; with their results", pp. 102–123.

21. Tarras mortar was made from "Dutch Tarras" or "trass", a pozzolanic material found on the Rhine at Andernach and near Frankfurt-on-Maine. A considerable trade from Holland flourished in the eighteenth century.

22. A volcanic ash from the Greek island of Santorini, similar in its cementing properties to pozzolana and trass.

Notes to Chapter III

1. In 1780 Smeaton drew up a list of mills built to his designs, *Reports*, **2,** 439; see Appendix III. Subsequent mills known to have been built are also listed in this Appendix.
2. Wilson, P. N. in his paper on "The waterwheels of John Smeaton". *Trans. Newcomen Soc.*, **30** (1955) 25–48, analyses all the watermill drawings in *Designs*. Technical details on the windmills are given by Wailes, R. "Notes on the windmill drawings in Smeaton's Designs". *Trans. Newcomen Soc.*, **28** (1953) 239–243.
3. Smeaton's Diary of his Journey to the Low Countries, 1755.
4. *Machine Letters*, 6 Feb., 1786.
5. *Reports*, **1,** pp. 248–251; 12 May, 1766.
6. *Reports*, **1,** pp. 313–316; 15 June, 1767.
7. "An Experimental Enquiry". *Phil. Trans.*, **51** (1759) 100–174.
8. *Machine Letters*, 24 Jan., 1787.
9. Wailes, R. *The English Windmill* (London, 1954).
10. *Reports*, **2,** pp. 422–423; 27 Nov., 1771.
11. *Machine Letters*, 7 Feb., 1782.
12. *Designs*, **1,** f. 101.
13. *Reports*, **1,** pp. 376–379; 15 Oct., 1770.
14. These were for Carron ironworks (1769), Hull oil-mill (1776), Long Benton winding engine (1777), Brooksmill (1778), Carshalton (1780), Warren Mill (1783) and Wandsworth (1789).
15. *Designs*, **1,** f. 96v.
16. *Reports*, **2,** p. 412; 15 Oct., 1770.
17. *Reports*, **2,** pp. 378–380; 23 Nov., 1781. For this mill at Deptford dockyard, Smeaton recommended that Boulton & Watt should supply the returning engine.
18. *Machine Letters*, 26 Feb., 1768.
19. Letter Book of 1764 (Inst. Civ. Eng. library). Smeaton to John Holmes, 13 Aug., 1764.
20. *Designs*, **2,** f. 146.
21. Farey, J. Article on "Water" in Rees' *Cyclopaedia*, Vol. 38 (1818).
22. Wilson, P. N., *loc. cit.*, p. 46.
23. *Reports*, **2,** pp. 367–372; 6 June, 1779.
24. *Designs*, **4,** f. 64.
25. *Reports*, **1,** p. 377; 15 Oct., 1770.
26. *Designs*, **2,** f. 95–108.
27. *Reports*, **2,** pp. 428–429; undated, but 1766.
28. *Reports*, **1,** p. 362; John Grieve to Smeaton, 10 July, 1769.
29. *Reports*, **1,** pp. 367–375; 31 July, 1769.
30. *Reports*, **1,** plate opposite p. 364.
31. This is the plate opposite p. 365 of *Reports*, **1.**

32. *Designs*, **2,** f. 76–79.
33. *Designs*, **2,** f. 91–94.
34. *Designs*, **2,** f. 56–58.
35. *Designs*, **2,** f. 111–112.
36. *Designs*, **2,** f. 63.
37. *Designs*, **2,** f. 62.
38. *Designs*, **1,** f. 32.
39. *Designs*, **2,** f. 56.
40. *Reports*, **2,** pp. 324–332; 13 Sept., 1776.
41. *Designs*, **2,** f. 123, l.s.
42. *Reports*, **2,** pp. 381–385; 5 Nov., 1779.
43. *Designs*, **1,** f. 18.
44. *Designs*, **1,** f. 8v.
45. *Reports*, **2,** p. 415; 29 Apr., 1774.
46. This plate is opposite p. 396 in *Reports*, **2.**
47. A drawing of Meikle's system is in *Designs*, **1,** f. 6v. which John Farey notes was sent to Smeaton 17 Mar., 1772.
48. *Designs*, **1,** f. 1–2.
49. *Reports*, **2,** pp. 396–397 [1782].
50. *Reports*, **2,** p. 414; 27 June, 1772.
51. *Reports*, **2,** p. 425 [1764].
52. Nicholson, J. *The Operative Mechanic* (London, 1853) p. 125.
53. For example, Kempe's *Engineer's Year Book* (London, 1919) p. 931.

Notes to Chapter IV

1. Smiles, S. *Lives of the Engineers*, Vol. 1 (London, 1861) p. 14.
2. Weston, R. H. *Letters and important Documents relative to the Edystone Lighthouse* (London, 1811). Hereafter referenced as *Letters*. The lease is given on pp. 257–262.
3. *Letters*. Weston to Smeaton, 6 Apr., 1756.
4. Smeaton, J. *A Narrative of the Building and a Description of the Construction of the Edystone Lighthouse* (London, 1791; 2nd edn, 1793; 3rd edn, 1813). Hereafter referenced as *Narrative* and by paragraph numbers in the (corrected) 2nd and 3rd editions.
5. Models of Rudyerd's lighthouse and its masonry courses are in the Weston collection at the Royal Scottish Museum, Edinburgh, together with some drawings; but most of the drawings (some possibly originals, others by Jessop and his predecessor John Holland) appear to have been retained by Smeaton as they are in the Royal Society (*Designs*, **5,** f. 193v, 193v l.s. (i)–(vii), and f. 194, the latter being incorrectly catalogued).
6. *Narrative*, paras 17–21 and pls 4, 5.
7. *Ibid.*, paras 34–54 and pls 6, 7.
8. *Ibid.*, para. 50.

9. *Ibid.*, para. 40.
10. *Ibid.*, paras 79–80.
11. *Ibid.*, para. 85.
12. *Ibid.*, pl. 13, fig. 6.
13. *Ibid.*, pl. 13, fig. 5.
14. *Ibid.*, para. 84.
15. *Ibid.*, para. 97 and pl. 7.
16. Josias Jessop (*c.* 1710–60) was the father of William Jessop, the eminent civil engineer.
17. *Narrative*, paras 117–118.
18. *Ibid.*, para. 174. See also Smeaton, J. "An Account of the effects of lightning upon the steeple and church of Lostwithiel". *Phil. Trans.*, **50** (1757) 198–204.
19. *Narrative*, paras 90, 130, 154, 167 and pl. 17.
20. *Ibid.*, para. 101.
21. *Ibid.*, para. 130.
22. *Ibid.*, para. 223.
23. *Ibid.*, para. 305.
24. *Ibid.*, para. 159.
25. *Letters*, Smeaton to Weston, 18 Jan., 1757.
26. *Narrative*, Books III and IV describe the progress of the works in considerable detail. There is a tabular abstract after para. 331.
27. *Letters*, Smeaton to Weston, 22 Mar., 1757.
28. *Narrative*, paras 313, 309.
29. Douglass, J. N. "Note on the Eddystone lighthouse". *Min. Proc. Inst. Civ. Eng.*, **53** (1878) 247–248, and Douglass, W. T., *Min. Proc. Inst. Civ. Eng.*, **75** (1884) 54–55.
30. Stevenson, R. *An Account of the Bell Rock Lighthouse* (Edinburgh, 1824).
31. Douglass, W. T. "The new Eddystone lighthouse". *Min. Proc. Inst. Civ. Eng.*, **75** (1884) 20–36.
32. *Narrative*, para. 81.
33. *Ibid.*, para. 30.
34. *Ibid.*, para. 246.
35. *Ibid.*, para. 244.
36. *Ibid.*, para. 245.
37. *Ibid.*, para. 274.
38. It was possible, for the first time, to carry out a valid *post facto* statistical analysis in 1742 in relation to observed cracking of the dome of St Peter's, Rome. No similar analysis of a structure yet to be built is recorded until 1771 in relation to what is now the Pantheon, Paris. See Mainstone, R. J. *Developments in Structural Form.* (London, 1975) pp. 283–292.
39. *Narrative*, Introduction.
40. Wren, C. *Parentalia* (1750); Price, F. *A Series of Particular and useful Observations . . . upon . . . the Cathedral-Church of Salisbury* (1753); Belidor,

B. *Architecture Hydraulique* (1737–1753). The source of the dovetail jointing is Vol. 3 (1750) pp. 200–201 and pl. 26, fig. 4.

41. *Narrative*, para. 75.
42. Mainstone, R. J. "Brunelleschi's dome". *Architect. Rev.*, **162** (1977) 156–166.
43. Douglass, W. T. "The new Eddystone lighthouse". *Min. Proc. Inst. Civ. Eng.*, **75** (1884), pp. 33, 36.
44. Report by Trinity House (1809) and reply by R. H. Weston, in *Letters*, pp. 282, 294. The usually quoted figure of about £40,000 seems to stem from an erroneous interpretation of this Report.

Notes to Chapter V

1. For the Upper Calder (later Calder & Hebble) Navigation, in its early days, see Hadfield, C. *The Canals of Yorkshire & North East England*, Vol. 1 (Newton Abbot, 1972) pp. 44–61.
2. Smeaton's printed report and map of 1757 are in *Designs*, **6,** f. 14 and 14 v.
3. *Journal of the House of Commons (JHC)*, 14 Mar., 1758. The locks in Flanders and Holland he had seen on his journey to the Low Countries in 1755; he had also studied Belidor's *Architecture Hydraulique*. The Act for the Upper Calder Navigation is 31 Geo. 2, c. 72.
4. Unless otherwise stated, details are taken from the Calder & Hebble Navigation Minute Books and Letters (PRO). See also ref. 1.
5. Smeaton's *Designs*, **5,** contains about 40 drawings for the Calder & Hebble.
6. Letter Book of 1764 (Inst. Civ. Eng. library). Smeaton to Grundy, 4 Sept., 1764.
7. Calder & Hebble Minute Book, 11 Apr., 1765.
8. For the Louth Canal, see Boyes, J. and Russell, R. *The Canals of Eastern England* (Newton Abbot, 1977) pp. 304–315.
9. *Reports*, **1,** pp. 22–25; 14 July, 1761.
10. House of Lords Committee, 14 Mar., 1763.
11. *JHC*, 16 Mar.; Lords Committee, 1 May, 1759.
12. *Designs*, **6,** f. 72.
13. *JHC*, 6 Feb., 1760.
14. *Reports*, **1,** pp. 26–35; 23 Nov., 1761.
15. Lords Committee, 14 May, 1762.
16. *Reports*, **1,** pp. 55–69; 16 Oct., 1762.
17. *Reports*, **1,** pp. 72–87; 31 Dec., 1782.
18. *Reports*, **1,** pp. 36–38; 21 June, 1762.
19. Boyes, J. and Russell, R. *The Canals of Eastern England* (Newton Abbot, 1977) pp. 62–75.
20. *Designs*, **6,** f. 77.

21. *Reports*, **1**, pp. 13–17; 11 July, 1761. *Designs*, **6**, f. 75.
22. Malet, H. *Bridgewater: the Canal Duke* (Manchester University Press, 1977) pp. 71–73. Dr Malet has kindly made available a copy of the Parliamentary evidence, now in the Huntingdon Library, California.
23. Farey, J. Article on "Water" in Rees' *Cyclopaedia*, Vol. 38 (London, 1818). See also Brewster, D. on "Hydrodynamics" in *Edinburgh Encyclopaedia*, Vol. 11 (Edinburgh, 1817).
24. Smeaton's reports of 1755 and 1758 are in the Boulton & Watt Collection, Birmingham Reference Library. For the 1758 plans, see *Designs*, **6**, f. 54–58.
25. *JHC*, 19 Feb., 1759; Lords Committee, 12 Apr., 1759.
26. For a general account of the Forth & Clyde Canal see Lindsay, J. *The Canals of Scotland* (Newton Abbot, 1968) pp. 15–51.
27. *Reports*, **2**, p. 73.
28. *Reports*, **2**, pp. 31–65.
29. He refers to it in his evidence on the Upper Calder Bill.
30. For the Languedoc Canal, see Skempton, A. W. "Canals and river navigations before 1750". *History of Technology*, Vol. 3 (Oxford, 1957) pp. 464–468.
31. *JHC*, 28 Apr., 1767.
32. *Reports*, **2**, pp. 73–97; 8 Oct., 1767.
33. Lords Committee, 25 Feb., 1768. The Act is 8 Geo. 3, c. 63.
34. All details of the Forth & Clyde Canal proceedings are from the Minute Books (West Register House, Edinburgh) and are given here by courtesy of Dr Jean Lindsay and Professor Skempton.
35. These reports were published in Edinburgh on 29 Oct., 1768. Smeaton's reply was printed in the following month.
36. *Reports*, **2**, pp. 98–120; 28 Oct., 1768.
37. Lords Committee, 21 Feb., 1771. The Act for the new line is 11 Geo. 3, c. 62.
38. Most of Smeaton's reports and some of his letters, written during the progress of the works, are copied into the Canal Minute Books, see ref. 34.
39. *Designs*, **5**, f. 2–37, and **6**, f. 59–68.
40. These and other key dates and statistics of the canal are given in appendices to the Superintendent's Report, 31 Dec., 1791 (West Register House).
41. Machine Letter Book (Inst. Civ. Eng. library). Smeaton to the Lord Provost of Edinburgh, 7 Mar., 1785.
42. *Reports*, **2**, pp. 125–127; 30 Nov., 1767.
43. *Reports*, **2**, pp. 128–130. For some details of the later work on the Calder, see Hadfield, C. and Skempton, A. W. *William Jessop, Engineer* (Newton Abbot, 1979) pp. 20–22.
44. *Designs*, **6**, f. 37.

45. Cross, A. "A Russian engineer in eighteenth century Britain: the Journal of N. J. Korsakov, 1776–7". *Slav. East Eur. Rev.*, **55** (1977).

46. The river is spelled "Lea", the navigation "Lee". For this navigation see Boyes, J. and Russell, R. *The Canals of Eastern England* (Newton Abbot, 1977) pp. 13–39.

47. *Reports*, **2**, pp. 155–163; 24 Sept., 1766. *Designs*, **6**, f. 85.

48. This estimate, dated 26 Feb., 1767, is revised upwards from that in the original printed report of 1766.

49. *JHC*, 15 Apr., 1767, Lords Committee, 3 June. The Act is 7 Geo. 3, c. 51.

50. *Reports*, **1**, pp. 282–294: three reports dated 27 Mar., 1771, 17 Apr., 1779, 12 Nov., 1782.

51. *Designs*, **6**, f. 79.

52. *JHC*, 2 Mar., 1767. The Acts are 7 Geo. 3, c. 93 and 7 Geo. 3, c. 96.

53. Hadfield, C. *The Canals of Yorkshire & North East England*, Vol. 1 (Newton Abbot, 1972) pp. 111–112.

54. *Designs*, **4**, f. 48.

55. *Reports*, **1**, pp. 310–312 on Linton Dam, undated but *c*. 1768; **2**, pp. 172–184 four reports on the works, May, 1770 to Jan., 1772.

56. For a general history on the Aire & Calder in the eighteenth century, see Hadfield, C. *The Canals of Yorkshire & North East England*, Vol. 1 (Newton Abbot, 1972), pp. 17–43.

57. *Reports*, **2**, pp. 131–140; 28 Dec., 1771.

58. *Reports*, **2**, pp. 151–153; 5 Dec., 1772.

59. For Smeaton's evidence, see *JHC*, 22 Feb., 1774 and 23 Mar., 1774.

60. Smeaton's plans of the new cuts and locks are in *Designs*, **6**, f. 16, 17, 18 and 19(ii).

61. More details of Smeaton's and Jessop's work on the Aire & Calder are given by Hadfield, C. and Skempton, A. W. *William Jessop, Engineer* (Newton Abbot, 1979) pp. 13–20.

62. *Reports*, **2**, pp 252–260; 6 Oct., 1773.

63. *Reports*, **2**, pp. 262–277; 3 Apr., 1775.

64. For Smeaton on the Grand Canal, see *Letters between Redmond Morres and John Smeaton* (Dublin, 1773) and Delany, R. *The Grand Canal of Ireland* (Newton Abbot, 1973).

65. The Greasbrough report is in Sheffield Public Library; the four reports of 1778 are in *Reports*, **2**, pp. 213–241.

66. Household, H. G. W. *The Thames & Severn Canal* (Newton Abbot, 1969) pp. 84–85. Smeaton's report of 14 Aug., 1789 is in Gloucestershire Record Office.

67. *Reports*, **2**, pp. 189–193; undated but 1771. Lords Committee, 15 Feb., 1771.

68. *Machine Letters*, 16 Sept., 1782. Smeaton to Meredith.

69. *Reports*, **2**, pp. 194–212; 16 Dec., 1782. For the complicated background

to Smeaton's proposals see Broadbridge, S. R. *The Birmingham Canal Navigations 1768–1846* (Newton Abbot, 1974) pp. 22–24.

70. *JHC*, 14 Feb., 1783.
71. Birmingham Canal Proprietors' Minute Book, 26 Mar., 1790.
72. *Aris's Birmingham Gazette*, 15 Mar., 1790. For the Worcestershire & Birmingham Canal, see Hadfield, C. *Canals of the West Midlands* (Newton Abbot, 1966).
73. Hutton, C. "Some account of the life of Mr John Smeaton". *Reports*, **1,** p. xx.
74. Lords Committee, 7 June, 1791.

Notes to Chapter VI

1. Smeaton's report on Lochar Moss is printed in Singer, W. *A General View of the Agriculture ... in the County of Dumfries* (Edinburgh, 1812).
2. *Designs*, **6,** f. 112.
3. *Reports*, **1,** pp. 1–6; 28 Nov., 1760.
4. Corporation of Doncaster Minutes, Vol. 4, 1755–1812 (Doncaster Archives Dept).
5. *Reports*, **1,** pp. 39–48; Sept., 1762.
6. We are indebted to Mr W. Bunting of Thorne for this point.
7. Tomlinson, J. *Doncaster from the Roman Occupation to the Present Time* (Doncaster, 1887) p. 237, contains extracts from an account book of 1762–72, now lost.
8. *Reports*, **1,** pp. 48–52; 23 Mar., 1764.
9. *House of Commons Journal* (JHC), Vol. 30. 16 Jan., 22 Feb., and 19 Apr., 1765. The Act (5 Geo. 3, c. 40; 19 Apr., 1765) gives no details of the method of drainage.
10. Skidmore, P., Dolby, M. J. and Hooper, M. B. *Thomas Tofield of Wilsic, Botanist and Civil Engineer* (Doncaster Museum, 1981).
11. *Reports*, **1,** pp. 52–54; undated, but probably June or July, 1765.
12. Details of the work from 1772 are in *Proceedings of the Trustees of Potteric Carr Drainage*. Permission and facilities for studying this minute book and various maps etc. were kindly granted by Mr J. A. Walker of Bawtry, Clerk to the Drainage Board. The works of the first stage can be deduced from those ordered to be done in 1772.
13. Doncaster Corporation Minute Book No. 4 refers to the new Rossington Bridge in September 1766, and an entry in April 1768 implies that the first stage of the works was nearing completion.
14. The Commissioners' Award, dated 1 Oct., 1771, signed by Tofield and four others, is with the Clerk to the Drainage Board.
15. A copy of Colbeck's map is in Doncaster Museum and Art Gallery.
16. Hadfield, C. and Skempton, A. W. *William Jessop, Engineer* (Newton Abbot, 1979) pp. 64–66.

17. Smeaton's letter of 27 Mar., 1770, with the letters from Tofield and Grundy, was published by John Farey, *Min. Proc. Inst. Civ. Eng.*, **4** (1845) 205–209.
18. Biswas, A. K. *History of Hydrology* (Amsterdam, 1970) pp. 262–267.
19. *Reports*, **1**, pp. 88–89; 12 Jan., 1764.
20. Minute Book of the Holderness Drainage Trustees, No. 1, 1764–68 (Humberside Record Office). For a plan and subsequent history of the scheme, see Hadfield and Skempton, *op. cit.*, pp. 69–74.
21. Smeaton's Letter Book of 1764. (Inst. Civ. Eng. library). Smeaton to Grundy, 3 Sept., 1764 and Grundy to Smeaton, 17 Sept., 1764.
22. One of Grundy's drawings of Holderness sluice is in *Designs*, **5,** f. 51.
23. *Reports*, **1**, pp. 90–98; 13 Dec., 1764.
24. *Reports*, **1**, pp. 199–206; 3 Dec., 1764.
25. "Observations from a View and a Report of the State of the Low Grounds in East Toft", in *Surveys, Reports etc by John Grundy of Spalding*, Vol. 2 (Inst. Civ. Eng. library).
26. 1764 Letter Book, see ref. 21.
27. "Plan from an Actual Survey describing the Low Grounds of Adlingfleet, Eastoft, Ousefleet, Haldenby & Fockerby, by Charles Tate, Surveyor, with a Scheme for Draining the same by John Smeaton, Engineer, 1764" (Leeds City Archives).
28. Smeaton's report reads as if the drain is to be dug at a gradient of 10 in./mile throughout its length, but the depths which he gives, relative to ground elevation, show the drain to be on a level from the sluice to point E. His depths are the same as those of the drain as built.
29. The petition for a Bill went to Parliament in January 1767 (*JHC*). The Act (7 Geo. 3, c. 40; 20 May, 1767) specifies that the main drain will run from Green Bank to Trent Falls.
30. Information on the works and proceedings is taken from the Commissioners' Minute Book (1767 ff.), their Award (1772) and the accompanying map. These were studied at Crowle by courtesy of Mr G. W. Haywood, Clerk to the Adlingfleet & Whitgift Drainage Board.
31. Grundy's report on Adlingfleet Drainage, 17 Dec., 1768 (Inst. Civ. Eng. library).
32. Korthals-Altes, K. *Sir Cornelius Vermuyden* (London, 1925).
33. Originally the Participants were allotted about 24,000 acres, but after all the ensuing legal disputes were settled the area was much reduced, as given in the text.
34. *Reports*, **1**, pp. 130–136; 19 Sept., 1764.
35. *Court of Sewers for Hatfield Chase*, Vol. 9. These records run from 1635 to 1858 in 23 volumes. They are included in the Hatfield Chase Corporation collection at Nottingham University library.
36. Gringley and Misterton carrs were originally in the Participant's land, but had later been transferred: see note 33.

37. Hadfield, C. and Skempton, A. W. *William Jessop, Engineer* (Newton Abbot, 1979) pp. 77–84.
38. *Court of Sewers*, Vol. 7. 13 Nov., 1761. George Forster was Surveyor of the Works from 1759 to 1771.
39. *Court of Sewers*, Vol. 9. 4 May, 1772.
40. Tofield, T. *A Scheme for effectually securing the Level of Hatfield Chace from being injured by the River Torn.* 20 Sept., 1773 (Nottingham University HCC/6166).
41. Matthias Scott was Surveyor of the Works from 1771 to 1783, first as a part-time appointment while still at Potteric Carr and from 1774 on full-time at £70 a year.
42. Recorded in Yeoman's report; see note 43.
43. Report by Thomas Yeoman to the Honourable the Participants of the Level of Hatfield Chace. 15 Dec., 1774 (Leeds Archives).
44. Report by Matthias Scott, 14 Oct., 1775 (Nottingham University, HCC/6214).
45. *Court of Sewers*, Vol. 9. 6 May, and 31 May, 1776.
46. "A Plan of all the Banks and Drains belonging to the Participants of Hatfield Chace... Surveyed in 1776" (Nottingham University HCC/9046).
47. *Reports*, **1,** pp. 299–315. 7 Oct., 1776. Longitudinal profiles of the ground and water levels along the Torne are in *Designs,* **6,** f. 100 and f. 101.
48. To calculate C we have assumed the entrance loss to be 20 per cent of the change in velocity head; friction loss in the sluice is based on Manning's $n=0.015$; the ratio of approach and discharge velocities is known from dimensions given by Smeaton.
49. *JHC*, Vol. 39, 12 Dec., 1782. The Act (23 Geo. 3, c. 13; 14 Mar., 1783) defines the leading dimensions of the cut and outfall sluice.
50. Contracts for the Keadby sluice, based on Foster's drawings, were advertised in December 1783. The sluice and cut were completed by April 1786 (*Court of Sewers*, Vol. 10).
51. For Foster's evidence on the Bill for the new works see *JHC*, Vol. 42. 15 Mar., 1787. The Act (27 Geo. 3, c. 53; 21 May, 1787) sets out in some detail what is to be done.
52. An order for the works to begin is recorded in *Court of Sewers*, Vol. 11. 30 June, 1787. They were finished by the summer of 1789.

Notes to Chapter VII

1. John Gwynn (1713–86), designer of bridges at Shrewsbury, Worcester, Oxford etc; not to be confused with Smeaton's resident engineer John Gwyn (*c.* 1733–89).

271

2. Ruddock, T. *Arch Bridges and their Builders 1735–1835*. (Cambridge, 1979).

3. *Mr Smeaton's Answer to the Misrepresentations of his Plan for Black-Friars Bridge*. 9 Feb., 1760 [London].

4. Smeaton, J. *A Review of Several Matters relative to the Forth and Clyde Navigation* (Edinburgh, 1768).

5. Gautier, H. *Traité des Ponts* (Paris, 1714).

6. Gautier, H. *Dissertation sur les Culées, Voussoirs, Piles et Pousées des Ponts* (Paris, 1717).

7. *Designs*, **4,** f. 94; undated, but probably 1754.

8. Ruddock, *op. cit.*, p. 85.

9. Emerson, W. *The Principles of Mechanicks*, 2nd edn (London, 1758).

10. Labelye, C. *A short Account of the Methods made use of in Laying the Foundations of the Piers of Westminster Bridge* (London, 1739).

11. Semple, G. *A Treatise on Building in Water* (Dublin, 1776).

12. Gautier, H. *Traité des Ponts*, 3rd edn (Paris, 1728).

13. Belidor, B. de F. *Architecture Hydraulique*, Vol. 4 (Paris, 1753).

14. Smeaton's drawing of the proposed Westminster cofferdam is in *Designs*, **4,** f. 172(i). A draft copy of his accompanying report is f. 172(ii).

15. Sheet piles with slanted points are shown on several drawings for the Calder & Hebble works of *c.* 1760 (e.g. *Designs*, **6,** f. 39v).

16. Perry, J. *An Account of the Stopping of Daggenham Breach* (London, 1721).

17. For references to Smeaton's drawings and reports on his bridges see Table 2.

18. A detailed description and analysis of the failure are given by Ruddock, E. C. "The foundations of Hexham Bridge". *Geotechnique*, **27,** (1977) 385–404.

19. Mr Smeaton's Memorial concerning Hexham Bridge [16 May, 1783]. *Reports*, **3,** pp. 299–320.

20. Figures given by Smeaton in his "Memorial" of 1783 show that he used the formula $v = C\sqrt{2gh}$ with $C = 1\cdot0$ precisely. A few years earlier when estimating flow through an outfall sluice, an analogous problem but with relatively low approach velocities, he took $C = 0\cdot95$ (see Chapter V). For the Hexham flood of 1782 a more correct value of C is about $1\cdot15$, assuming that the energy loss is 20 per cent of the change in velocity head; or even higher if the loss is smaller. If $C = 1\cdot15$ then the average velocity between the piers is about 20 ft/s. It is interesting to note that a similar result is obtained by adapting a semi-empirical analysis published by John Robertson in his paper "Concerning the fall of water under bridges". *Phil. Trans.*, **50** (1758) 492–499.

21. For details see Ruddock, *loc. cit.* (1977).

22. Ruddock, E. C. "Hollow spandrels: a historical study". *Struct. Eng.*, **52** (1974) 281–293.

23. Ruddock, E. C. "William Edward's bridge at Pontypridd". *Indust.*

Archaeol., **11** (1974) 194–208.
24. *Reports*, **1**, p. 339.
25. Ruddock, E. C. "The building of the North Bridge, Edinburgh, 1763–1775." *Trans. Newcomen Soc.*, **47** (1976) 9–33.
26. *Reports*, **3**, pp. 218–222.
27. The Perth spandrels were built, according to Smeaton's design, in 1770 (Commissioner's Minutes, 1765–1868. City of Perth District Council Office).
28. Phillips, J. *General History of Inland Navigation*, 3rd edn (London, 1795) p. 317.
29. Coldstream Bridge Trustees' Minutes 1762–72 (Northumberland Record Office).
30. *Machine Letters*, 26 Nov., 1790.
31. Perth Bridge Commissioners' Minutes (*loc. cit.*) 15 Aug., 1770.

Notes to Chapter VIII

1. Rolt, L. T. C. and Allen, J. S. *The Steam Engine of Thomas Newcomen* (Hartington, 1977).
2. *Designs*, **3**, f. 5.
3. *Reports*, **1**, pp. 223–229. *Designs*, **3**, f. 8–9. This is not Smeaton's experimental engine as often, but quite erroneously, assumed.
4. Dickinson, H. W. *Water Supply of Greater London* (Newcomen Society, 1954) pp. 65–67 for extracts from Smeaton's unpublished report of 29 Mar., 1766, modifications to the design, and engine performance. The original drawings are in *Designs*, **3**, f. 10–20.
5. Letter from Smeaton to Boulton & Watt, 5 Feb., 1778 (B & W Collection, Birmingham Ref. Library).
6. Farey, J. *Treatise on the Steam Engine* (London, 1827) pp. 233–235. Hereinafter referred to as *Treatise*. Farey had access to Smeaton's papers (see Chapter XI).
7. Dickinson, H. W. and Jenkins, R. *James Watt and the Steam Engine* (Oxford, 1927) pp. 352–357. For Smeaton's measurements of the power exerted by horses, see Chapter II of the present book.
8. Farey found Smeaton's paper on the Cornish engine tests after completing the *Treatise* and included it in the 2nd volume which had reached page proof stage at the time of his death. The proofs have long been in the Science Museum Library and are now published (Newton Abbot, 1971). The test results, given on p. 92 of Vol. 2, have to be corrected to allow for the bushel being reckoned at 94 lb in Cornwall.
9. *Designs*, **3**, f. 3, f. 6. The engraving by Wilson Lowry, reproduced here, is based on the original drawings and comes from Farey's article "Steam

Engine" in Rees' *Cyclopaedia*, Vol. 34 (1816).

10. A summary and analysis of the experiments from Smeaton's tabulated results and calculations are given in *Treatise*, pp. 166–172.

11. For Smeaton's table of engine sizes and performance, see *Treatise*, p. 183.

12. Dates and test results on the old and new engines at Long Benton are given in *Newcastle Courant*, 5 June, 1779.

13. Full details are provided in *Treatise*, pp. 172–182. Original drawings in *Designs*, **3**, f. 73–83.

14. The duty of 9·1 million, like all others quoted in this chapter, is based on the useful work performed. Farey includes the work done in pumping injection water, when the duty becomes 9·4 million.

15. *Treatise*, pp. 232–233. For the Walker engine see J. Sykes, *Local Records*, Vol. 1 (1824) p. 240.

16. *Treatise*, p. 204.

17. *Designs*, **3**, f. 112–125.

18. *Reports*, **2**, pp. 347–359.

19. *Treatise*, pp. 190–192.

20. Farey quotes from Smeaton's letter and gives much information on the Kronstadt engine. It was erected by one of the Carron engineers who went to Russia for the purpose.

21. *Reports*, **2**, pp. 360–361. Drawings in *Designs*, **3**, f. 99–111.

22. *Designs*, **3**, f. 160–175. The estimates and letter are in *Reports*, **2**, p. 375 and pp. 345–348.

23. *Treatise*, pp. 297–305. The engraving by Wilson Lowry reproduced in Fig. 43 is based on several of Smeaton's drawings. It comes from Farey's article "Winding Engine" in Rees' *Cyclopaedia*, Vol. 38 (1818).

24. *Designs*, **3**, f. 157–160.

25. *Designs*, **3**, f. 176–186. *Treatise*, pp. 305–306.

26. Smeaton's Journals for 1782 and 1783 (Trinity House, London).

27. *Treatise*, pp. 278–281. *Designs*, **3**, f. 40–60.

28. *Treatise*, pp. 251–257.

29. *Reports*, **2**, pp. 343–345. See also *Trans. Newcomen Soc.*, **37** (1963) 91–94 and **39** (1967) 145–150.

30. Dickinson, H. W. and Jenkins, R. *James Watt and the Steam Engine* (Oxford, 1927) pp. 107–115.

31. Letter from Smeaton to Boulton & Watt, 5 Jan., 1778. (Birmingham Ref. Library).

32. Letter from Smeaton to Boulton & Watt, 5 Feb., 1778. (Birmingham Ref. Library).

33. Dickinson and Jenkins, *op. cit.*, p. 136.

34. Letter from Smeaton to Boulton & Watt, 30 March, 1778. (Birmingham Ref. Library).

35. *Treatise*, p. 338.

36. *Reports*, **2**, pp. 378–380.

37. John Farey. Article "Mill" in Rees' *Cyclopaedia*, Vol. 23 (1813). Drawings for the millwork and mill house in *Designs*, **1**, f. 130–135.

Notes to Chapter IX

1. On harbours Smeaton wrote about 45 reports and there are well over 100 drawings in the Royal Society collection. With few exceptions these fall into two periods, 1762–83 and 1787–91.
2. *Reports*, **1**, pp. 295–300; 25 Oct., 1766. *Designs*, **5**, f. 165–170.
3. Information from Mr Cyril Noall, Curator of St Ives Museum, 1979, and Mr R. Glossop and Dr R. D. Slack, 1980.
4. Smeaton, J. *Narrative of the Building . . . of the Edystone Lighthouse* (London, 1791) p. 181.
5. *Reports*, **1**, pp. 302–305; 2 May, 1767. *Designs*, **5**, f. 98–101.
6. Turner, T. "The works of John Smeaton". *Trans. Newcomen Soc.*, **50** (1978), 37–54.
7. *Reports*, **3**, pp. 60–67; 18 May, 1770. *Designs*, **5**, f. 81–83, 87.
8. Turner, *loc. cit.*
9. *Reports*, **3**, pp. 68–73; 6 Jan., 1774. *Designs*, **5**, f. 84–86.
10. *Machine Letters*, May–June 1782 and *Designs*, **5**, f. 86v.
11. Turner, *loc. cit.* The completion date of 1778 is given in the *Select Committee on Post Office Communication with Ireland*, 1842.
12. Rennie, Sir John. *The Theory, Formation and Construction of British and Foreign Harbours*, Vol. 2 (London, 1854) pp. 187–189.
13. Letter to John Smeaton, Esq. Engineer, 23 May, 1768. Letter Book of Outgoing Letters (Town House records, Aberdeen).
14. *Reports*, **3**, pp. 38–46; 19 Feb., 1770. *Designs*, **5**, f. 56, 60, 63.
15. Outgoing Letters, 17 Mar., 1770.
16. Letter Book of Incoming Letters. Gwyn to the Lord Provost, 9 Feb., 1774 (Town House records).
17. Shore Works Accounts (Town House records).
18. *Ibid.*
19. Incoming Letters. Gwyn to the Lord Provost, 29 Dec., 1779.
20. Shore Works Accounts.
21. North Pier Ledger, 1768–80 (Town House records).
22. *Designs*, **5**, f. 57A. Survey by Andrew Mackay. The soundings are comparable with those of 1769 as depths further upstream are practically identical in the two surveys.
23. *Reports*, **3**, pp. 47–50; 22 Mar., 1788. *Designs*, **5**, f. 58, 62. A covering letter sent by Smeaton with his report is printed in *Reports by Smeaton, Rennie and Telford upon the Harbour of Aberdeen* (Aberdeen, 1834); it mentions that he and his assistant Henry Eastburn spent 8 days on the drawings.

24. *Designs,* **5,** f. 170v. Smeaton's report, dated 19 Dec., 1772, is printed in *Tidal Harbours Commission, Second Report* (London, 1847) Appendix C. pp. 303–304.

25. Gwyn's estimate [1773] is given in Arbuthnot, J. *An Historical Account of Peterhead* (Aberdeen, 1815) pp. 103–107.

26. Neish, N. *Old Peterhead* (Peterhead, 1950) p. 82.

27. For a general history of the harbour see Buchan, A. R. "The engineers of a minor port—Peterhead". *Indust. Archaeol. Rev.,* **3** (1979) 243–257.

28. Memorials from the Magistrates of Peterhead in 4th and 6th *Reports of the Commissioners for Highland Roads and Bridges* (London, 1809, p. 51 and 1813, pp. 56–57).

29. *Designs,* **5,** f. 71–73. No report has been found.

30. *Designs,* **5,** f. 75.

31. *Machine Letters.* Smeaton to Gwyn, 1 Apr., 1783 and 4 June, 1783.

32. Turner, *loc. cit.*

33. Smeaton recorded all letters sent and received between these dates in his "Minute Book" (see Chapter XI).

34. Turner, T. "John Gwyn and the building of the North Bridge, Kingston upon Hull". *Transport Hist.,* **3** (1970) 154–163.

35. Hull, Guildhall MSS. Smeaton to the Town Clerk, 4 Jan., 1785.

36. Information from Trevor Turner, 1977.

37. Smeaton, J. *An Historical Report on Ramsgate Harbour* (London, 1791), reprinted in *Reports,* **3,** pp. 74–128.

38. Matkin, R. B. "The construction of Ramsgate harbour". *Trans. Newcomen Soc.,* **48** (1977) 53–71.

39. The Report of John Smeaton, Engineer, upon the Harbour of Ramsgate. 24 October 1774. (Ramsgate Public Library; hereafter referenced as RPL). *Designs,* **5,** f. 121.

40. A further Report on Ramsgate Harbour, 12 Feb., 1777. (Rennie Collection, National Library of Scotland; hereafter NLSR). *Designs,* **5,** f. 123 and 124.

41. Letters from Smeaton to Mr Evans, Secretary to the Trustees; 5 Jan., 13 Mar. and 3 May, 1783 (NLSR) together with An Explanation of the Design for the New Gates for the Bason of Ramsgate Harbour. 5 Jan., 1783 (RPL). *Designs,* **5,** f. 125 and 127 (gates) and *Designs,* **5,** f. 141 and 143 (dock).

42. Account of Mr Smeaton's time upon the business of Ramsgate Harbour. 24 May, 1783 (NLSR).

43. The Report of John Smeaton, Engineer, upon the Dock lately erected. 12 Dec., 1787 (NLSR).

44. The Report of John Smeaton, Engineer, upon the matter of his late Journey in December 1787. 9 Jan., 1788 (NLSR).

45. *Designs,* **5,** f. 132, 133 and 134.

46. *Designs,* **5,** f. 139 and 140, sketches f. 138v.

47. *Machine Letters.* Smeaton to Gwyn, 27 Feb., 1788, and Smeaton to Mr Evans, 28 Feb., 1788 (NLSR).
48. Smeaton to Mr Evans, 21 May, 1788 (NLSR).
49. *Designs,* **4,** f. 146.
50. *Machine Letters.* Smeaton to Gwyn, 4 Aug., 1788.
51. The Report of John Smeaton, Engineer, upon the progress of the Works of Ramsgate Harbour in the year 1788. 9 Dec., 1788 (RPL).
52. Smeaton to Mr Evans, 15 and 24 Jan., 1789, replying to letters from Gwyn and Cull (RPL).
53. Smeaton to Gwyn, 24 Apr., 1789, with enclosed drawing of flap valve for the dock (RPL).
54. Rennie's Notebook No. 3 (NLSR). In the *Historical Report* Smeaton says the method of levelling the chalk bottom was introduced by William Etheridge in 1752.
55. *Designs,* **5,** f. 144 l.s. iv.
56. Mr Smeaton's Estimate of future Works [1791] (RPL).
57. Trustees of Ramsgate Harbour, Minutes (PRO).

Notes to Chapter X

General For further details see Smith, D. "The professional correspondence of John Smeaton", *Trans. Newcomen Soc.,* **47** (1976) 179–188.

1. *Reports,* **1,** p. 290, 12 Nov., 1782.
2. *Reports,* **1,** p. 211, [1764].
3. *Reports,* **3,** p. 32, 4 May, 1782.
4. *Machine Letters,* 1 Oct., 1782.
5. *Machine Letters,* 5 Apr., 1783.
6. *Machine Letters,* 5 June, 1783.
7. Smiles, S. *Lives of the Engineers,* Vol. 2 (London, 1861) pp. 74–75.
8. Dixon, Mary: in *Reports,* **1,** pp. xxvi–xxvii.
9. Austhorpe Journal, 8 Aug., 1781 (Trinity House Library). The mill referred to was near Austhorpe Lodge.
10. *Reports,* **2,** p. 101, 28 Oct., 1768.
11. 1764 Letter Book, 1 Aug., (Inst. Civ. Eng. library).
12. *Machine Letters,* 22 July, 1791.
13. Farey, John: note in *Designs,* **1,** f. 1 written in the 1820s.
14. *Reports,* **2,** p. 385, 27 Feb., 1775.
15. Hadfield, C. and Skempton, A. W. *William Jessop, Engineer* (Newton Abbot, 1979) pp. 12–15.
16. That Eastburn arrived at Austhorpe as a pupil in 1768 is clear from several of Smeaton's letters. It is certain he had left Austhorpe by the

beginning of 1789 (*Machine Letters*, 11 Feb., 1789) but he probably went nearly a year before this.

17. *Machine Letters*, 15 Jan., 1783. Letter to Samuel Galton.
18. *Letters between Redmond Morres, Esq; one of the Subscribers to the Grand Canal, and John Smeaton, Esq; Engineer, and FRS* (Dublin, 1773) p. 13. We are indebted to Miss Julia Elton of Weinreb Ltd for photocopies of this very rare publication.
19. *Ibid.*, p. 18. Smeaton to Morres, 29 Feb., 1772.
20. Letter from Smeaton to Boulton & Watt, 30 Mar., 1778 (Birmingham Ref. Library).
21. Stockton Bridge Order Book (Durham County Record Office), Smeaton's Account for work done in 1760 and 1762.
22. Printed statement issued by Smeaton 12 May, 1767 (Science Museum, Trade Card V, 36).
23. *Machine Letters*, 28 Aug., 1782.
24. *1764 Letter Book*, 30 Jan.
25. *Machine Letters*, 1 Oct., 1782.
26. *Machine Letters*, 28 Aug., 1782.
27. *Machine Letters*, 26 Mar., 1786.
28. *Machine Letters*, 1 Oct., 1782.
29. Dixon, Mary, *loc. cit.*
30. Letter to Boulton & Watt, 30 Mar., 1778.
31. Towards the end of his career Smeaton charged 10 guineas a day or 50 guineas a week, but this was "rather to save time than acquire money" (*Machine Letters*, 21 July, 1787). Such fees were quite exceptional and had no influence on the profession.
32. Personal communication from Professor Skempton based on an unpublished study of engineers' fees, salaries and living expenses in the eighteenth century.
33. *Reports*, **2,** p. 386; 19 Feb., 1780.
34. *Reports*, **2,** p. 178; 19 Jan., 1771.
35. *Reports*, **1,** p. 305; 2 May, 1767. More rarely Smeaton would allow 20 per cent for contingencies.
36. *Reports*, **2,** p. 236; 27 Jan., 1778.
37. *Reports*, **2,** p. 153; 5 Dec., 1772.
38. *Morres–Smeaton Letters*, p. 26; 19 Sept., 1772.
39. *Reports*, **2,** p. 122; 14 Mar., 1768.
40. *Morres–Smeaton Letters*, pp. 29–38; 12 Dec., 1772.
41. *3 Douglas's Reports, Kings Bench 1782*, pp. 157–161. Folkes v. Chadd and others.
42. *Ibid.*, p. 160.
43. *Encyclopaedia Metropolitania*, Vol. 14 (London, 1845) p. 609.
44. Smiles, S. *Lives of the Engineers*, Vol. 2 (London, 1861) p. 86.
45. *Ibid.*

Notes to Chapter XI

1. Minutes of the Trustees of the River Lee, 30 Sept., 1766 (PRO). More typically 500 copies were printed: Skempton, A. W. *Early Printed Reports and Maps in the Library of the Institution of Civil Engineers* (London, 1977).
2. Letter from John Rennie to the bookseller Peter Elmsley, *c.* 1796 (BM: B.276b).
3. It is hoped to publish full details in a bibliography of civil engineering works before 1840.
4. Thomas Mortimer's *Universal Director* (London, 1763).
5. For the publishing history of *Reports, Miscellaneous Papers* and the *Edystone* book, see Skempton, A. W. *Notes Rec. Roy. Soc.*, **26** (1971) 135–155 and Woolrich, A. P. *Notes Rec. Roy. Soc.*, **35** (1980) 131–133.
6. Banks' manuscript list of Smeaton papers is in the Sutro Library, San Francisco.
7. Lot 941 in Sotheby's auction sale commencing 11 Mar., 1886. Adolph Sutro, through dealers, bought several lots from this sale, one of which presumably included the list of Smeaton's papers noted above.
8. *John Smeaton's Diary of his Journey to the Low Countries*, edited by Arthur Titley (Newcomen Soc., 1938).
9. Rowatt, T. "Notes on original models of the Eddystone Lighthouse". *Trans. Newcomen Soc.*, **5** (1924) 15–21.
10. The 1764 letter book was presented to the Institution of Civil Engineers by Sir Alexander Gibb & Partners in 1972. It had been acquired through bookdealers.
11. Letter to Samuel Smiles (Leeds Archives), transcribed by Michael Lee. In *Lives of the Engineers* (London, 1861) Vol. 2, p. 77 Smiles embellishes the story.
12. Weston's Eddystone collection was given by his son to the Earl of Morton. After her husband's death in 1827 the Countess of Morton presented it to the Royal Society of Edinburgh, whence it came to the Museum in 1859; see ref. 9. Help in studying this material has been given by Mr Allen Simpson of the Museum.
13. Mr A. P. Woolrich has generously provided much information on John Farey. He points out that so early as 1808 Farey had permission from Banks to copy some of Smeaton's drawings for illustrations in *Pantologia* (London, 1802–12).
14. In his article on "Water", Rees' *Cyclopaedia*, Vol. 38 (1818), Farey says that Smeaton "never completed a design which he formed, to publish a collection of practical hydraulic machines founded on his own experience. Among his manuscript papers which have been lent to us by Sir Joseph Banks, we find an outline for this work, of which we have availed ourselves in this article".
15. Obituary in *Min. Proc. Inst. Civ. Eng.*, **11** (1852) 100–102.

16. Will of Edward Farey: probate 4 Nov., 1913. This has been discovered by Mr Woolrich. Edward also bequeathed his father's copy of the *Edystone* book to the Royal Society.
17. *A Catalogue of the Civil and Mechanical Engineering Designs 1741–1792 of John Smeaton*, edited by H. W. Dickinson and A. A. Gomme (Newcomen Soc., 1950).

Index

Notes and References, on pp. 259–279, are not included in this Index.
Italic figures, at the end of some entries, indicate page numbers of illustrations.

Printed in the United States
94388LV00006B